SOLDIERS MADE ME LOOK GOOD

MAJOR-
GENERAL **LEWIS MACKENZIE**
(RET'D)

A LIFE IN THE SHADOW OF WAR

SOLDIERS

MADE ME LOOK GOOD

Douglas & McIntyre

VANCOUVER / TORONTO / BERKELEY

Douglas & McIntyre Ltd.
2323 Quebec Street, Suite 201
Vancouver, British Columbia
Canada V5T 4S7
www.douglas-mcintyre.com

Library and Archives Canada Cataloguing in Publication
MacKenzie, Lewis, 1940-
Soldiers made me look good : a life in the shadow of war / Lewis Mackenzie.
Includes bibliographical references and index.

ISBN 978-1-55365-350-9

1. MacKenzie, Lewis, 1940–. 2. Canada. Canadian Army—
Officers—Biography. 3. Canada—History, Military—20th century.
I. Title.
U55.M33A3 2008   355.0092   C2008-903616-6

Editing by John Eerkes-Medrano
Copy editing by Ruth Wilson
Jacket photograph courtesy of Lewis MacKenzie
Uncredited photographs courtesy of the author
Text design by Naomi MacDougall
Printed and bound in Canada by Friesens
Printed on acid-free paper that is forest friendly (100% post-consumer
recycled paper) and has been processed chlorine free.

Distributed in the U.S. by Publishers Group West

We gratefully acknowledge the financial support of the Canada Council for the Arts,
the British Columbia Arts Council, the Province of British Columbia through the Book
Publishing Tax Credit, and the Government of Canada through the Book Publishing
Industry Development Program (BPIDP) for our publishing activities.

THIS BOOK IS DEDICATED to the Canadian soldier of today, a member of a tiny army fighting well above its weight on the international stage and bringing much credit to Canada as the rest of us safely observe from the sidelines.

"We were pragmatic to the extreme, and we thought every problem could be solved by an equation or by adjusting the numbers. Not one of us had any education in the humanities— even Hitler fancied himself an architect, in spite of his lack of formal training. While serving twenty years behind Spandau's walls I constantly studied the humanities, and I'm convinced that if a few of us within Hitler's inner circle were so educated at the time we could have made a positive difference."

ALBERT SPEER, speaking to Canadian students in West Germany, 1976

Contents

Introduction

IN 1993, THANKS to the curiosity and support of a large number of Canadians, I was fortunate to be the author of a national #1 bestseller entitled *Peacekeeper: The Road to Sarajevo*. No one was more surprised than I was, and I assumed that writing a book was a one-time experience, sort of a "been there done that but don't push your luck" type of thing.

What I did not anticipate was the somewhat flattering interest from publishers hoping for a second book. I was leery of the suggestion and kept thinking of Michael J. Fox's disappointing film, *Back to the Future, Part II*. I had really enjoyed the first *Back to the Future* but the sequel was a bit of a flop, and I had heard that it was basically a montage of clippings gathered from the editing-room floor after the first movie had been completed. It seems the producers of the sequel assumed they could reap rewards from the positive legacy of the first movie during the distribution of the second. It didn't work, and I was concerned that I might suffer the same experience if I wrote another book. So I resisted the overtures.

We retire from our chosen Profession of Arms pretty young. Let's face it, we don't need some fifty-five-year-old turning around and shouting "follow me!" to a thousand armed nineteen- to twenty-five-year-olds as they storm the enemy on a hill in some faraway land. I took off my uniform a month before my fifty-third birthday in 1993.

To my considerable surprise, life did not come to a shuddering halt when I turned in my military ID card and ventured out the door and onto civvy street. During the past fifteen years I seem to have been on fast-forward and involved in a significant number of interesting and—most of the time—satisfying experiences. I have written about them all: returning to Somalia; involvement with the release of Canadian hostages in Bosnia; multiple appearances before U.S. Congressional committees and dealing with accusations of rape and murder from the Bosnian prosecutor that followed; heading up a team to restructure the Irish Armed Forces; running in the 1997 federal election; hosting an award-winning documentary on the UN; helping CTV cover NATO's bombing campaign against Serbia from Belgrade; assisting a small Canadian NGO founded by a fellow soldier with its humanitarian work in Africa; commenting on military and foreign affairs, initially for the *National Post* and later for the *Globe and Mail;* maintaining my love for (obsession with) motor racing by continuing to race Formula Fords and anything else I'm offered and, along the way, speaking to well over a million people in eight countries on the professional speaking circuit.

Two chapters of this book are dedicated to what will probably be controversial subjects. One deals with Carol Off's biased, highly critical and error-ridden personal evaluation of my performance as the UN commander in Sarajevo in 1992. The other chapter analyzes the probable genesis of a serious disagreement between Senator Roméo Dallaire and me regarding leadership priorities.

If I wanted to start this book at the beginning, describe how I ended up in the military and then jump to my post-military career, I had a problem. I would have to account for the thirty-three-year-gap, and I couldn't describe the most interesting experiences I had in uniform because I had already done that in *Peacekeeper*. I thought about various options on and off for the last few years, and I've come up with what I hope is a satisfactory solution.

Rank progression in the military is frequently inexplicable to those both inside and outside the Profession of Arms. Many factors come into play: some within an individual's control, such as performance, knowledge, fitness and commitment. In many instances, though, other factors are well outside the individual's control: timing, exposure, an articulate boss and the severity of the challenges at work, all of which come under the general heading of *Luck!* There are many highly talented people in uniform who might have performed to an outstanding level well beyond their current rank, but the absence of luck in their careers has denied them the opportunity. For those of us fortunate enough to benefit from Lady Luck's smile, our success is due in no small part to those talented people who work for us and who—with all their experience and talent, but less luck—make us look good. I decided I would cover my military career by describing the events that I thought were the most responsible for the good fortune and satisfaction I experienced in my thirty-three years of commissioned service. Not surprisingly, I emphasize the large role played by luck in each anecdote.

It would be inappropriate to conclude this book without discussing the two subjects that dominate my time at present:

Afghanistan and leadership. I feel compelled to write about our sincere efforts to help the Afghan people get their country back to a secure state under their own control. I will offer some comments about how we got there and what we are achieving. My visits to the country have me longing to be back in uniform, but I realize that the current generation of our soldiers has moved on to establish their own enviable reputation as second-to-none. They make us all look good, at home and abroad, in spite of the few critical rants to the contrary. Any of them who pick up this book will be bored to tears reading about the experiences of a one-time Cold War soldier, considering what they have experienced on the post–Cold War battlefield.

This book comes from a soldier who spent most of his career training for a big fight with the Russian-led Warsaw Pact. Fortunately for all of mankind, it never materialized. Lurking around the corner was a new and equally challenging international threat to peace and security, waiting to fill the vacuum once the Berlin Wall came down. Our current generation of solders is in the thick of that campaign, doing something about the threat, while too many Canadians try to wish the problem away. I look forward to reading the books they will write about their experiences. *They* certainly won't be boring!

4

SOLDIERS MADE ME LOOK GOOD

PART ONE

COLD WAR GRUNT

1: Small-Town Canada

"Lewis is a disrupting influence in the classroom. With his capabilities of leadership, he should be setting a much better example."

MISS SHAVER, GRADE SEVEN TEACHER

I WAS AN UNLIKELY candidate to be a soldier. I was born in Truro, Nova Scotia, the site of the hospital nearest to our tiny village of Princeport. I'm not sure if Princeport still has the official status of a village today. In the 1940s you needed a church to qualify, and we had that, along with a one-room, eleven-grade schoolhouse a scant twenty-five yards away on the same piece of property. Unfortunately, amalgamation fever was alive and well even in the 1960s, and both buildings disappeared beneath the blade of a bulldozer when it became obvious that a population of just over fifty souls could not sustain them.

Princeport consisted of a collection of relatively small farms overlooking the junction of Cobequid Bay and the Shubenacadie River. My grandparents on my father's side lived there, and my father, Eugene Murdock ("Connie") MacKenzie, the third of four boys and two girls, lived a few hundred yards away at the end of a seasonal lane—"seasonal" meaning that it was easily passable only during the hot, dry summer months. My father had left school after grade eight to help support his family, like so many of his generation. The Great Depression saw him searching for work throughout the province, ultimately landing a steady job with the Mersey Paper Company in Liverpool, Nova Scotia.

When I first saw the light of day on April 30, 1940, the Nazi Blitz was on against London and my father was training at Camp Petawawa, two hours west of Ottawa. He and two of his brothers had joined up at the outbreak of hostilities; these brothers joined the air force and navy, and Dad went to the army's combat engineers. The youngest brother had suffered a serious gunshot wound from a hunting accident that prevented him from joining his brothers at the Halifax recruiting depot.

My mother's family, the Whartons, were originally from Nova Scotia's south shore town of Liverpool. Mum's name was Shirley, and her father, Newman Wharton, was a master sea captain of considerable renown. He operated his schooner, the *Jean and Shirley*, from the world-famous fishing and shipbuilding port of Lunenburg, an hour northeast. The Jean in the *Jean and Shirley* was Mum's older sister.

My grandfather, like most of his colleagues, enjoyed racing back to Lunenburg from the Grand Banks off Newfoundland once his boat had taken on a full load of fish. One of his closest friends was Angus Walters, the skipper of the legendary *Bluenose*, and one of my first recollections is my mother telling me that Angus had said my grandfather had twice beat him racing back from the Grand Banks, "fair and square." These unofficial races took place with boats carrying a full load of fish and using conventional sails; however, when the fast schooners ventured forth against the world's best in competition, they mounted racing spars and purpose-built sails.

My grandfather was tempted to try his hand at professional racing, but the fate of his brother, Lewis, haunted my grandmother. Lewis Wharton had been captain of the schooner *Columbia,* a highly successful racer sailing out of Gloucester, Massachusetts, in the 1920s. In order to qualify for the International Fisherman's Trophy, an entrant had to have been a working fishing boat for at least one year. Tragically, during the great August gale of 1927, the *Columbia* was lost with all hands in the Atlantic graveyard off the coast of Sable Island. The drowning of its twenty-six crew members was the largest single loss of of life on any ship sailing from Gloucester harbour in over four centuries. My grandmother inaccurately blamed the loss on racing modifications to the *Columbia* and would not tolerate the thought of any similar modifications to the *Jean and Shirley,* so my grandfather was forced to limit himself to unofficial races back from the Grand Banks. Thirteen years later I was named after my late, great uncle, Lewis Wharton.

My mother was smart and excelled in school. Her parents were strict disciplinarians, and it rubbed off on their offspring. We spent every summer during the war at my grandparents' home in Liverpool, Nova Scotia. It was a real treat to live and play, if only temporarily, in what to me was a sprawling metropolis. They say that the sense of smell is the greatest trigger of nostalgia. I tend to agree, as every time I detect a whiff of a pulp and paper plant I think of the war and my summers in Liverpool, played out under a sulphur-rich, yellow cloud generated by the Mersey paper plant, close to the centre of town.

My mother ruled with an iron hand, frequently wrapped in velvet, when we visited her parents. Her father was a kind and extremely quiet man, quite the opposite of the stereotypical master seafarer, while her mother was misemployed in life: she would have made an excellent sergeant major or drill sergeant. You spoke when you were spoken to, and that was that. My grandfather now stands out in my mind as someone who proved beyond a doubt that you don't have to rant and rave to be a successful leader. He established his reputation by his deeds, not by the volume of his rhetoric.

My dad, much to his frustration, never made it overseas during the war. While engaged in a training exercise, he had a finger blown off, which kept him in Canada. The fact that he was stuck in Petawawa, Ontario, as an instructor while the war raged on weighed heavily on his mind and was to have a significant impact on our lives within a few years. In 1945, following the end of the war, he was demobilized and returned to Princeport. He had reached the rank of warrant officer first class, or chief warrant officer in today's terminology. This was a significant achievement, considering his lack of formal education.

Fortunately for the family, my father was good with his hands, missing finger notwithstanding. On his return home, he worked at various jobs, depending on the season. He built his own boat and knitted his own nets for fishing on the Shubenacadie River, a scant hundred yards from our back door. In the winter he was employed as a sheet metal worker and took on steeplejacking whenever the opportunity arose. He was probably one of the original "ambulance chasers." Lightning strikes were a major problem in Nova Scotia in those days; barns and churches were tall and attracted lightning like a magnet—at least that was my dad's line, and he kept to it. Any time there was a report of a lightning strike in the province, he would be off in a cloud of dust to speak with the neighbours of the strike victim about immediately mounting protective rods on all their tall buildings. Churches that had been struck generated by far the most business for us. Anyone who lived nearby assumed that if God's natural forces could target a church no one was safe, so they'd better put up some rods. Dad was standing by to oblige.

The installation of lightning rods was an expensive proposition, primarily because of the outrageous cost of copper wire in post-war Canada and the requirement to work at some pretty significant elevations. But my father was unafraid of heights, and one of my favourite snapshots shows him standing on his head on the peak of the roof at the Dorchester Penitentiary in New Brunswick—where, I hasten to add, he was working under contract to repair the smokestack.

As the years passed and I reached all of ten years old, I began to help Dad with the really high work, because he was becoming less and less comfortable with heights. The change was a result of a different lifestyle that Dad had adopted during his five-year stint with the army; he had become a weekend alcoholic.

A weekend alcoholic is someone who follows the old and much-quoted adage, "Work hard and play hard." Once the soldiers were out of the field, where drinking was tightly controlled, they routinely "tied one on" with their mates at happy hour on Friday evenings. Because they were away from home, they had no compelling reason to sober up on Saturday, so they carried on partying into Sunday. About noon on Sunday—or later, depending on their constitution—they cleaned up their act and dried themselves out so that they would be ready to go, bright and early, on Monday morning.

This affliction was common in Dad's time and continues to this day, although its occurrence is greatly reduced, thanks to changing attitudes. I myself frequently followed the route as a young, single officer. Fortunately, however, I spent a lot of time in the field, so drinking didn't develop into a conditioned reflex as soon as 4:30 PM rolled around on Friday. My dad, on the other hand, had five years to practise, without the intensity of surviving the battlefield to break the routine. In hindsight it was a pretty impressive performance—drink for a day and a half, don't touch another drop for the next five and a half days, then repeat. At the time it caused a lot of tension in the house, as my mother was not a drinker, nor did she enjoy going anywhere with my father when he was imbibing. Out of the house Dad was a good, even outstanding, party person. He was gregarious and generous to a fault, and he loved to dance. He was popular and always good for a laugh; yet, with the benefit of hindsight, I think he secretly resented the fact that he never got overseas, and he found some solace in alcohol.

Sharing space in our modest farmhouse was my sister, Katheryn, six years my senior and smart as a whip. Fortunately for me she was destined to be relatively short, so she beat me up only until I was nine, when to my considerable surprise and pleasure I noticed that I was looking down at her. "Tap," as she was known back then (there were so many Katheryns in our family and the area in general that you needed to nickname them to keep track) excelled in school, which made life more difficult for me, particularly as we were all crammed into the same schoolroom. When I entered grade one, Tap was already in grade seven. Since a lone teacher had to deal with eleven grades at the same time (wouldn't today's teachers' unions have a ball with that!), the more senior students would frequently be called upon to teach the rest of us, and—you guessed it—I was occasionally taught by my sister. She must have been pretty good at it and must have benefited from the experience because, some five years later, when she went to the Colchester County Academy in Truro to complete grade twelve, she won the province's Governor General's Award for academic excellence.

The independence and freedom inherent in a rural upbringing in the 1940s and '50s had a lot going for it. Our home was
surrounded by forests, except for a few fields of hay, so with
a few quick steps I could disappear from the watchful gaze of
my mother, standing sentry at the kitchen window. The nearby
sheer, two-hundred-foot riverbanks were a magnet; their almost
vertical slopes rested on the edge of the Shubenacadie River,
which retreated twice a day when the world's highest tides
receded from the Bay of Fundy. The banks and the exposed
river bottom and, for that matter, the river itself, were a deep
rusty-red colour—the result of an extremely high iron content,
a legacy of the Triassic geological period that produced the
rich soil so common throughout Nova Scotia (take one geology
course in college and you become an expert!). The red mud had
the consistency of chocolate pudding, so if you ran as fast as
the footing would permit and dove head-first into the ooze, you
could slide for a good fifty yards, the mud providing the ultimate lubricant.

Twice a day, thirty-foot-plus tides would build in the Bay of
Fundy, pushed by the Atlantic. The resulting onrushing wall
of water would encounter the deluge of the Shubenacadie River
heading for the bay in the opposite direction. When the two met,
the tidal water would initially dominate, and the river water
would be pushed back up the river against its normal direction. The resulting turbulence was referred to as the tidal bore,
and in spite of it having taken on a mythical status as a tourist attraction over the last twenty years, I've always considered
the bore to be appropriately named. Perhaps if we had stayed
in Princeport, we could have constructed some bleachers overlooking the river and sold tickets. However, in the absence of
any material benefit from the tidal bore during my time there, it
merely provided another source of concern for my mother. She

was convinced that one day I would be trapped at the base of the bluffs and drown when the tide came in.

At seven years of age, I enjoyed disappearing into the forest alone with my first .22 calibre rifle. Shooting at cans was necessary in the beginning, to prove to my father that I was capable of aiming, but after overcoming that hurdle I was hunting with a purpose. There was a good supply of food in the surrounding woods, and rabbits, partridges and particularly deer were a godsend. The deer required the use of Dad's .303 Lee-Enfield, which I was not permitted to carry by myself. Fortunately, unsuspecting deer frequently wandered along the treeline a hundred yards from our porch. I would sit in a chair and aim the rifle while my mother held me from behind to help control the recoil, and then I would squeeze the trigger. It worked on two occasions, and I can still remember waiting for my dad to return from work in Truro and seeing the look of surprise on his face as he was led to the carcass by his two lawbreakers. (There was some obscure regulation that said you were not permitted to fire a gun from the confines of your residence with the intent of hunting; we arbitrarily decided that our porch did not qualify as "confines.") With venison and an inexhaustible supply of fish, which my father cured in the smokehouse he had built, we ate pretty well—although like most kids, my sister and I expressed a dislike for anything that wasn't bought in a store.

On most Friday nights we all took the trip to Truro to buy groceries, with me in the back of our Fargo. There was always an argument over how many five-cent comics I could buy, but early on I discovered *Classics Illustrated* comics, which in spite of their fifteen-cent price were a much better deal than three of the normal variety. To this day I occasionally give the impression that I have read all the classics, from the *Iliad* through *David*

Copperfield to *Moby-Dick*. I owe the illusion to those fifteen-cent *Classics*.

Today we pride ourselves in keeping up with the latest news by way of the Internet. Those who lived in the country in the 1940s had an equally efficient tool for staying on top of local happenings and gossip: the telephone party line. Everyone in the community had their own distinctive series of rings; ours was three long and two short. Every family knew every other family's code, and listening to other people's trials and tribulations was an important part of the day's entertainment. Unfortunately, whenever someone surreptitiously picked up their receiver to eavesdrop, there was a modest but noticeable electronic drain on the line and the volume of the ongoing conversation was reduced for everyone. Occasionally, when a discussion was particularly long and juicy, so many listeners would join the audience that the two people having the conversation would no longer be able to hear each other. This usually resulted in one of them exclaiming, "For God's sake! Would all you eavesdroppers please hang up so we can start over again!" The fact that we were the most isolated home in the community meant that my mother felt a moral obligation to the family to remain as current as possible (at least that's what she told us!), so she spent a good deal of her time with her ear glued to the receiver.

While my daughter, Kimm, was growing up, I probably bored her more than once describing how I had walked for miles through two feet of snow to get to that one-room school in Princeport. It was a bit of a shock to discover during a recent nostalgia visit home that it was under a half mile, but at least it was an entertaining half mile. It's not a bad start to a day when you walk through a forest alive with the sounds of animals and birds too numerous to count. Emerging from our woods, it

was a clear run across an open pasture past my grandparents'
home, always a warm refuge in the winter when the temperature dipped below zero (that's Fahrenheit!). My grandmother
could dry frozen mittens and snowsuits faster than anyone—
and without igniting them! Then down the hill, past the swamp
on the left of the lane—it was impossible not to stop each and
every time, to and from school, because the swamp offered an
advanced biology course if you paid attention. The passing
of the seasons was revealed by the changes in the bog and its
inhabitants. The frogs' eggs, tightly packed together like tapioca
pudding, virtually overnight were transformed into thousands
of minute tadpoles that soon grew tiny legs, and ultimately the
bulging eyes of an adult frog would appear. As winter neared,
the summer's vocal sentries would make their way to the muddy
bottom before November's ice presented us with a modest skating rink a few feet above their resting place.

The single schoolroom's routine was a team builder par
excellence. I didn't realize it at the time, but those female school-
teachers—including a particularly attractive one, Margaret, who
married my youngest uncle—were my first leadership role mod-
els. They managed to get more out of us than the sum of our
parts, and more often than not they made learning an enjoyable experience. We, their team, restricted to one spartan room,
helped each other learn. I didn't understand synergy then, but
that's what I was witnessing.

If every life has a dominating turning point, mine occurred
when the North Korean army swarmed south over the 38th parallel into South Korea on June 25, 1950. Two months earlier, I
had celebrated my tenth birthday.

Following the Second World War, Canada was ranked the
fifth-largest military power in the world, behind the United
States, the Soviet Union, Great Britain and China. Over one

million men had served in the war, 708,500 of them in the army. However, the euphoria of total victory, combined with unrealistic optimism for the future—particularly after the signing of the United Nations Charter on June 26, 1945—saw almost total demobilization. By 1947 the Canadian Permanent Force, as it was known at the time, numbered a mere 8,000 souls. As the Cold War intensified, even Canada was aroused from its new and comfortable isolation. In 1949, threats to our north justified the creation of the Mobile Strike Force, whose title was significantly more impressive than its operational capabilities. Even as the force was exercising for the first time "north of 60," Canadian politicians and military thinkers were focusing their attention on Europe. Czechoslovakia was taken over by the communists in 1948, and the Soviets blockaded Berlin in June that year. Shortly thereafter, the Soviet Union's 1949 nuclear test made the idea of a land defence of Canada's north dated, to say the least. The western European countries got together and formed a defence union to face down the Soviets. Canada led the way in turning the union into a trans-Atlantic club, and ultimately, in April 1949, into the North Atlantic Treaty Organization (NATO). With the creation of NATO, Canada could exercise its new stated policy to "defend Canada from as far away as possible." Participation in NATO required that some dues be paid, and by the end of 1949 the strength of the regular army had grown to just over 20,000 and that of the militia to 37,000.

The outbreak of the Korean War created a problem for Canadian decision makers. While Canada had no obvious self-interests threatened in Korea, it had been an outspoken supporter of the United Nations' responsibility for maintaining "international peace and security" when the UN Charter was signed four years earlier in San Francisco. At the same time, Canada's modest military was required to help defend North America and, if necessary, to deploy (albeit very slowly) to help the Europeans in the event of Soviet aggression. Thus, it looked like Canada would have to recruit an additional force for deployment to Korea.

On August 7, 1950, Prime Minister Louis St. Laurent went on national radio and announced that a Canadian Army Special Force would be recruited to be available to meet Canada's obligations to the UN and NATO. A scant few minutes after the prime minister's pronouncement, only the dust from my father's 1942 Fargo truck lingered in the air as he left our view on his way to the army recruiting station in Halifax, a good two hours away.

With my father heading towards the recruiting depot, I soon discovered that our rural lifestyle, in all its simplicity, in concert with a solid educational foundation and everyday country activities like running, throwing and roughhousing, would be of considerable value when a Cold War conflict halfway around the world dictated our next stop. To my father's considerable surprise, when the army recruiters found his old file and saw that he had been senior instructor when he was released in 1945, they offered him the rank of warrant officer second class, one rung lower than his wartime rank. It was a heck of a deal, considering the number of ex-soldiers who were lining up to get back in, and with no hesitation Dad signed on the dotted line. What followed was six months of menial jobs at the Halifax garrison, which permitted visits home on the weekends while the "system" debated what to do with him. In January of 1951, Sergeant Major MacKenzie was posted to the Royal Canadian School of Military Engineering, at Vedder Crossing, just outside Chilliwack, British Columbia. To his chagrin, however, he ended up helping to train others on their way to Korea and missed yet another opportunity to serve overseas in an operational theatre. To further complicate matters, since the army was not yet sure how it would employ its new crop of ex-soldiers and, indeed, how many of them would adjust to military life outside of a world war context, it decided that families would not accompany the new "recruits" to their initial retraining.

Our isolated farm on the near edge of nowhere was not the ideal location for a growing family while Dad went off to the other side of the country, and it was decided that after I completed grade five we would move to Truro, the Las Vegas of Nova Scotia, or so it seemed from ten miles out in the country. The town was referred to as the "hub" of Nova Scotia because of the junction of rail- and roadways within its town limits. The resulting frantic level of activities promised to make life interesting for a transplanted eleven-year-old. We rented a small apartment on the second floor of a modest house on Young Street. One of our neighbours was the combined police and fire hall, and the other was the Nova Scotia Teachers' College. Directly across the street was a large and imposing funeral home, a stark contrast to the open field and treeline I'd grown accustomed to.

Soon after arriving in Truro, I made the short walk to Central Elementary School and reported in for grade six. It was a significant change to have only one grade in the same room and only one teacher to look after thirty or so ten- to eleven-year-olds. My new teacher was an unforgettable character: I'm usually terrible with names, but I certainly remember Miss Bruce-Payne. She was British, authoritative, impatient, caustic and yet totally dedicated to her charges. What set her apart from everyone else I had met so far was the fact that she had survived the German bombing blitz on London ten years earlier, during the Second World War, and she never let us forget it! Throughout the year I spent at Central, whenever things got a bit boring in class, all one of us had to do was ask Miss Bruce-Payne about the Blitz: "What was it like? Were you scared? Did you see anyone killed?" The subject of the current period would immediately be forgotten, and Miss Bruce-Payne became our personal Second World War tour guide, taking us on mental excursions into the London Underground, where we shared the horror of air raid after air raid and the joy of each "All clear!" I never forgot Miss Bruce-Payne, and for years afterwards I paid her a visit whenever I returned to Truro.

Truro has a significant black population. During my country upbringing I had seen black people only from a distance on the Friday night grocery runs to Truro, and racial prejudice was unknown to me. I was more than a little surprised when our grade six schoolyard activities were unofficially segregated along racial lines. At times there was virtual warfare between blacks and whites, and since the blacks were greatly outnumbered they usually got the worst of it—despite the fact that, one on one, they were usually superior when it came to physical confrontation. For some reason, even as a child I preferred to side with the underdog. It's tempting to claim that I instantly recognized the stupidity and cruelty of discrimination, but more likely it was the excitement of picking a fight that I knew I would have to work particularly hard to win. And though I call it excitement today, it was more likely fear. Whatever it was, it produced the adrenalin rush I needed to help me survive.

And it helped me make a few friends among the school's black students. This fact soon raised the ire of the white bully in our class. I certainly was not going to be *his* friend. One day, early in the school year, he and his partners in crime saw fit to chase me home after school. Fortunately, I was fast enough to beat them by a respectable margin to my front door. Unfortunately, though, I used the extra time to run upstairs to our apartment, grab my air rifle and take up a firing position just inside our open living room window. When the bully and his buddies appeared, I got off a few shots at their lower extremities before they beat a hasty retreat screaming something about seeing me the next day. In the fear of the moment, I'd forgotten that I wouldn't be able to avoid meeting them at school for the next year or so.

I didn't sleep that night. I knew I had bitten off more than I could possibly chew and that I might live to regret it (if I lived). I considered running away, but the proximity of the police station was intimidating enough to keep me inside. The next morning I put on my sneakers, in case speed might be necessary to contribute to my survival, and headed off to school. (At the time, I thought I was sick to my stomach from fear; now, having experienced a similar sensation hundreds of times during my adult life, particularly while being shot at or in the cockpit of a race car just before the flag drops, I realize that it is merely a good dose of adrenalin working its way through my body to help me cope with a situation I should never have gotten myself into!)

When I arrived at school the next morning, I was approached by the bully's delegation and advised that a fight had been scheduled for 3 PM that afternoon in an alley just across the street from the our schoolyard. I spent the entire day contemplating my fate. Being new to the school, I didn't have a lot of folks aligning themselves with me, although I did receive words of encouragement from some of my black classmates. It seemed that 3 PM arrived much earlier than usual that day, and I made my way into the crowded alley. I saw that the bully and his ever-increasing gaggle of supporters were blocking the far exit, so I made the slow walk towards them—it was like a scene out of the movie *High Noon*. I didn't know anything about boxing, but my country upbringing had prepared me to wrestle all day if need be, and I understood the importance of surprise. Twenty feet from the bully, I broke into a sprint and let out a scream. Convinced that I had gone mad, he stood there (frozen with fear?) until my leap was complete, and I knocked him to the ground. I wrapped my right arm around his neck and proceeded to squeeze, hard. About thirty seconds later, when his resistance had all but disappeared and his gallery of supporters were looking more than a little concerned, I asked him if he wanted to give up. I interpreted his bulging eyes and his barely audible moan to be a yes, and I relaxed my hold. It was all over. I had survived the first of many ill-conceived confrontations.

During the days immediately following this minor schoolyard showdown, a few of my black friends invited me to their neighbourhood, located on the hill at the south end of Young Street. I had heard some white folks refer to the area as "Nigger Hill," and I was told by the same people that no white kid ever went there. You can appreciate my surprise when I discovered the friendliest neighbourhood in town: there was an open space at the top of the hill, and in the winter the residents created a natural skating pond where I was told I would be welcome come first freeze-up. It was always a source of pride to me that I was welcomed there.

I made a lot of friends at school after that ridiculous fight, so I was more than a little disappointed when my mother told me that Dad had called and we were to join him in Vedder Crossing, British Columbia, as soon as my school year was finished. But I have to admit that the thought of a train trip of some three thousand miles from one coast to the other was enticing, to say the least.

During the glory days of Canadian rail travel, you could board a train on one side of the continent and not get off until you arrived at the other side. In between, you were coddled by a dedicated and efficient staff while being treated to a moving panorama of the second-largest country in the world and geographically one of the most diverse. Long stretches of wilderness were interrupted by tiny settlements where it seemed everyone, regardless of age, waved at the passing train. Since they'd taken the trouble to do so, I felt an obligation to wave back at every one of them. As a result, I spent most of my time glued to the window, awaiting the next sign of civilization and the next friendly greeting. My mother and sister merely watched the unfolding canvas of colours and shapes, oblivious to my higher calling as the train's designated waver.

When the trans-Canada trains reached the West, there were two routes available through the Rocky Mountains. As a rule, Canadian National took the northern option, which entered the mountains at Jasper, while Canadian Pacific opted for the southern route, which had Banff as its entry point. I presume we were on Canadian National, because just before experiencing one of the most traumatic moments of my young life I remember seeing a sign on the railway station announcing "Jasper, Alberta."

My mother loved ice cream, particularly in a cone. It was not available in that form on the train, so when she saw a sign above one of the doors on the train station that exclaimed "Double scoop 5 cents!" the temptation was overwhelming. Our conductor had told us there would be a ten-minute stop and that we were welcome to get off and stretch our legs if we were so inclined. I was given fifteen cents and told to bring back cones for the three of us, and not to dawdle as I only had a short time. I rushed into the station. There was only one person in front of me, and he was being served. So far, so good. Within no more than five minutes, I had my three cones and rushed out the door—to an empty siding. Our train was gone!

I looked up the track, expecting to see a trail of smoke disappearing into the mountains. Nothing. I looked back down the track. Empty! It didn't take me long to conclude that I'd been abandoned, perhaps intentionally. A quick check of my surroundings was not encouraging. In 1952, Jasper was, to put it mildly, isolated. The train station was tiny and there was no living body in sight, though I presumed the ice cream man was still inside. I knew I was in Alberta, but that didn't do me a lot of good because I was not sure where Alberta was in relation to where I was headed. And I was completely broke. So I started to eat the ice cream cones as fast as I could, before they melted, assuming that this might be my last meal—ever.

As I was finishing the third cone, I heard a noise to my left, coming from down the track. Lo and behold, a train was slowly approaching. As it pulled into the station, I desperately scanned the windows, looking for a familiar face, but I was not convinced that it was in fact "my" train. Then, to my considerable relief, I saw two females frantically gesturing from the other side of their window. Both my mother and my sister looked panic-stricken—until they saw my pitiful face, covered with ice cream, and they started to laugh. I was not amused.

My mother told me that moments after I jumped off the train, it had started to back down the track. Mum had accosted the poor conductor, reminding him that he'd said we would be stopped for ten minutes and advising him in no uncertain terms that her son was still in the station. He reassured her that they were merely going to a siding for a few minutes to change tracks and that they would soon return to the station. Mum never let me off the train again until we reached our destination of Chilliwack the next day.

Military housing was, and continues to be, a problem for the Canadian Forces. Today it is generally inferior to equivalent civilian homes, which should come as no surprise, considering that most of them were constructed in the 1940s and '50s. Since that time, a conservative estimate would suggest that the rent collected from their military occupants has paid for each and every building at least fifteen times over. Not one cent of that rent has gone back into maintenance; rather, it has found its way into successive governments' general revenues, with the predictable result that military housing has not kept pace with that in the surrounding civilian communities.

In the 1950s, the problem was somewhat different. Permanent married quarters (PMQS) were allocated geographically by rank. Senior officers—that is, all ranks of major and above—were in one area, while junior officers were in another. Non-commissioned ranks were segregated as well, with privates (sappers, in the case of the military engineers) and corporals in one area, sergeants and staff sergeants in another, and warrant officers first and second class in yet another. It was expected that each rank group would socialize only among themselves, and that unofficial rule applied to families as well. Consequently, promotion caused a good deal of friction, particularly for the kids, as they were expected to change their friends when their father was elevated in rank.

The military also dictated the maintenance of these temporary homes. For example, they mandated when the grass had to be cut and what type of fence could be erected. This was all too much for my father, so we rented a small cottage in the beautiful summer resort settlement of Cultus Lake, a few miles from my dad's military base at Vedder Crossing and inside a B.C. provincial park. The village's population was about four hundred during the winter, but as soon as the good weather arrived, the number exploded to five times that. Every year, folks from Vancouver and smaller urban areas swarmed to their summer homes beside one of the most beautiful lakes in Canada. I thought I'd died and gone to heaven.

Starting with junior high school, kids from Cultus Lake and the other settlements in the area had to take a bus to one of two schools in Chilliwack. Since we had arrived three weeks after the school year had begun, I was more than a little intimidated on my first day of classes. On the positive side, I was taller than most of the other grade seven students—most of the grade eights, too, for that matter—and this gave me a degree of false self-confidence.

On my very first day at school, I dug myself a hole that would take me months to get out of. Halfway through my class, a plane flew over our school at a very low altitude. It sounded like it was going to come through the building, and at the peak of its engine roar, and thinking of Miss Bruce-Payne and the Blitz, I yelled: "Everyone down! The Germans are bombing!" I thought it was funny, but absolutely no one joined me in my laughter. Then I felt a sharp pain in my ear as the teacher, Miss Shaver, grabbed me by the lobe and marched me to the principal's office. Miss Shaver went inside and spent a few short minutes with the principal. The door opened, and I was gestured inside.

What ensued was a one-way conversation that enlightened me to the fact that the majority of the farming population in the Chilliwack area were immigrants from Germany, some of whom had arrived before the war and others after. They were hard-working, dedicated new Canadian citizens, and I had just insulted them and at least half of my classmates. Today I might be quick enough to say that I meant to yell, that "the Nazis " rather than "the Germans" were bombing us, but back then all I could do was live with the mortification.

Being the new guy, and naive as well, I fell into the trap of confusing popularity with success. I quickly became the class clown and played to an audience of my peers. Miss Shaver was very perceptive, and at the end of our first term, to the horror of my parents, she probably described me better than any other teacher did during the next four years: "Lewis is a disrupting influence in the classroom. With his capabilities of leadership, he should be setting a much better example. He has a keen mind and an enthusiastic attitude, but he does not realize that for success in the future he must build a good foundation today. He wastes time. Lewis must also develop self-control. He allows his enthusiasm to control his actions. Certain formalities are required in a classroom, and until Lewis realizes this and settles down to work, of which he is capable, he will not achieve the results of which he is capable. Perhaps because he started school late this term and came from a different province he has felt that popularity is most important. However, next term I expect much better from Lewis." Miss Shaver didn't pull her punches.

If anything can be credited with dragging me off the path of self-destruction in school, it was team sports. In Princeport, the closest thing to organized sport was the annual egg-and-spoon race at the school picnic. Truro was not much better, except for the foot races to and from the bullies at school. Chilliwack, though, was different. The area was known for its sports teams, with soccer, basketball, volleyball and baseball at the head of the list. Hockey was on the horizon, too: the civic motto "Let's skate in '58" optimistically predicted the construction of an ice arena. When I left Chilliwack in 1956, the cry had changed to "Let's try again in '67," so I never did get a chance to engage in the national pastime.

The second week into my stint at Chilliwack Junior High, all the students were gathered together in the gym to be selected for the various intramural sports teams. I had never played any of the sports then being organized, but since I was one of the tallest students in the crowd I was chosen in the first round for one of the basketball teams. When I explained to the team captain that I had never held a basketball, let alone played the game, he replied: "Look, Lewis, you see that key-shaped area painted on the floor in front of each basket? Just park yourself in there for three seconds at a time, and when we get the ball to you, put it in the basket. That's all there is to it!" I took his advice, and during our first game I scored all our points—and we won! Almost immediately it began to dawn on me that, rightly or wrongly, popularity was somehow linked to athletic ability. Fellow students treated you differently; even teachers were friendlier, and your group in the schoolyard during breaks was bigger. Unfortunately, this increased attention had its downside as well: there was a tendency for the jocks to rule the roost, and many people must have thought we were a royal pain in the butt. At the time, though, it was a great way to fit in. I ended up playing all the major sports and became the captain of most of our teams. If anything, athletic success came too easily for me. Without trying too hard, I could perform well enough to be on the school teams. It would take a few years before the game would become more important to me than the hype and attention it brought my way.

Even at that early age, it seemed to me that there was an obvious link between athletic ability and leadership. This is not to say that every good athlete is a good leader, or that every good leader must have athletic ability. However, if the leader is good at team sports in particular, this gives him or her an advantage in motivating subordinates. This is particularly true in the military, where the Profession of Arms is a form of extreme competition with potentially deadly results when played for real. Recent research has shown a direct correlation between effective leadership and two disparate activities: the study of philosophy and team-sport athletic ability. I can't say I'm surprised.

My four years in Cultus Lake, when I was between the ages of twelve and sixteen, were memorable, to say the least. But I wouldn't be surprised if every older adult thinks of that period as something really special. What made Cultus Lake different from the other places I'd lived in were its summers, when all that decadence arrived from the big city of Vancouver—at least I thought it was decadence, and revelled in the thought.

There was no shortage of summertime employment there, and I worked during the daylight hours as an assistant lifeguard and at night as a skate cop at the local roller-skating rink. Both jobs brought me into daily contact with the 1950s version of the rich (anyone with a car) and famous (anyone we recognized who did not live in our community). Both jobs paid a dollar an hour, plus tips at the roller rink, which probably provided me with my life-time-high discretionary purchasing power. I spent it on all the right things—girls, movies, junk food, bootleg liquor and gas for my older friends' cars.

The only machine I'd operated before moving west was a neighbour's tractor in Princeport, when I must have been no more than ten years old. I enjoyed the sensation of covering rela-tively long distances without any physical effort. Since I had to walk at least a mile to see any of my friends in the village, the idea of driving from point A to point B was particularly appeal-ing. Thanks to the tutelage of my new brother-in-law, Donnie Chisholm—who'd left Old Barns outside of Truro, joined us in Cultus Lake and married my sister shortly after his arrival—I was a pretty good baseball pitcher. Following a couple of no-hit-ters in the Chilliwack's under-sixteen league, I was invited to play for an under-twenty-one team in which virtually all my teammates had their own cars or drove their father's. A couple of the more adventurous players let me drive their cars away from the main roads. It was not long before I was bitten by the automobile bug.

In 1954, we had a tiny 1949 four-cylinder Ford Anglia for family transport. Today that car's body is a popular choice for motor-sport enthusiasts to wrap around a 1,000-horsepower engine on their way to the drag strip. Unfortunately, ours had 975 fewer horses and struggled up some of the hills between Chilliwack and Cultus Lake. To me, however, this represented a learning opportunity—as long as I was prepared to accept some risk. My father always attended happy hour on Friday nights and usually got home around 8 PM. He would have a quick nap and then, once a month, my mother would accompany him back to the Sergeants' Mess at the military camp in Vedder Crossing, some three miles away. They would go with a friend or by taxi because my mother didn't like to operate any car with a manual transmission and Dad knew he would be in no condition to drive later that night.

One day, as soon as they had left, I found the keys to the Anglia and eased it onto one of the many dirt trails that ran through the woods just behind Cultus Lake's built-up area. This first attempt was a disaster: every friend's car I had driven so far had an automatic transmission, and I obviously had not paid enough attention to what my father had done behind the wheel with a manual gearbox. I attempted to sneak out of the neighbourhood without being seen or heard, keeping the car lights turned off, but the crashing and grinding of gears foiled my clandestine efforts. Our neighbours peered from their windows to see where the hellish grinding noise was coming from, but fortunately, the back alley where Dad had parked the car was pitch black, so no one recognized me. Not that it would have made any difference; I was overcome with the euphoria of "flying solo" and was committed to making it to the trail through the woods, a mere hundred yards and multiple missed shifts away.

I was not deterred by this first solo fight, and at least once a month thereafter I'd head out to the woods. After an hour or so of negotiating the forest trails, I would make my way back to our lane. Because it was slightly downhill, I'd push the car to our back door. Usually the temptation to venture out in the car again would get the best of me, and I would repeat the process two or three more times the same evening. The Anglia didn't use much gas, but with all the miles I was putting on it I started to hide a container in the woods adjacent to the soccer field, directly opposite the only gas station in the village. I would park the car at the far end of the field, in the dark, and top up the tank to its original level after each foray. I guess Dad didn't keep a close eye on the mileage because he never seemed to notice that once a month there was a significant increase in the Anglia's odometer reading.

On my sixteenth birthday I was standing in front of the Chilliwack Driver's Licence Bureau—a good hour before opening time. And an hour after opening time, a written and driving test later, I was on my way to a life of increased mobility.

A few weeks later my father was assigned to Fort Belvoir, south of Washington, D.C., for a one-month course with the United States Army Corps of Engineers, and he left the Anglia in my hands for safekeeping(!). Whenever bad weather closed down the swimming dock and the roller rink, I would take off in the car and cruise the main highway outside of Chilliwack for hitchhikers. I would pick up the first person or couple with their thumb out. They would ask, "Where are you going?" and I would respond, "Where are you going?" The reply was invariably "Vancouver," some sixty miles away, and I would say, to the hiker's delight: "I'll take you!" Frequently I made the return trip without a passenger, but fortunately for my dad, when I did pick up someone leaving the city, no one ever said "Winnipeg" or "Toronto"!

At the age of thirteen I had lied about my age and joined the Air Cadets, primarily because quite a few of my friends were already members of the local squadron in Chilliwack. Each summer we went off to camp at the Abbotsford air base, just twenty miles down the road towards Vancouver. The highlight of the month was a flight in a twin-engine Expeditor on a flight plan that always took us over Cultus Lake. By the time my third camp rolled around, I was appointed the NCO in charge of the British Columbia contingent—an appointment I held for about six hours. An overly keen staff officer did some quick calculations and determined that if I was fifteen then, for me to have two previous camps under my belt I must have lied about my age when joining the cadets two years earlier. I was immediately relieved of my first command.

Soon after that third summer camp I left the Air Cadets, lied about my age again, and joined the town's militia unit, a squadron of the Royal Canadian Engineers. I was now wearing the same uniform as my father, and following my first parade I was promoted to lance-corporal! I wish I could say that my rapid advancement to the first rung on the leadership ladder was the result of demonstrating skills in that regard, but I have to admit that it was strictly due to my height. The unit was scheduled to compete in a militia drill competition to be held in Vancouver in two months, and during my first night with the unit I was assigned to the team. As the tallest member I had to be the "right marker"—that is, the individual the other team members align themselves with when they form up—and the right marker had to be a lance-corporal, in accordance with the rules of the competition. During my next thirty-seven years in Her Majesty's uniform, the criteria for subsequent promotions would prove to be somewhat more demanding.

During my four years in the Chilliwack area, I witnessed racism directed against yet another segment of Canadian society. In Truro, the victim was the black community; in Chilliwack, it was the Native population. There was a reserve (today the progressive Soowahlie First Nation) between Cultus Lake and

Vedder Crossing, and every morning our bus picked up Native students at the reserve stop on the main highway on the way to school. Although there was no open hostility to the Natives, sarcasm directed their way clearly separated us into two distinct groups. The segregation was more evident when we got to the school, with its relatively large urban population. The self-imposed segregation and derogatory comments came from a small group of ignorant underachievers. Nevertheless, the way they treated the Native students reminded me of my year in Truro. Making friends with the Native students seemed like a good idea.

One of them, Leonard Fisher, was better than I was in just about every sport we played, and the two of us spent hours every day practising one or two sports, depending on the season. We became close friends. I became welcome on the reserve and, thanks to Leonard, played a few games as goalie for the Tzeachten all-Indian team in the Fraser Valley adult soccer league. Leonard and I had a falling-out over some minor issue just before my dad was posted back to Nova Scotia in 1956. It bothered me that we never crossed paths again for over thirty years. In 1993, when I was invited to pay a nostalgia visit to Chilliwack High, I was delighted to see my old friend Leonard looking so well. He had served in the navy for a period, and after he left he took on a cook's position at my dad's old base in Vedder Crossing.

My four years in Cultus Lake were also made enjoyable by teenage romances, each one in its infancy publicly declared to be "the one and only." Being a jock made it easier for me to convince the opposite sex to give me a chance, and my friends and I thought we were pretty cool, jumping from one intense relationship to another. But my final romance in the area was to have a pretty significant influence on my life two years hence. Pat Spears was the daughter of the local ranking RCMP officer in the region. Pat was tall, slim, beautiful, athletic, smart—and uninterested in me. I was of course determined to change her mind, but in the midst of my campaign Dad advised us that he was being posted to Halifax and that we would be leaving in two weeks. I was devastated. I had never seriously considered moving anywhere again until it was time for me to leave home for good. So, leaving my friends, in general, and Pat, in particular, three thousand miles behind was a definitely a low point in my life.

On the plus side, my father advised me that we would be driving to Halifax in our new Vauxhall Viva Deluxe. By now, you must be starting to question my father's taste in automobiles. The Vauxhall was maroon in colour, with two massive and totally non-functional chrome strips on each side of the hood; however, it was a new car, and the transmission was undoubtedly in better shape to take on an extended trip than the one I had "christened" in the Anglia. We would traverse the continent by following Route 2, which winds along the top of the northern United States through Washington state, Idaho, Montana, North Dakota, Minnesota, Wisconsin and Michigan. In the northeast corner of Michigan, we would cross over the border to Sault Ste. Marie and carry on through Ontario, Quebec and New Brunswick to Nova Scotia—and according to Dad, I would drive the whole way! I thought I'd died and gone to heaven for a second time.

The trip was surprisingly uneventful, and the Vauxhall's reliability, if not its comfort, exceeded everyone's expectations. I got my fill of driving but never tired of the enjoyment associated with finding my way from one coast to the other. However, what we were to do when we reached our destination was still unclear. There was a possibility that Dad's posting to Halifax would be temporary and that he might be assigned to Sydney, Cape Breton, in a few months. It was decided that Mum and I would bunk in with my sister, who following her marriage to Donnie Chisholm in Cultus Lake had moved to Old Barns, his home near Truro. Dad would commute from Halifax on weekends until his employment was confirmed.

For some obscure reason, kids from Old Barns and the surrounding rural areas attended Brookfield Rural High. Athough Colchester County Academy in Truro was only five miles away, the powers that be decided that those of us in the country would benefit from the fifteen-mile school bus ride to Brookfield. To my considerable surprise, they were right! Brookfield was a village that produced some of the best sports teams in the province and, more than once, in the nation. It was famous for its fastball, baseball and hockey teams, which dominated any league they entered. A good deal of the credit for the teams' success was attributable to the efforts and athletic skills of the local Henderson family. All seven of the Henderson kids were outstanding athletes, as their father had been before them. The son closest to my age was Ned, who on graduation chose a career in the Canadian Forces instead of an offer from the Boston Bruins of the National Hockey League. Ned became one of Canada's all-time top fighter pilots, but tragically he was killed just before he was to be promoted to the rank of general.

Shortly after I started grade eleven in Brookfield, Dad was posted to Sydney, as we had anticipated. I was able to convince my parents to leave me behind at my sister's for a few months so that I could finish the soccer season with our school team. We were leading the Nova Scotia Headmaster's Provincial Championship, and with Ned and me working together as right outside and centre forward, respectively, we were piling up the goals. We went on to win the championship—ironically, against a team from Cape Breton, my new home.

2: Welcome to Cape Breton

"MacKenzie, you score thirty-five points a game for
our basketball team, and we don't care what you are!"
MONSIGNOR MACLENNAN, PRESIDENT, XAVIER JUNIOR COLLEGE

ARRIVING IN THE city of Sydney in the early winter of 1956 was a bit of a shock. It was much larger than any place I had ever lived, and its high school, Sydney Academy, was old, big and intimidating. The city was dominated in more ways than one by its single large business, the DOSCO steel plant, whose smelter constantly spewed an impressive cloud of red iron-ore dust. On some days, if you stood still for too long outdoors you would be blanketed with a thin film of dust, just like everything else was. But after a few days you stopped noticing it—though I doubt that the same could be said for the folks who actually worked at the coke ovens.

My parents rented a small apartment only a stone's throw from the school, and I started the second term of grade eleven. It was immediately obvious that this school was different from the ones I was familiar with. The student body seemed to be segregated into more self-created groups. They didn't qualify as gangs, in the current pejorative meaning of the term, but there was definitely a pecking order. Fortunately, it was relatively easy for me to fit in because the basketball season was just starting, and the skills I'd learned in Chillwack allowed me to hold my own with the best players.

There was so much new and enjoyable for me to do in Sydney that I studied only enough to get by. I have to say that the superior performance of the teachers at Brookfield during my first term in grade eleven prepared me very well for the rest of the school year. So, in spite of the seductions of city life, I managed to maintain a good grade average.

Some three decades later, when I worked for a year in the military's personnel directorate, I was concerned about the absence of "roots" for soldiers' kids as a result of their families' constant moves. The sons and daughters of Canadian Forces personnel undergo more turbulence and disruption while pursuing their education than any other group I can think of. My challenge of dealing with a mere five schools was modest compared with the number of schools that soldiers' kids have to deal with today. For example, my daughter Kimm attended eight schools in four countries and three provinces, and her experience was, regrettably, closer to the current norm. Our Personnel Directorate conducted some surveys and discovered that for the rest of their lives, the majority of soldiers' kids call the place where they went to high school "home." I can relate to these results, because the friends I made in Sydney in the three years I was there were as close as any I made over the next forty-five years.

One of those friends in my group was Gerry MacNeil, tall, slim and a gifted athlete. He was the academy's "girl magnet," so he was a good guy to know: the spillover effect ensured that all his friends had dates. He and I were forwards on the basketball team and usually accounted for most of the points our team scored.

Gerry spent a career with the Department of Indian Affairs and Northern Development, ultimately retiring in Ottawa.

Leo Wall was the character of our group. Blessed with tight-curly blond hair and an infectious smile, Leo was totally unpredictable and got us into more hot water with authorities than we thought was possible. Leo wasn't a great basketball player, but what he lacked in natural ability he made up for in semi-controlled energy. Not surprisingly, he was much better at hockey. You sure didn't want to get in his way once he reached top speed. Leo later went into teaching and retired in Sydney.

Gordie Morrison was the "grandfather" to us all, in that he was a good two years older than the rest of us. (When you're only sixteen, that's a big gap!) Fortunately, his advanced age brought some much-needed maturity to the group, not that it trumped our Leo-led antics. He also contributed some steadiness on the basketball court and contributed badly needed outside shooting skills. Gordie became a pharmacist, and when I last spoke with him, he was living in Mississauga.

Our "gang" had the (exaggerated) reputation of being the wildest collection of characters, so we worked hard to live up to it. Although our social lives revolved around the basketball schedule, our after-game activities became the genesis of legends. In spite of our tender age, we all drank—some more than others, we were to find out. We were too young to fake our way into the liquor store, so we approached the most popular bootlegger in the part of Sydney known as the Pier. Once we had accumulated enough cash to make the purchase and one of us had convinced his father, usually by using his mother as an intermediary, to give us the family car for the night, we would strike out for the Pier. We would make our purchase, find a back street or park overlooking Sydney's infamous "tar ponds" and commence to drink.

For the first few months of this Friday night routine, we removed the brown paper bag before passing the bottle around. That way, we could see how much each of us consumed—the logic being that no one would take more than his share. The bottle's contents were usually gone in about five minutes. But following one such purchase midway through the school year, someone suggested that we leave the paper bag on the bottle. To our amazement, the bottle was passed around at least twice as many times as usual before it was declared a dead soldier. Obviously, there were some among us who did not want to drink as much as the rest, and with the bag hiding the contents of the bottle we could fake drinking and get away with it. I wish I could report that the person who proposed the change to our routine went on to become a renowned psychologist, but this was not the case. Following the appropriate dose of Dutch courage, we routinely ventured into an unsuspecting Sydney. I'm relieved to report that our exploits never harmed anyone outside our own group.

There are very few unbending straight segments of highway in Cape Breton. One of the longest is a one-mile straightaway, dubbed the Yazar Stretch, on the main highway between Sydney and the town of Louisbourg, some eighteen miles down the coast and, since 1960, the site of the megaproject that reconstructed the eighteenth-century French fortress. We would regularly drive to the beginning of the stretch and play our own version of "over the top." The rules were simple: As the driver accelerated onto the straight and brought the car to sixty miles per hour, the challenge would be to exit through one rear side window and slide across the roof of the car, re-entering through the window on the opposite side. Getting out of the car and onto the roof was relatively straightforward. Sliding along the roof, however, presented some unique challenges if you were short because you had to release your grip on one side before grasping the other. I, fortunately, was able to maintain at least a one-hand grip during the exercise.

The serious problem arose when re-entering the vehicle. This phase of the undertaking usually occurred when the approaching corner at the end of the straight seemed only a few yards away and was rapidly closing in. This impression, coupled with the all-too-frequent closing of both side windows by the car's occupants just as the hapless victim was attempting to gain entry, elevated the level of hilarity for those safely inside. Cars approaching from the opposite direction flashed their lights as if to tell the driver of our car that he unknowingly had a passenger on the roof. Every-one managed to survive, but a few of us have permanent scars from landing in the ditch on the outside of that corner, fortu-nately a lefthander, at the end of the stretch. Looking back now, I think the patron saint of idiots was watching over us.

We regarded schoolwork as a constant interference in our social lives, but since we needed to maintain decent marks to remain on the academy's sports teams, we all did just enough studying to get by. In spite of coming from another school, and before that, another province, I managed to maintain an eighty-five per cent average with relatively little effort. I was pleased to get by with dedicating so little time to my studies. It was only many, perhaps too many, years later that I realized I'd probably wasted a golden opportunity to grow intellectually. There was certainly no shortage of teachers expressing the common opin-ion: "Lewis, you are not working up to your potential!" But at the time, doing so would have seriously impaired my lifestyle, including my basketball playing.

Our basketball team was loaded with talent, and we were dominating the Cape Breton league. Occasionally we would play a couple of very good adult teams from Sydney and New

Waterford to help elevate the level of our play. They would frequently beat us, but our level of fitness allowed us still to be competitive. Mind you, my first game playing for Sydney Academy provided me with a rude awakening.

Our high school league got off to its start in 1956, with our team making the fifteen-mile trek to Glace Bay to play St. Anne's High. Their school gym was in the lower level of a hall, and as we ran onto the floor to start our warmup, something didn't seem right. But I was unaware of what it was—until I attempted my first layup. The backboards for the baskets were virtually bolted to the wall, with no space for a player to land after taking off for a layup. If you approached the basket in a conventional manner at a running pace, you could find yourself splattered against the wall after releasing the ball. Having learnt the game in British Columbia, which was renowned for its basketball teams, I thought I was pretty hot stuff and proceeded to hot dog it more than was required by the game. Gerry and I worked well together up front, and with Gordie feeding the two of us passes at just the right times, we dominated the game. I was warned by our guys that Cape Breton basketball could be a bit rough, but the few elbows that were thrown my way were no different from what I was used to and I managed to give as good as I got.

When the final whistle had gone, confirming our win by a substantial margin, the spectators came onto the floor. One diminutive lady approached me at a brisk walking pace. I didn't recognize her and assumed that she must be from Glace Bay and wanted to congratulate me on an outstanding game. Turning to face her, I held out my hand to acknowledge her approach. By now she was getting closer to me and accelerating. With one fluid motion, she drew back her right arm—which I now noticed had a death grip on a large leather purse—and swung it, with amazing accuracy, at the side of my head. I could have used a couple of stitches to close the wound, but I opted for tape instead. As it was being applied, I could hear that madwoman screaming as her purse rocketed towards my ear: "Don't you ever elbow my son again, you British Columbia smartass!" As we left for the team bus, Gerry greeted me with: "Welcome to Cape Breton basketball, Lew." And all along, I thought they meant the opposing players would be rough!

After completing grade eleven at the academy, I assumed that come autumn I'd return for grade twelve. Since the next year's education was never a general subject of conversation for me, it came as a surprise midway through the summer when I discovered that most of my friends would be taking their senior matriculation at Xavier Junior College (now Cape Breton University) in Sydney, then an extension of St. Francis Xavier University in Antigonish, on the Nova Scotia mainland. Gerry, Leo and a few others encouraged me to make the move to the college with them. But there were two problems. First, you had to pay tuition to attend the college. At that time it was somewhere close to three hundred dollars, not a small amount for my father, who was probably clearing in the neighbourhood of three hundred dollars a *month*. The second hurdle was more sensitive. At the time, universities in the Maritimes were segregated along religious lines. St. Francis Xavier, and St. Mary's in Halifax, were bastions of Roman Catholic education in Nova Scotia, whereas Acadia in Wolfville appealed to those of the Baptist faith—and so it went on throughout the three Maritime provinces. Xavier Junior College was a Catholic institution and I was a Protestant—not that I knew what that really meant. I had attended the United Church and Sunday school during my early years in Princeport and Cultus Lake, but it never occurred to me that religion would ever influence my education or my choice of friends.

I decided to pursue the Xavier Junior College option and was pleasantly surprised when my family agreed to foot the bill. I had worked during the summer at a local soft-drink bottling plant and had managed to save a few dollars, which would help to offset the significant cost of books on top of the tuition. I submitted my application to the college, very aware that I was applying to enter first-year university only having completed grade eleven. Since Nova Scotia's high school system was completed with grade twelve, unlike the British Columbia school system, which had thirteen grades at the time, many students went directly to first-year university after completing grade eleven. If you stayed in high school and completed grade twelve, you had a good chance of being accepted into second-year university, with the potential to obtain a bachelor's degree in three years.

A few days after I'd dropped off my application, my mother was told by phone that I should report to the college president's office the following day. I called Gerry and Leo to see if they knew what was going on, but they both pleaded ignorance. They did, however, assure me that the president did not make a habit of interviewing students before they got into trouble.

I reported to the president's office ten minutes early, wearing my only tie. At the appointed hour, the door opened and an imposing figure emerged. Dr. Malcolm MacLennan (God rest his soul) was a large man, well over six feet tall, but in spite of his advancing years he moved with the grace of someone who had been a fine athlete in his day. He introduced himself as "Monsignor MacLennan" and motioned me into his office. I approached the seat directly in front of his desk, but I stood there nervously, and could not sit down until he had done so. Our initial conversation was one-sided as Dr. MacLennan asked me about my background and where I had gone to school. He seemed genuinely interested in my family and in where my parents were from. He asked me if I was interested in philosophy, and did I think I would be able to fit in some classes on the subject, in spite of my request to study engineering? When he mentioned the subject of religious classes, I had a sinking feeling in the pit of my stomach: he didn't know that I was not a Catholic. Summoning up all the courage I could, I blurted out, "Of course, Monsignor, you realize I'm Protestant!" Dr. MacLennan looked me squarely in the eye. Without missing a beat, he said: "Young MacKenzie, you score thirty-five points a game for our basketball team, and we don't care what you are!" (Unfortunately, I managed a thirty-five-point game only once in the next two years.) Our conversation then completed, the good president welcomed me to Xavier Junior College and its basketball team.

My old gang from the Academy was still intact, thanks to basketball, and we still had an exaggerated (in our minds) reputation to uphold. In October 1957, the Soviet Union launched *Sputnik,* the world's first orbiting satellite. Its passage overhead was clearly visible during the hours of darkness, providing the weather co-operated. Following one of our Friday brown-bag starts to the weekend, someone suggested that we would get a clearer view of the satellite if we observed it from the highest spot in town. We decided that this ideal location would be the top of the local TV broadcasting tower, which was located on a prominent hill in the south end of the city.

When we arrived at the base of the tower, we began to question the wisdom of our plan. The tower was twelve feet in diameter at its thickest point, about fifteen feet above ground level. From that point, unfortunately, it tapered to a relatively narrow point, where it embraced a massive ball bearing, which in turn rested on a ground-based fitting. We decided that the purpose of the bearing was to let the three-hundred-foot tower sway a certain amount with the wind, thereby reducing the stress on the entire structure. This might have been good engineering, but it made reaching the first leg of the attached steel ladder a little difficult. Ingenuity prevailed, and I found my way up to the bottom rung via the backs of a slightly unsteady human pyramid.

Flashback extract from Miss Shaver's grade seven second-term report card, dated March 28, 1953: "Lewis has a tendency to show off." Mid-way to the top, I realized that this engineering marvel was extremely compliant with the wind, swaying back and forth, and that if I wasn't careful I would suffer from motion sickness. Physics dictated that the swings became greater the closer I got to the three red lights mounted on the tower's summit. I picked out a star in the night sky and kept my eyes focused on that one spot in the universe, ignoring the slurred words of direction and encouragement emanating from below. It helped.

Somewhere near the summit, I sobered up. My timing was not great. Whenever you steeplejacked, even during the 1940s, volumes of safety regulations dictated that you must wear the right kit with a safety line as a first priority. It was a little late to do anything about it at this stage, so with a death grip on the metal ladder I decided to wait for *Sputnik* to appear. Fortunately it was not long appearing, and it was worth the effort.

The night was clear, and the Soviets' winning entry in the space race flashed its way yet again across the sky, to the great consternation of the Free World. Nevertheless, for a few minutes on that tower, I marvelled at the sight of something man-made circling our planet at inconceivable heights. Ten minutes and a pair of sore arms later, I was back on solid ground with my friends—and I was the only sober one in the bunch.

Meanwhile, back on earth and with my feet planted firmly on the ground, I selected an engineering major for my first year at the college. My best marks in grade eleven had been in science and math, and—you guessed it—most of my friends were going into engineering. I suppose we thought we could excel with a minimum of effort. As the year progressed, everyone started to make plans for the summer. Obtaining good, worthwhile summer employment was, and still is, by all accounts, a challenge for most college students. A few of my friends had joined the Canadian Officer Training Corps (COTC), whose mission was to produce army officers for the militia. During the academic year there were only a few training nights dealing with subjects like military law, tradition, organization and so on. The real treat came during summer break when you went off to your chosen corps for almost three full months of concentrated officer training before returning for the next academic year—and you got paid for it!

When I scanned the list of the available corps and the location of their schools, I couldn't believe my good fortune. If I selected the Corps of Royal Canadian Engineers and was accepted, they would send me to Vedder Crossing, my dad's old camp in British Columbia. And, no less important, I would be five miles from Chilliwack and the love of my life from grade ten, Pat Spears. I signed on the dotted line and became the lowest form of humanity in the army, next to second lieutenant: an officer cadet.

Even I was surprised, because I had never been a big fan of the military. During my school years in Chilliwack, I had seen only one side of a soldier's life, and even that view was restricted to the activities of those who ventured into town on paydays. They normally made the return trip on the last bus, as did I on my way to Cultus Lake, and more often than not they were well and truly pissed. The fact that they didn't represent the majority or that perhaps they had earned the right to blow off some steam before being shipped off to Korea never entered my mind.

My opinion of the military had been eroded even more while attending Chilliwack High. The military camp's soldiers, particularly the sapper apprentices, who were school-age soldiers training for full-time employment in the regular army when they were of age, were our competitors for the affections of the local girls. It wasn't a fair fight; it all boiled down to the fact that they had money, limited as it was, and we did not. Frequently the school's public address system would blare: "A dance will be held at the military camp this Friday evening. Any girls who wish to attend, please leave your name at the office. Transportation will be provided, and it will leave the gym's front entrance at 7 PM on Friday. Have a good time!"

On hearing this announcement, every red-blooded male student felt like he had been run over by a truck. Without an opportunity to offer even token resistance, our dates for the weekend had been enticed from our poverty-stricken grasp. Worse, they would disappear behind the enemy's gate to suffer, in our minds, untold indignities.

On the positive side, the soldier's apprentices came to our rescue more than once. Cultus Lake, one of the more popular summer destinations in the Vancouver area, was a magnet for all kinds of unsavoury characters. At the head of the line was a large and despicable Vancouver motorcycle gang that invaded Cultus Lake at least twice a year. For twenty-four hours they would pin down the small local police detachments, block the highway in and out of the town, and terrorize tourists and locals alike. Once the word had gone out that a large police contingent was on the way, these tough guys would put their tails between their legs and slink back to the city. Most of them, like their brethren in terrorist organizations, were cowards. Nevertheless there is nothing more ruthless than a bunch of cowards targeting a defenceless victim.

We were no match for this collection of rejects, but as our intelligence gathering improved and the jungle drums told us the goons were about to visit us again, we passed the word to the sapper apprentices down the road at the army camp. With the unofficial concurrence of the camp commander, scores of soldiers—easily distinguishable by their short-cropped hair— would show up and blend into the weekend influx of tourists. The motorcyclists would roar into Cultus Lake, and within minutes one or more of them would be involved in a confrontation with a tourist. By then, a contingent of soldiers would have violently removed the gang's roadblock and would have established their own about a mile down the sole road leading from Cultus Lake, sealing off the resort. They would gather together in small groups and, with bicycle chains, brass knuckles and web belts, which sported a large metal buckle, proceed to deal a formidable beating to the weekend invaders. Inexplicably, the gang members did not immediately get the message. Each year they would increase their numbers, not realizing that the army had an immediate and relatively inexhaustible source of reserves only minutes away. After a few years of humiliating defeats, the bikers gave up on Cultus Lake and went on to easier pickings. It's probably just as well, because in today's more sensitive environment the local military commander would be court-martialled for allowing his folks to get involved. Pity.

3: Just a Summer Job?

"Mr. MacKenzie, are you the owner of a 1947
Chevrolet, licence number A3849?"

CORPORAL DOWNEY, ON BEHALF OF THE RCMP

MY EARLY INVOLVEMENT with the military had been dictated
more by self-interest than by any great affection or respect for
the institution. I had followed my friends into the Air Cadets and
the militia, and now I had signed up for army officer training just
to get a free trip across the country to see an elusive girlfriend—
not exactly in the same league as God, Queen and country, as far
as motivation goes. Whoever said that God doesn't have a sense
of humour never studied the backgrounds of soldiers before they
walked through the front door of the recruiting office. A good
number of us arrived by very circuitous routes.

Fortunately my friend Gerry had also signed up, and we
made the trip out west together. Despite my father having served
at the Royal Canadian School of Military Engineering (RCSME) in
Vedder Crossing for more than four years, I had rarely ventured
through the front gate of the camp. My first impression was one
of absolute cleanliness and efficiency. The camp being the school

for army engineering, there was no shortage of expertise when it came to beautifying it, and the result was truly impressive. The grass was manicured, the roads were spotless and every building looked like it had just been painted. We were quickly escorted through the main built-up area of the camp to a corner close to the Vedder River and the highway leading to Cultus Lake. The open sandy lot was the site of about thirty sandy-coloured "bell" tents, each of which would accommodate two people. There were whitewashed rocks everywhere, delineating the paths between the tents. The area was separated from the main road by an eight-foot-high plywood fence that had been painted dark green.

Before Gerry and I reported to the base, we had made a quick visit to my old stomping grounds in Cultus Lake. Riding on the bus, as we passed the camp, I noticed that someone had painted "DO NOT FEED THE ANIMALS!" in poorly drawn, large white letters on the tall green fence, which obscured the view of a field packed with two-man tents. The penny dropped, and I realized that my successors in Chilliwack High were probably expressing their opinion of the heredity of this summer's crop of first-year officer cadets. It felt more than a little unusual to be on the other side of the fence—literally.

In any recruit training course it is important to convince a bunch of individuals that their effectiveness is directly proportional to their ability to work as a team. Before anyone can lead, he or she must demonstrate an ability to follow and, in doing so, to support the designated leader and the objectives of the group. There is no place for "doing your own thing." To the uninitiated—this includes the participants themselves in the early stages of their training—the concept can appear rigid and demeaning. Slowly, as the group ceases to resemble a mob and becomes a team capable of conducting the dirtiest job a country can ask of its citizens—to kill on demand in support of a just cause—the participants begin to realize the importance of their individual contribution to the team's success.

To reinforce this concept with the first-year officer cadets, the RCSME organized their training along infantry lines rather than strictly combat engineering skills, which would be taught in the following three summers. The infantry's role provides the best context in which to develop leadership skills as its component building blocks at the lowest levels, ten-man sections and thirty-man platoons, and provide many opportunities for cadets to practise command appointments. The emphasis on infantry skills was in keeping with the Engineer Corps' strongly held view that every engineer is a warrior first and a combat engineer second. Their casualty rate during the two World Wars, the Korean War and recent operations in the Persian Gulf, the Balkans and Afghanistan provides ample proof that they practise what they preach.

Once we learned how to salute and march from one point to another as a group without running into anything or anybody, we moved to the field to begin our infantry training. To help them conduct this training, the engineers had two infantry instructors assigned to the RCSME for that very purpose. Both infanteers were members of the Princess Patricia's Canadian Light Infantry (PPCLI), which most of us knew by the reputation they had earned as a result of their outstanding performance during the Korean War, where their 2nd Battalion was awarded the U.S. Presidential Unit Citation for bravery at the battle of Kapyong. Lieutenant Mel Canfield, the senior instructor, looked and acted the part. With his maroon jump boots, beret and starched khaki "bush clothing," he could have doubled as a recruiting mannequin. His second-in-command was a Korean War vet, Sergeant Major Shaw, known as "Boy" Shaw by his friends because he had been one of the youngest sergeants to serve in Korea. Sergeant Major Shaw was short, burly and gruff, and he was held in complete awe by each of us. Within days of our first encounter, the word circulated that he had walked through the front door of his home in Canada, weeks after he'd been reported killed in action in Korea, wondering what all the fuss was about. It didn't matter that someone had embellished a story based on more than a few half-truths—we were impressed! Assisting Canfield and Shaw was a Corporal Downey of the engineers, who we all agreed was undoubtedly an infanteer at heart, considering his performance. It was a stroke of good fortune that these three individuals would have such a substantial effect on my immediate future.

Our training soon became a blur of marksmanship (shooting), field craft (seeing and not being seen), navigation (map reading), section tactics (ten guys practising together to kill the enemy) and digging and more digging (the safest place to be when under fire is underground). We moved from one training location to another on the run, so those who were not fit on arrival soon caught up or packed it in. During those early days I certainly didn't understand leadership and what it involved, but I remember what impressed me and why I would have gladly followed some individuals and not so willingly some others. Confidence itself was high on the list of the most desirable characteristics. Those instructors who read the script of their lesson plan word for word did themselves no favour. It was hard to trust that someone was professionally competent if he could not lift his eyes from a prepared text. This concern was frequently reinforced during question time if the instructor had difficulty thinking on his feet. On the other hand, instructors like Sergeant Major Shaw and Corporal Downey knew what had to be taught and went out of their way to make the learning process both enjoyable and effective. It was also quite obvious that a

few instructors looked upon their responsibilities as an incon-
venience, to put it mildly. Once the class was over, they would
disappear from sight until the next day. The real leaders, however, would make a serious effort to get to know us and would
fine-tune their efforts to address our weaknesses. Almost forty
years later, I still remember the names of those self-confident
leaders who took the time to treat us like individuals even in the
context of the team. The others, I have long since forgotten.

Unfortunately the summer's training was not without incident. On arrival we were confined to barracks (tents!) for two
weeks, presumably because we were too undisciplined to be
trusted in public. As the Friday of our first liberation approached,
I phoned every girl I had known well during my days at Chilliwack High and pleaded with them to get their dad's car and, at
precisely 7 PM on Friday, to park on the outside of the high green
fence that separated our compound from the main highway. At
the appointed hour, at least twenty of us trainees scrambled over
the fence and dove into the waiting cars. Ten minutes later, we
arrived at Cultus Lake and arranged the boy-girl pairing. Since
only a dozen girls had showed up, some of our colleagues went
off to the roller rink to try their luck. The couples stayed with
the cars and embarked on a summer of romance restricted to
infrequent days off, the quality of our liaisons more than com-
pensating for quantity.

But this desire to squeeze every ounce of enjoyment from
our free time almost ended my career before it started when
Gerry and I determined within the first twenty-four hours of
our initial forty-eight-hour pass that we had to have a car to
take maximum advantage of the local social opportunities. We
recruited two other trainees to invest in the $250 down pay-
ment, and purchased a 1947 straight-six, four-door Chevy with
a vacuum-operated clutch and a column-mounted three-speed

transmission—in my name! Payments were $90 a month, but since we never actually made a monthly payment, the amount was academic. The Chevy logged over four thousand miles during the next three months and never let us down. We couldn't afford auto insurance, so in accordance with military directives we had to park the vehicle outside the camp.

During the last week of its summer training, our troop spent most of its time on the main parade square, under the direction of Corporal Downey, rehearsing for our graduation parade. Midway through the week, we had just reformed on the square after a five-minute break when I noticed a police car with RCMP markings slowly drive by directly in front of us. Less than a minute later it returned and stopped, and two police officers, accompanied by a military policeman, got out and approached the parade square. Corporal Downey was facing us, with his back to the officers; however, everyone in the troop was staring straight ahead, watching the drama unfold. It was at least a minute before Corporal Downey turned and noticed the three spectators. He gave us the commands "Stand at ease—stand easy," and marched off in the direction of the police. From our vantage point, we could see an animated conversation taking place, with more than a few gestures in our direction. After a few minutes of suspense, Corporal Downey turned, faced us and bellowed: "Mr. MacKenzie, front and centre on the double!" I responded with "Corporal!" and took off in his direction, arriving a few seconds later. Standing rigidly at attention, I wondered if someone in my family had died or been seriously injured. My curiosity was immediately satisfied. The RCMP corporal asked, "Mr. MacKenzie, are you the owner of a 1947 Chevrolet, licence number A3849?"

It seems the owner of the used car lot from whom we (I!) had purchased the car was a little upset that he had yet to receive a monthly payment, some two and a half months after the deal had been consummated. Fortunately for me, the survival of the local business community depended on maintaining good relations with the RCSME. The lot owner merely wanted his car back. Recognizing my good luck, I was quick to agree and returned to the troop praying that my uniform trousers concealed my shaking knees.

You may be wondering what transpired between me and Pat Spears, the original object of my affection and the reason I joined the army officers training corps in the first place. When I arrived in the Chilliwack area that summer, I discovered that the judges of the Fraser Valley Apple Blossom Festival, displaying eminent good taste, had chosen Pat as their queen for 1958. I managed to accompany her to a few events, and each time we would be introduced as "Ladies and Gentlemen, Miss Apple Blossom Festival Pat Spears—and escort!" The events were pretty staid, and obviously Pat had to be on her best behaviour—which was, frankly, in conflict with my own priorities. Gradually we saw less and less of each other, and I never had a chance to thank her for providing me with the impetus to join the army. Hopefully I just have.

Following our graduation parade, I was called to the office of Captain Mills, the commandant of all cadets undergoing their first summer of training. I had seen him only a couple of times from a distance, and he seemed to go out of his way to avoid me. On my entering his office, he motioned me to sit down. A smile crept across his face, and then he spoke: "Lewis, you might not know this, but your father and I are good friends. I was commissioned from the ranks a few years ago, and before that I was a sergeant major working with your dad during the time you were going to high school in Chilliwack. I even remember you pitching the odd game for our sapper apprentice baseball team. I didn't want to make the fact that I knew your dad obvious to

your fellow cadets because it might have made things more difficult for you. I want to tell you that you have done very well this
summer, particularly during the leadership assignments. You
should give serious consideration to transferring to the Regular
Officer Training Plan (ROTP), which will qualify you for commissioned service in the regular army. Your university education
will be paid for, and you will be paid a few bucks every month
for spending money. You can remain at Xavier Junior College for
now and go to St. Francis Xavier in due course. You would return
here next year for second-phase officer training and start learning how to be a combat engineer officer." I asked, "What will
next summer's training involve?" Immediately he responded,
"Lots of bridge building, road construction, demolitions, things
like that."

Now I was really confused. The idea of free education with
some spending money as a bonus was more than a little attractive, and although I did not intend to join the regular army on
graduation I naively assumed that I could always leave the university training plan whenever I wanted. The problem was the
engineers. I had been a lance-corporal in the Royal Canadian
Engineers militia squadron in Chilliwack a few years earlier. I
had attended a summer concentration in Wainwright, Alberta,
and built so many temporary bridges that we actually built one
blindfolded, to mimic doing it in the dark, as part of an engineer
competition. It was all good fun and challenging, but compared
with the almost three months of infantry that we had just completed it seemed a little tame. Lieutenant Canfield and Sergeant
Major Shaw had not only trained me, they had also inspired
me. If the purpose of an army was to fight, those two were the
type of leaders I would follow—not to ignore the fact that they
also looked the part, with their airborne regalia. With a good

deal of trepidation I responded, "Captain Mills, I really enjoyed my summer here and I'd like to apply to ROTP. But I'm not sure about becoming an engineer officer. My highest marks this summer were in all the infantry subjects, and I really enjoyed all the leadership roles, especially patrolling. Doesn't that mean I should give serious consideration to transferring to the infantry?" Captain Mills stared at me, smiled and nodded slowly. "You're probably right. Your father will never forgive me!"

Soon after my return to Sydney, I reported for an interview to apply for ROTP infantry. The word on the street suggested that current affairs were an obsession with all the interviewers, so I read the daily paper from cover to cover for a week before my appointment. No more than ten seconds after the interview began, the captain from the recruiting depot in Halifax asked me what I thought about the Marshall Plan—did I think it was a good idea? I didn't have a clue what the Marshall Plan was, but he had asked me for my opinion. I had at least a fifty-fifty chance of hitting the right answer—if there was one. I blurted out something like "I know there's a good deal of controversy about it, but I'm in favour of what it is trying to do." The captain knew I was tap dancing, and he put me out of my misery by dedicating the remaining time to determining why I wanted to join the infantry.

Three weeks later, my ROTP acceptance certificate arrived in the mail, along with my first cheque, for $69—a princely sum for a destitute college student. As Captain Mills had foretold, my father was not impressed with my transfer to the infantry and, with his tongue firmly implanted in his cheek, referred to my decision as "going slumming!" But what the hell, it was Friday, so Gerry, Leo and I went off to the bootleggers' in the Pier and subsequently celebrated our newfound wealth.

Now that I had transferred to the infantry, there was no compelling reason to continue with the study of engineering. To my surprise, I discovered that I preferred college subjects like logic, philosophy, history and even English to my old high school favourites of math and science. The fact that it took less effort to do well in these non-technical subjects probably had more than a little to do with my decision the next year to transfer to the arts program.

Years later, while serving in Germany with Canada's NATO contingent I shared a table with Albert Speer, Hitler's minister of wartime production.* As the only defendant at the Nuremberg Trials to admit to his share of guilt in the crimes of the Third Reich, Speer had been sentenced to twenty years in Berlin's Spandau jail. He was released in 1966. Some ten years later, the Canadian high school in Lahr, West Germany, which looked after the education of our children, invited Speer to speak to the student body. I was invited to the dinner that concluded the evening. I found it more than a little humorous when Speer was asked by a very confident grade eleven student: "Mr. Speer, how could a group of talented people like yourself be convinced to follow a madman like Hitler?"

Speer was quiet for a few seconds, giving the impression he had never been asked the question before. Then he responded, "Young lady, probably because we were all trained as engineers! We were pragmatic to the extreme, and we thought every problem could be solved by an equation or by adjusting the numbers. Not one of us had any education in the humanities—even Hitler fancied himself an architect, in spite of his lack of formal training. While serving twenty years behind Spandau's walls

---

* When I was introduced as the executive assistant to the commander of Canadian Forces in Europe, Speer looked me in the eye and said: "Hmmm, interesting. Executive assistants are dangerous. I remember Martin Bormann."

I constantly studied the humanities, and I'm convinced that if a few of us in Hitler's inner circle had been so educated at the time, we could have made a positive difference."

It was nice to have some justification, albeit from an infamous source, for my questionable decision seventeen years earlier.

4: The School of Foot

"Washing and defecating within a few feet of each other may seem bizarre, but to the infanteer it is often par for the course."

THE FOLLOWING SUMMER, in 1959, I made the train journey to Barrie, Ontario, where I and many others were met by a three-ton truck with ample room in the back for us and our kit. I had no idea that this would be one of my last rides for the next three months, and that by the end of the summer a similar ride would seem like a holiday trip in a Rolls-Royce. We were about to report to the School of Infantry, or as it was more appropriately described by its students, "the school of foot."

Camp Borden, ten miles west of Barrie, was an important training centre for the army, and to a lesser degree the air force, for most of the twentieth century. At the time it was home to the Armoured Corps School and the School of Infantry, as well as some service support schools—the Royal Canadian Service Corps School being the largest of them. Adjacent to the camp's built-up area was the field training area, which closely resembled a massive sandbox. In areas where the topsoil had been removed by the frequent passage of tracked armoured vehicles, large sandy patches dotted the landscape. We foot-borne infanteers soon came to despise the training area. For every two steps we went forward, we slipped back at least one, and digging a slit trench (foxhole, for those conditioned by U.S. television) was virtually impossible because the walls of our new home below ground would collapse before we had a chance to reinforce them.

We were unceremoniously dropped in front of a large barrack block that had "Normandy" inscribed over its main entrance. Our infantry training began immediately.

In any army, it's the infantry that does the dirtiest work. This is not to suggest that the other members of the combat fraternity—the Armoured Corps, the artillery, the engineers and the signallers—have an easy time of it; on the contrary, at various times in any battle they can find themselves worse off than the infantry. But for grinding, seemingly endless physical demands and gut-wrenching tension, combined with ever-present fatigue and hunger, the infantry soldier takes the prize, a prize that is usually limited to an infrequent hot meal, a few hours of shut-eye and the occasional pat on the back.

During the 1950s, if you aspired to be a leader in the army in general and the infantry in particular, you had to prove to a collection of war-hardened vets that you had the potential to survive the physical and mental challenges of the World War II and Korean War–type battlefields. A number of our instructors had been in combat as recently as six years earlier, and they knew where to place the emphasis in our training. With no human rights legislation, no access to information and no government-imposed social experimentation to distract them from their responsibility to produce junior leaders for the infantry, they had a free hand to do what they knew was necessary from experience.

Our first few weeks of instruction, dealing with the basic elements of infantry work—map reading, field craft, small arms
training, military law—was dominated by what we affectionately referred to as "chickenshit." It was designed to rid us of any
notion that any one of us was more important than the group. If
one of us screwed up, we all paid. We were quartered four to a
room, and daily inspections of our surroundings were routine,
culminating every Friday with the platoon commander's surgical
evaluation of our progress. The floors of each room were waxed
to a brilliant gloss that was maintained by each occupant skating
his way around his area on two grey wool socks that acted like
modern-day skateboards—without wheels. Woe betide anyone
who dared to walk on our floor without first mounting the wool
skids at the entrance to the room. Beds were made to a standard
that would have pleased any nurse. Hospital corners were the
norm, and the tension of the top blanket had to be such that a
coin would bounce clear of the bed when dropped from a modest height by an inspecting non-commissioned officer (NCO).
Obviously, there was a choice to be made: you could make your
bed to an acceptable standard on Sunday and sleep on the floor
for the rest of the week, thereby gaining a few extra minutes of
peace and quiet each morning, or you could opt to make your
bed daily. Most of us chose the former. Occasionally a no-notice
inspection would find us sound asleep on the floor, whereupon
the instructors would gleefully tear our beds apart as we stood
rigidly at attention.

At the time, the purpose of the constant hassle by the instructors was lost on us. However, when I returned as an instructor
on the same course five years later, I could see that some candidates expended too much energy sweating the small stuff
and were unable to identify the important issues. Any theatre
of operations is full of distractions, and to be effective a leader

has to know which issues are critical and which are superficial, and treat them accordingly. Mind you, there were a number of benefits that justified an apparent obsession with neatness, cleanliness and order. Living under field conditions during operations is a filthy business for any army—TV and movie images of war notwithstanding. During defensive operations, the safest place to be is underground in a hole you have dug yourself, while during the offence, more often than not you will find yourself on your belly moving towards the enemy at night and in the worst possible weather. Ablutions take a back seat to sleep, unless the importance of proper sanitation is drilled into your brain. Washing and defecating within a few feet of each other may seem bizarre, but to the infanteer it is often par for the course. It was blatantly obvious to us all within a few days that if we were going to survive and not receive the dreaded "pink slip" that would put us on our way home and out of the army, we had to get our act together and perform as a team. Patrolling and small-unit tactics would come soon enough. During those first few weeks we had to work together, even if the only result was the shiniest floors and toilets in the barrack block.

For the first half of the summer, we made it to the field for only a half a day of practical training a few times a week. More often than not, we thought the only reason we were driven to the field training location in the back of a truck was to give us a starting point for the run back to camp with a full kit and a weapon a few hours later. We grew to hate running and marching in the sand but, if nothing else, it probably made us fitter than we would be at any other time in our lives. Occasionally we stayed out overnight to gain some rudimentary skills in night patrolling, but we never deployed to the field for more than a few days.

As we neared the last half of the summer training, rumours circulated about a one-month killer exercise that all second-phase infantry cadets underwent in Meaford, a remote training area about fifty miles to the northwest. The third-year cadets who had experienced the exercise the previous summer and who lowered themselves to speak to us told stories of endurance tests that resulted in sixty per cent attrition rates, with cadets quitting the exercise—and the army—every day.

Resigning or quitting was the potential culmination of a psychological game between instructors and cadets. Most of the instructors were NCOs—corporals, sergeants or warrant officers—first class or second class. The fact that "officer cadet" appeared on the rank chart above "warrant officer first class" and just below "second lieutenant" was more than a little misleading. Simply, officer cadet was not a rank but a species resting at the bottom of the military food chain. We had no authority, and our lives were in the hands of our NCO instructors.

Fortunately, it was in the interest of the NCOs to do the very best job possible of training each cadet in the skills needed to help him qualify as commissioned officer. If they permitted an underskilled or wimpish cadet to progress through the system, he could end up being their boss in the not-too-distant future. With the Cold War hot and heavy and memories of Korea fresh in everyone's minds, the instructors knew that a future battlefield might be just around the corner, and they didn't want to be caught under fire with a weak and or incompetent junior officer. Therefore, they made it extremely easy for anyone to quit. In fact, they encouraged it. When the going got a little rough and sleep was at a premium and a cadet was heard to complain, he was told: "Well, Cadet, why don't you put yourself out of your misery and quit!" The invitation had the most appeal during tests of physical endurance. Midway into a ten-mile march and run in the driving rain, after twenty-four hours without sleep and carrying a kit plus some common platoon items like mortar bombs or a radio, the enticement of "Mr. MacKenzie, you're looking a little tired. Why don't you throw your kit up here into the truck and pack it in? You say the word, and we'll drive you into camp and deliver you to your quarters" held a certain attraction.

Some officer cadets took advantage of the offer. By the time the rest of us arrived back at our rooms, all evidence of the "quitter's" presence in the platoon was gone. It was as if he had never existed. Even his bedding had been removed, as if anything that belonged to him would contaminate the group. Those cadets who understood the game being played found it a good deal easier to meet the mental challenge and actually used the knowledge to increase their endurance, whereas those who took everything personally had a very difficult time withstanding the pressure. What happened next, however, tested everyone's endurance, mental and physical.

5: Field Training

"You've earned a rest. I just wanted to tell you
how proud I am of every one of you. You could
have quit and you didn't. Well done."

COLONEL "JIMMY" DEXTRAZE

FOR AN ASPIRING infantry officer in the early days of the Cold War, excellence in the classroom was important. If some of us failed a particular test, though, there was a good chance we would be given more instruction before trying it again. No such compassion was evident when we started the practical field exercises. The NCO instructors had an obligation to the current generation of soldiers to protect them from incompetent officers, and the best opportunity to weed out weaklings soon presented itself when we mounted up and headed northwest to the Meaford training area.

The route from Camp Borden to Meaford meanders through some of the most beautiful countryside in Ontario. The view was impressive even from the crowded back of a two-and-a-half-ton truck, particularly when we made our way through the Blue Mountain resort area. The Meaford training area occupies a peninsula jutting out into Georgian Bay. Its northern limit stops at sheer cliffs overlooking Cape Commodore. During the Cold War, heavy weapons were fired from the cliffs at targets in the bay.

As we drove through the training area, we viewed the barren landscape with some apprehension. Our friends in the Armoured Corps had done a good job of tearing up virtually every inch of terra firma with their Sherman tanks, and as a result deep ruts ran in every direction, as far as the eye could see. These furrows might not impede the tanks, but to an infanteer with sixty-five pounds on his back, walking at night and with no moonlight, they were a frustrating obstacle.

Somewhere in the middle of nowhere, the trucks stopped and we dismounted with our kit. A single instructor appeared, and he explained that war was imminent and that we had been assigned a defensive position in this area. It was essential that we dig in as quickly as possible and be prepared to defend the area from all directions.

The next few days rapidly degenerated into a full-time battle merely to stay awake. Days lost their structure as daytime digging in and nighttime patrol rehearsals were followed by the patrols themselves and in turn by more digging in. Arguments ensued over what day it was as we all fought the effects of chronic fatigue. Throughout this period, each of us was indiscriminately yanked out of the "follower" role and placed in a leadership position. We all knew that failure as a student leader would result in banishment from the course, so a burst of adrenalin dissipated our fatigue—for about ten minutes.

We practised a combat decision-making technique called the Battle Appreciation. *Mission* was considered first, and was given to us by our immediate superior. Next we looked at the *Enemy Forces*—their strength and location. Then *Friendly Forces*— in other words, what we had available to do the job. Next was *Ground*. In the attack, this normally boiled down to attacking the enemy position from the left, centre or right. Finally, *Time and Space,* the consideration of which was usually interrupted by the sergeant instructor asking: "Well, what the hell are you going to do about that enemy fire that is trying to destroy your platoon?" Whoever was in charge had only a few minutes to make up his mind while the platoon returned fire. When the time came for the leader to issue brief orders to the three fellow officer cadets filling the subordinate section commander appointments, their burst of adrenalin had worn off and they had returned to their zombie-like state. And so it went.

Making matters worse—or more challenging, with the benefit of hindsight—was the fact that we couldn't really dig in, but at the same time we had to get below ground. The red clay I remembered from my home in Nova Scotia had somehow also appeared in Meaford, except that in travelling between the two locations a perverse mutation had occurred and it was now the consistency of dried cement. There wasn't a shovel in the world that could dent it. Picks were useless, so we unsheathed our bayonets and literally chipped away to create our two-man trenches. One foot down per night was considered pretty good going. When it rained, the ground couldn't absorb the moisture, so we bailed our trenches of muddy water as millions of infanteers had done before us.

Food was a luxury and rarely showed up as scheduled, if at all. The instructors knew that reduced calorie intake would increase our fatigue and thus would enhance their ability to assess our performance under pressure. Combat, after all, is fatiguing, and regular meals in the front lines during the Second World War and Korea had been a rare luxury for most of our instructors. Now, in 1959, these war vets took pleasure in strolling through our filthy positions, sucking on a Dairy Queen milkshake and munching on a burger, making all the appropriate sounds of pleasure—just excruciating. A few cadets failed to appreciate the aim of the exercise and quit on the spot. They were whisked away within minutes, never to be seen again in uniform.

This exercise was scheduled to last six weeks. Halfway through the fifth week (as far as we could tell), a rumour shot through the platoon that it was ending a week early. Our spirits soared, and they went even higher when we were ordered to show up with all our kit at the instructors' camp at noon the following day for a special announcement. Before leaving the positions we had chipped in the ground, we were ordered to fill them in.

At noon precisely, we stood in three ranks facing the instructors' tent lines. There was a light breeze and a wonderful smell of food in the air. To our right was a sixty-foot-long ditch, about five feet deep and three feet wide. During the previous few weeks we had dug it as punishment. The ground at this location was mercifully soft, so progress was much faster than it had been back at our trench positions. Very early in the exercise, we christened the trench the "dinosaur latrine." Anytime someone was caught sleeping on duty or doing something equally serious, he was sentenced to digging time in the trench.

Directly in front of us were about five six-foot folding tables. They were draped with spotless white sheets. The instructors approached as a group, took up positions around the tables and, as one, grabbed the sheets and whipped them away, revealing . . . food! There, before our bulging eyes and growling stomachs, was a smorgasbord of monumental proportions. Turkey, chicken, ham, salads, fresh fruit, cheesecake and pitchers of ice tea accounted for only a portion of what our brains could register. The senior instructor explained: "You will be departing for your barracks in Camp Borden in a few hours, but before you do, we thought you would appreciate a decent meal for a change—it's all yours!" We lurched forward like Labrador retrievers chasing scraps that were falling from the table.

As we reached the object of our desire, our mumbles of enthusiasm were shattered by a scream: "STOP!" This, from every instructor. We froze. By this time the senior instructor had jumped the obstacle and was directly in front of us, with the ditch and the smorgasbord between us. "Gentlemen," he started. "We have just been advised of a nuclear strike a few miles from here. All the food has been contaminated. Push it off those tables, into the trench, and get that trench filled in immediately!"

For a moment we were dumbfounded, but an order is an order, and most of us realized, in spite of our fatigue, that we had been set up. This was yet another test of our endurance. And what the hell, we were heading back to the barracks in a few hours anyway.

It took a good hour before dinosaur latrine disappeared. You could still smell the turkey, even after burying it some six feet under. We collapsed in a heap when the last shovelful had been tramped back in place. We figured by then it must be about time for the trucks to show up and take us "home." The instructors approached again. "Gentlemen (I grew to hate that greeting, and still do), it appears that some of you suffered radiation poisoning as a result of the recent attack, and Mr. MacKenzie, you have died as a result. The rest of you will conduct a field burial and graveside service. Carry on."

Now, months earlier, we had taken a period of classroom instruction on temporary field burials, but we never thought we would actually have to do one until the next war—whenever that might be. I took up my "dead" position on the ground. Someone found a roll of hessian sack material, and I was wrapped in it from head to toe. Heavy-duty coated wire, normally used for connecting field telephones, was wrapped around my ankles and up to my knees, waist, chest, neck and finally head, at eye level. All the lateral wraps were then connected by a single strand running lengthwise along my body from top to bottom. I was now trussed up like a ham hock and getting mighty hot! It was a good 30°c that day, and the two layers of hessian pressed against my nose were interfering with my breathing, although the odour wasn't all that bad. (Years later, the smell of the fireproof Nomex lining in my motor racing helmet reminded me of that pungent odour, and I actually liked it.) For some reason, everyone had disappeared and I was baking in the hot sun by myself, able to wiggle only my toes and fingers for mild relief. I found out later that my fellow students were off digging my grave, close to the buried smorgasbord.

What seemed like an eternity later, I could hear voices approaching. By this time, my sweat had mixed with the hessian, and the resulting mixture was burning my eyes. It was now impossible for me to distinguish shapes through the material, no matter how hard I tried.

The next thing I knew, I was lifted off the ground, dropped on what was probably a stretcher and transported over rough ground by presumably tired colleagues. About a hundred yards later, I was lifted off the stretcher and lowered into a comfortably cool place. Not bad, I thought, until I heard the service start. "We are gathered here to wish farewell and godspeed to our fellow soldier, Lewis MacKenzie." That's about all I remember comprehending, as I decided to concentrate on maintaining my composure. I assumed that as soon as the service was over, this particular exercise would end. A shovelful of dirt on my chest soon convinced me otherwise. Subsequent shovelfuls convinced me that this was getting serious and that I had better work harder at not panicking. I told myself that if they killed me, surely someone would get into serious trouble—so they would stop in time, wouldn't they? They did, but then they left me to speculate about my fate in complete silence for a good fifteen minutes before lifting me out of my grave and unwrapping me. Later I was told that a number of my fellow cadets had wept during the service—not, presumably, because of their affection for me, but because the combination of fatigue, the recent "food" experience and their immersion in the role-playing of one soldier burying another had quite unravelled them.

A senseless exercise? Far from it. The instructors knew that much more demanding challenges awaited their student officers in the next war. What I had been subjected to didn't even rate on their scale of mental endurance. One of them, Sergeant McPherson of the Royal Canadian Regiment, when he was a sniper in Korea, had spent up to three days in no man's land camouflaged and unable to move a muscle while visually tracking the Chinese lines searching for a kill.

We didn't realize that things were about to get worse.

It was pretty close to the time that we had been told we would depart for Camp Borden, more than fifty miles to the south. At the appointed hour, three two-and-a-half-ton trucks ground to a stop about fifty yards away from us. We could feel those soft beds waiting for us back at the barracks. It was Friday, so they might even give us the weekend off to recover!

Just as we started to gather up our kit and put on our webbing and packs, the instructors appeared from behind the trucks. "Gentlemen, the war has not gone well. The territory between here and Camp Borden has been captured by our enemy, the Fantasians,* and they are attacking the approaches into Borden as we speak. It will be your job to infiltrate on foot through

---

* As far back as the 1950s it was considered politically incorrect to call our enemies by their real name, the Soviets, so Fantasians had been introduced as a pseudonym.

the Blue Mountains to Camp Borden, as quickly as possible, to reinforce the garrison there. You will have to move primarily by night to avoid capture. As an exercise point, anyone who is caught will be interrogated and brought back here to start over again. You have ten minutes to form yourselves into groups of six and to reorganize your kit before you depart. By the way, our intelligence folks tell us the Fantasians are aware that you will be trying to infiltrate their positions, so over a hundred of their special forces and numerous police units will be looking for you day and night. Good luck, gentlemen!"

So much for a free weekend. Aching muscles and joints were now facing their biggest challenge of the summer. Sure, the month in Meaford had been physically demanding; but platoon attacks and patrolling had been followed by time in our defensive positions when there was some respite from carrying all that kit along with our rifles. Now we'd be spending the next four or five days, according to the most optimistic estimate, sneaking through the woods and valleys at night and presumably lying low but alert during the day to avoid capture.

Some of the cadets failed to see the point of the instructors playing yet another mind game with us. Later, after having conducted similar dirty tricks when I returned as an instructor myself, I understood that they were looking for cadets who said to themselves, "Screw you bastards. You aren't going to break me, no matter how hard you try. Once I pass this course I might leave the army voluntarily, but you can't make me quit!" Or words to that effect.

For the next five nights we hobbled south along the slopes of the Blue Mountains, avoiding the valleys with their built-up areas and the mountain crests that would reveal our silhouettes and make us ripe for ambush and capture. During the day, when we took a few hours to sleep in rotation, we'd frequently curl up close to a herd of resting cows—they were excellent natural sentries, easily spooked by any approaching Fantasian patrol. We discovered that the Fantasians were actually a hundred-man company of the Royal Canadian Regiment from London, Ontario. They were dead keen on their role-playing as soldiers and were competing to capture officer cadets and put them through the wringer while they had the chance.

Northeast of Camp Borden and its adjacent town of Angus lies the Minesing Swamp. Measuring some twenty square miles, it presents a considerable challenge to anyone on foot, especially if silence is essential to avoiding capture; the sound of sucking boots being extracted from the muck can be heard for a considerable distance. Added to that challenge is the potential presence of Ontario's only deadly reptile, the massasauga rattlesnake, in its natural habitat—something that would dissuade anyone from dozing off on an elevated dry spot.

Just before we entered the swamp, our accompanying instructor and assessor told us that if we made it through to the other side by 1600 hours on this, the sixth day of our infiltration, we would be met there by trucks from Camp Borden. We would be driven the last two miles to our barracks.

Our progress was good, considering the conditions. We could hear other groups from our platoon off to our flanks sucking their way along parallel routes. Occasionally someone would cry out in discomfort or pain as he tripped or stepped in a hole and slipped beneath the gooey surface of the swamp. No Fantasians were anywhere to be seen. Contrary to rumour, soldiers aren't masochists; why hunker down in a swamp for a day when you don't have to?

At 1530 hours we approached the point where we were told the trucks would be waiting. Anticipating an ideal location for an ambush, we approached the crossroads carefully, only to find the area completely unoccupied except for a number of our fellow cadets who had arrived before us. "Where the hell are the trucks?" someone asked.

"Gone," replied one of the earlier arrivals. "When we got here thirty minutes ago, all we found was this note on a stake at the crossroads which accuses us of being late and advising us that we have to march the rest of the way to the barracks."

This was a considerable blow to our morale and our aching bodies. I was told that the cadet who had been designated the company commander for the final day of the exercise had been injured and that the appointment was now mine: I was to get everyone organized and march them to the barracks. By this time we were all so tired and punchy that none of them questioned any order; they just sleepwalked into a ragged line. When everyone was accounted for, we stepped off in the direction of the camp, the pavement more than a little uncomfortable under our flattened feet and soggy boots.

Within the hour we arrived at the main gate of Camp Borden. From that point we were under the scrutiny, intentional or otherwise, of the cadets and staff from the other corps schools located at the camp. The Armoured, Intelligence, Medical and Service Corps all ran officer training courses during the summer. As far as we were concerned, they had it pretty easy, physically at least, and there was no way we were going to give them the satisfaction of seeing us in pain. So everyone sucked it up and managed to stay in step, more or less. Another forty-five minutes and we turned the corner towards the parade square in front of our Normandy barrack block. I came to a halt, and when the first platoon of the company was in position I gave the order, "Halt!"

The normal procedure followed on hearing such an order—given when the right foot passes the left—is for the right foot to complete its step, the left foot to take a shortened step, followed

by the right foot slamming down with as much noise as possible
to align with the left. (Probably the reason most army vets suffer
from lower-back problems later in life!) Unfortunately, no one
in the two platoons had received a parade square order for more
than five weeks while we were in the field. This fact, combined
with flat feet, muscle cramps, shin splints and being on autopi-
lot with fatigue, resulted in one of the most pathetic attempts to
stop a group together previously seen on that sacred ground of a
parade square. (It's used as a parking lot today, which cuts me to
the quick when I visit.) Some cadets tried to halt, but their legs
refused to respond to their brain; while others just slowed down
and took shorter and shorter steps until they came to a stop a
good three yards beyond where they had intended. A few sleep-
walkers just kept marching until I gave the halt order one more
time. With some effort, we formed up into two platoons in three
ranks facing our barrack block.

Immediately a black staff car approached from the right and
stopped on the road directly between the parade square and the
barracks. The right rear door opened and an officer appeared,
resplendent in his starched bush field dress, red tabs on his collar
indicating (even from a distance) an officer of colonel or general
rank. He wore a forage cap with the hat badge of the Royal 22nd
Regiment, the Van Doos. As the officer marched towards us we
could make out the two pips and the crown of a full colonel,
along with a chest full of Second World War and Korean War
medals. I came to attention and gave the order to the company
to do the same. The odd groan, accompanied by grunts of pain,
told me that some of us were having as much problem in coming
to attention in unison as we had earlier had in halting.

I now recognized Colonel "Jimmy" Dextraze, the commandant of the Infantry School and a legend in his own time. Soon
to be General Dextraze and ultimately the chief of defence staff,

Colonel Dextraze had earned the Distinguished Service Order (DSO) for his leadership and bravery following the Normandy landings, had returned to the army to command a battalion in the Korean War and was awarded the Commander of the Most Excellent Order of the British Empire in 1964 for his initiative and fearlessness as a UN "peacekeeping" commander during the brutal civil war in the Congo. I had no idea how many cadets were behind me, so I made up a number and reported, "Thirty-eight cadets on parade, sir; remainder are accounted for. Do you wish to inspect, sir?"

What followed was one of those few moments in my life that I will never forget. The war hero many times over in three campaigns, the decorated Canadian who had witnessed the carnage of combat up close, teared up and didn't turn away. "No," he said, "you've earned a rest. I just wanted to tell you how proud I am of every one of you. You could have quit, and you didn't. Well done." And with that, he saluted and turned away before I could respond.

I'm not sure if it was that split-second experience, where I witnessed a tough, charismatic and proven leader unashamedly show his emotions, that affected my own personality, but to this day I am more emotional when watching someone excel than when I see them suffering a tragedy. When Nadia Comaneci, the Romanian gymnast, scored her perfect 10 at the Montreal Olympics, and when Gilles Villeneuve, the champion racing driver, won the Canadian Grand Prix in Montreal, I had to leave the room to hide the tears. And yes, on innumerable occasions when Canadian soldiers did more than I ever asked them to do, and did so to an unequalled standard, I had a lump in my throat. So, more than forty years ago, on that parade square, "Jimmy" Dextraze taught us that if you loved your chosen profession you should never be ashamed of having strong emotional attachments to those who share it with you. We were learning that there was a lot more to soldiering than just thinking of it as a summer job between school years.

Life back at Xavier Junior College was relatively tame after the summer of intense military physical and psychological evaluation I'd experienced at Borden. Now that I was firmly committed to the infantry rather than to the combat engineers, I didn't need an engineering degree to stay in the ROTP. I took the easy way out—a less than desirable personal trait I had at that time in my life—and transferred to the arts program. I loved philosophy, perhaps because I was the only Protestant in the class and was always being asked: "Well, what does our resident Protestant think about Saint Thomas Aquinas's view of (fill in the blank)?" I had no idea what the proper response should be, as I was rapidly learning a good deal about the Catholic faith without a good foundation in my own—a cross between my mother's Anglican and my father's United Church affiliations. With little risk, I offered my personal opinions on Saint Thomas and every other Catholic thinker offered up by Father Charlie, our much-loved philosophy professor.

To my surprise, I developed a new confidence in class, no matter how ill-founded, often debating issues beyond my competence. My close Catholic friends tolerated my views from the dark side, and I experienced the most enjoyable academic year of my life. I must have disagreed without being too disagreeable, though, because the college generously awarded me the Birks Medal for academic achievement and student leadership at the 1960 spring graduation ceremony. I think that receiving the medal was in itself an education for me. I didn't always have to agree with my peers in order to be taken seriously by them.

Basic infantry officer training during the late 1950s and '60s was intended to eliminate cadets who failed to demonstrate the "right stuff" during phase two—the second summer of training for university students like me. Having survived that phase the previous summer, I returned to Camp Borden and the School of Infantry in June 1960 for the final training. Success would bring commissioning as a second lieutenant in Her Majesty's Canadian Army and assignment to an infantry regiment once I'd completed my university degree.

Phase three training saw us treated more like "gentlemen" than as wasters of rations and quarters. The classes were oriented more towards military law, administration and planning, culminating in the delivery of orders to tactical groupings up to company (approximately hundred-soldier) level. The cadet attrition rate was extremely low compared with the previous summer's rate, and most of those who left did so of their own accord, convinced the military was not for them.

During a rare free weekend, good friend and fellow cadet Chris Smith asked me if I would like to accompany him to a motor race at a track near Jarvis in southwestern Ontario. Chris had joined the PPCLI as a private soldier a few years earlier. On his promotion to corporal, the regiment decided Chris had considerable potential, so he was enrolled in the Officer Candidate Plan (OCP) at Camp Borden. The OCP candidates crammed their three phases of infantry training into one year, rather than the three summers taken by those of us at university. It was universally agreed that the OCP guys had the harder course. For one thing, they trained throughout the winter, whereas the rest of us had the luxury of three summers, longer days and decent weather.

Chris, having drawn a salary as a soldier for a couple of years while the rest of us were bumming off our parents, had cash flow and a car—and not just any car. Parked behind our barrack block was his blood-red PV544 Volvo, a 47 Ford lookalike and Sweden's version of what a practical sports car should be and do.

I've often contemplated what my life would have been like if I'd turned down Chris's invitation. I had no idea that this one day trip would have an almost immediate impact on my military career.

We were about a mile or so from the Harwood Acres racetrack when the short hairs on the back of my neck sprang to attention. I had no idea why. In retrospect, after having many similar experiences over the years, I realize I was responding to the king of senses—smell. Most race car engines in those days were lubricated with castor-based motor oil. When this oil was abused by a high-revving engine, what emerged from the exhaust had a strong pungent odour that was extremely persistent and settled at ground level at the track and surrounding areas. To most non-motor racing enthusiasts it was disgusting. To the rest of us, it was Chanel No. 5.

Minutes later we were in line, waiting to purchase our tickets, when yet another sense was triggered—hearing! In my twenty years I'd never heard the exhaust note of an unmuffled, free-flowing race car engine. I felt weak, nervous and excited, all at the same time. Obviously, a race had started because I could hear at least twenty engines screaming in unison. I ran a few hundred yards to a pathetically flimsy wire fence a few feet from the track and stood in awe as a lifetime passion was planted, nurtured and born in the presence of Porsches, Austin-Healeys, MGs, Jaguars and even Volvos, all driven by new heroes as they flashed by at over one hundred miles per hour.

I was smitten. In a moment, all my life's priorities (such as they were) were subordinated to sports cars, preferably race-modified sports cars.

Chris and I returned to Camp Borden, and for the last few weeks of our phase three training I daydreamed much too often about sports cars and how I could arrange my life to afford one.

Fortunately, my inattention to what was being taught at the time did not have a terminal effect on my training results: I managed to graduate, along with the twenty other cadets in our platoon who had survived three summers or the equivalent of tough, challenging infantry training. As the years passed and infantry officer training included more advanced subjects and less physical and psychological testing, our collective response was: "We might not have been be all that smart on graduation, but we could lick anyone who tried to keep us from doing our job!"

To our considerable envy, those OCP candidates who graduated with us were immediately promoted to second lieutenant and posted to a battalion within an infantry regiment. There were six regimental possibilities. The Royal Highland Regiment, the Black Watch, was stationed in Gagetown, New Brunswick; the Royal 22nd Regiment, the Van Doos, had battalions in Valcartier and Quebec City, Quebec; the Canadian Guards were located in Picton and Petawawa, Ontario; the Royal Canadian Regiment were in London, Ontario; the Queen's Own Rifles of Canada, although originally a Toronto regiment when formed in 1860, were in Calgary, and the Princess Patricia's Canadian Light Infantry's home was in Edmonton. To complicate matters, a game of "musical bases" was frequently played when the three Canadian infantry battalions, on an average of one per year, rotated into or out of Germany for service with our standing brigade-group commitment to North Atlantic Treaty Organization (NATO). For example, if a battalion left Calgary for a three-year tour with NATO, there was no guarantee that the unit would return to Calgary three years hence.

All of this was germane because for some new officers, a preferred geographical location for a good portion of the rest of their career was more important than which regiment they joined. For others, a combination of family tradition, regimental history and reputation, or the regiment of the most respected instructors, would subordinate location in the selection process. For the majority of the cadets, though, it was a moot point because only the top few graduates actually got their first choice of regiment.

For those of us who still had university to complete, it was back to school. In my case, a combination of skipping senior matric and transferring to arts from engineering meant that I still had two years of academics facing me before commissioning, joining a regiment *and* receiving a salary! The military wasn't quite sure what they would do with me the next summer while I was waiting for my senior year at St. Francis Xavier. Most of the speculation indicated that I would probably be sent to a battalion that was short of officers as a temporary fill-in for three months.

I was still obsessed with getting a sports car, and the thought of waiting another two years was daunting. For the past three summers, I had been drilled to practise methodical and quick decision making, which is absolutely necessary when leading soldiers in operations. I had learned that a good strategist considered the advantages and disadvantages, weighed them and went with the option that provided the best chance of success. I ignored everything I'd been taught and acted on impulse. I quit university.

6: Working for a Living

"I see your 'X' ring. Did you room with Brian Mulroney

or Frank McKenna?"

ALMOST EVERYONE THE AUTHOR MEETS

SINCE MOST OF the infantry regiments were short of junior officers, the powers that be kicked into overdrive and I was advised that I had but one option. I could take my release from the ROTP and the Canadian army and, minutes later, accept re-enrollment as a second lieutenant with a five-year short-service commission. If I agreed, I would immediately join the 2nd Battalion of the Queen's Own Rifles of Canada, the QOR of C, in Calgary. The unit had just returned from a three-year tour in Germany. A short-service commission meant that in five years the army would look at me and I would look at the army, and if one of us wished to sever the relationship there would be no option but divorce. Compared with two more years in the classroom, two years of guaranteed regular monthly paycheques seemed like a good idea. I signed on the dotted line.

It took a few years for me to understand the negative implications of my rash decision. Taking my release—albeit for only a few minutes, if that—meant, according to the fine print buried somewhere in the bowels of the Queen's Regulations, that I had given up all seniority credit for the time I'd spent in COTC and ROTP, including the eleven months spent on three phases of practical officer training at the Royal Canadian School of Military Engineering in Vedder Crossing, B.C., and at Camp Borden, Ontario. The moment I accepted my commission, my seniority was identical to that of some civilian walking past the recruiting office in downtown Toronto who stops, turns around, enters and says to the recruiter, "I'd like to join the army and train to be an officer." What made matters worse, and slightly more ridiculous, was that if I'd known the implications of my one-minute release from the army, I could have stayed at the university, deliberately failed all my courses and been commissioned as a second lieutenant with full seniority credit for all the time I'd spent on training, including the three months I'd devoted to failing my last semester. In a delightful touch of irony, proving that God has a sense of humour, some fifteen years later I was the military assistant to the author/enforcer of that regulation, and ten years after that I was the officer in charge of that regulation, which then mysteriously disappeared forever. Seven years after that I was invited back to St. Francis Xavier to give a convocation address and accept an honorary doctorate. During the ceremony I was presented with the famous and highly recognizable university "X" ring, which I have proudly worn ever since, responding "no" to people when they say: "Oh, I see your 'X' ring. Did you room with Brian Mulroney or Frank McKenna?"

Before boarding the train in Sydney for Number 1 Army Personnel Depot in Halifax, where the commissioning would take place, I made my farewells at home. My father, the sergeant major with the tough façade, for the first time ever got emotional over something I was doing and reminded me that I always had a home with them if things didn't work out. My mother, having said goodbye to her first-born some six years earlier, was looking at an empty nest. Having now experienced that moment myself, I know how she must have felt. At the time, however, I couldn't wait to get on the train, break away from life at home and find my own way somewhere.

The ceremony in Halifax was short and sweet. With one pip on my shoulder, indicating my rank of second lieutenant, I was accorded a status a little lower than a snake's belly. While my rank was saluted by non-commissioned ranks as part of military protocol, any genuine respect for the holder of the rank would have to be earned. At least my first day as an officer was easy, as that evening there was a mess dinner scheduled at Royal Artillery Park, adjacent to Citadel Hill in the centre of Halifax, and I was invited. The attendees, all very senior to me, were collegial and welcoming—a pleasant surprise to someone who had been an officer cadet for the previous three years, a rank that made the snake's belly seem sky-high.

I arrived in Calgary three days later. I was picked up by a fellow QOR junior officer, Dennis Murphy, who had experienced some "personality differences" with his first Black Watch of Canada commanding officer in Gagetown, and as a result had rebadged QOR of C, which brought him back to his hometown of Calgary.

I noticed on the drive to Currie Barracks, in Calgary's southwest corner, that the bus line terminated at the "loop," about 300 yards short of the camp's front gate. When I returned for a second tour in 1970 there were over thirty avenues beyond the camp gate, and when I returned yet again in 1977 as the commanding officer it seemed the sprawling city stretched halfway to the Rockies, sixty miles to the west. If only I had bought some property there in the 1960s...

7: German Patrol

"Murphy and MacKenzie, I'm sending you to Germany.
Now get out of here and behave yourselves."

LIEUTENANT-COLONEL DAN OSBORNE

FORTUNE SMILED ON me more than once in my thirty-three
years of commissioned service. Looking back on those years with
20/20 hindsight, I can now see that a few key events must have
given my career a boost. In today's world, similar career boosts
are often and quite properly related to demonstrating leadership under enemy fire. During the Cold War we trained and
waited for such opportunities, but in the more stable years that
followed—when the Warsaw Pact nations had been deterred—
those occasions were rare or non-existent. One had to make one's
mark either during training exercises or behind a desk. I was
fortunate—lucky—mostly to be able to experience the former.

There must have been more incidents than I can remember,
but the key "lucky" events that I can pinpoint occurred in three
places: West Germany, Libya and Wainwright, Alberta. And
the German luck began with a slightly embarrassing incident
in Calgary in 1962. The first year of service with my regiment

in Calgary was on fast forward seven days a week. We trained hard and played hard. Most of the senior leaders of the battalion, including the senior non-commissioned members, were veterans of the Second World War, and many had also seen action in the Korean War. They were confident and relaxed because they had nothing to prove. Those of us who were young and inexperienced lived under their imposing shadows and did our best to live up to their expectations. Though we realized our limits during training, on most weekends we tended to go overboard and tried to outdo the vets' wild behaviour during their times out of the front line—or at least the stories they'd told us about their exploits. A combination of fast cars, alcohol, live ammunition and the opposite sex soon brought us into a collision course with the authorities outside our regimental family. Three of us—Dennis Murphy, who had met me at the train station in Calgary, Second Lieutenant Bill Minnis and I—partied together. Bill was a year senior to me; he had been commissioned in 1959 and also had the advantage of having served in Germany with the battalion immediately after his commissioning. He was tough, talented and very much respected by his soldiers and NCOs.

We three created our own brewery in a bathtub on the second floor of the Officers' Mess, near our rooms. Since all of our last names began with the letter M, we made up labels reading "Triple M Brewery—bottled under the supervision of government employees." As the brew was fermenting in the tub, I recalled (incorrectly, as it turned out) that my dad would add some raisins to his homebrew a week or so before bottling. Then we received word that our commanding officer, Lieutenant Colonel Dan Osborne, would be inspecting our single officers' quarters in forty-eight hours. We moved the desired bottling date ahead a week and stacked the fifty or so bottles in a closet in the hallway.

The colonel arrived on a Friday morning. Halfway through his inspection, the dignity and relative silence was broken by a machine-gun-like staccato. I can only assume that the raisins were not done with their fermenting when we bottled the brew. The sound of beer bottles exploding in a confined space filled our ears. A dark fluid appeared beneath the door just as the colonel was passing by. Colonel Dan, being the type of soldier he was, just looked at us and shook his head. Fortunately, he didn't look behind the closet door. The bottles that survived were opened that evening and the brew consumed by the dozen living-in officers. I did my best to look puzzled as everyone complained about the raisins and wondered who'd had that dumb idea.

The brewery incident, combined with a good deal of live ammunition being fired in and around the Officers' Mess on the weekends and our speeding through the camp in our three sports cars, convinced the colonel that he needed to split up the Triple M Brewery for our own good. We were called to his office on a Monday morning and told in no uncertain terms that our future in the army was threatened unless we cleaned up our act. He went on to say, "Our sister battalion in Germany, which replaced us last year, needs two reinforcement officers. Minnis, you had a year in Germany, so you're staying here. Murphy and MacKenzie, I'm sending you to Germany to join 1 QOR of C. Now get out of here and behave yourselves. Wait a minute, MacKenzie. You stay behind." I was petrified, fearing what was coming next. Colonel Dan stared at me for a good minute and then said, "Lewis MacKenzie, some day in the future I would like you to invite me to be a member of your mess. That's all, dismissed."

I was so junior and so inexperienced that I didn't immediately comprehend what my commanding officer had just said. The penny dropped after I left his office: by saying "your mess," he meant that he foresaw the day when I would be a lieutenant colonel battalion commanding officer, with my own battalion officers' mess and in a position to invite outsiders to be associate or honorary members. Making this comment to a twenty-year-old second lieutenant certainly indicated a degree of confidence in my potential not displayed by anyone else, including me. It was with immense pleasure, sixteen years later, when I returned to Calgary as the commanding officer of the 1st Battalion Princess Patricia's Canadian Light Infantry (1 PPCLI), that my first call was to Colonel (retired) Dan Osborne, offering him honorary membership in "my" mess. He accepted, providing the odour of stale beer in the upstairs hallway had dissipated in the past sixteen years.

When Dennis Murphy and I arrived at 1 QOR of C in northern Germany, just outside the village of Deilinghofen, the battalion had been there for a year and had completed an annual training cycle. The other two Canadian infantry battalions in the brigade had been there two and three years, so our new unit was the rookie group. Competitions within the brigade were intense, with the annual track and field meet giving bragging rights to the winning unit for a year. Close behind in prestige was the annual platoon patrol and defence competition. Under supervision from the brigade, each unit would pick two of its platoon commanders' names out of a hat—one for the patrol, and the other for the defence competition. Each infantry unit, including ours, had about twenty platoon commanders. Never having won anything before, I was surprised to hear the results of the draw: "Defence, Mr. Murphy. Patrol, Mr. MacKenzie." To this day, I think it was a setup, and that somehow the draw had been rigged to give the two new guys their baptism by fire.

My platoon consisted of thirty-three soldiers, an unbelievably large number by today's standards. My platoon sergeant and second-in-command was Huey Graham, and that presented a problem. Huey was fairly young, in fact he was an acting sergeant, because he still needed an additional course to be confirmed in rank. The rules for the competition stated that to create a competitive level playing field, we could replace anyone who had an acting rank with someone who had a confirmed rank. The unit decided to replace Acting Sergeant Graham with a more experienced sergeant. If I knew anything about human nature at the time, I knew that anyone who is told he can't do the job can't wait to prove the skeptics wrong. Sergeant Graham and I got along well; he knew his job, and our soldiers trusted him. Through my company commander, Major John Probyn (John flew a glider into Arnhem during World War II's Operation Market Garden) I asked to see the commanding officer, Lieutenant Colonel Hank Elliot (Hank went ashore at Normandy as a platoon commander on the June 6, 1944). Colonel Elliot heard my plea and said "OK," and that was the end of the exchange. Graham would stay with the platoon.

Patrolling is one of the most challenging and enjoyable tasks undertaken by the infantry. There are a number of types of patrols, all primarily carried out at night, and the more miserable the weather the better. On the small size are recce patrols, four or five soldiers using stealth to spy on the enemy and pinpointing their positions so that they can be dealt with by artillery fire, air strikes or a ground attack later. Fighting patrols can and have been up to battalion size (eight hundred soldiers) but are usually around thirty soldiers strong. In between are "snatch" patrols, dispatched to capture prisoners, and escort patrols, which accompany someone with a particular expertise, such as explosives, to a target.

Fighting patrols are the ultimate test of essential infantry skills: stealth, navigation, initiative, endurance, camouflage and weapons discipline. If a unit can produce good patrollers, it's undoubtedly a good unit. With a platoon of over thirty soldiers to be evaluated, there was little doubt that our competition task would be a fighting patrol. Having only a week to prepare for the competition, we focused on the basics. Everyone was extremely fit to begin with, but we increased the length of the daily runs and added extra weight to our packs. We spent a good deal of time in making all of our kit quiet. The ends of the straps on our webbing were taped down, as were any buckles, lest they make some noise when tapped by a rifle or other metal object. Water bottles presented a challenge: once you'd taken a drink, you could hear the water sloshing around in the metal canteen. At night, with thirty of us sneaking through the German countryside, anyone would be able to hear us coming for miles.

The solution rested with something I remembered from my first platoon a year earlier. Whenever we went to the field, more than a few of my soldiers would be inebriated within a few hours. They were mostly Korean War vets—outstanding, tough soldiers—and training exercises were a bit of a bore for men who'd killed Chinese communists. Although I carried out many inspections of them and their kit, I'd never found anything resembling alcohol. It was the smell of rum on their breath that ultimately gave them away. I recalled that when I tasted the contents of their canteens many of them were full of Coke, which was perfectly OK, because you could substitute pop for water if you wished. However, the next time I inspected I took a pencil and shoved it right to the bottom of one of the suspect canteens. Sure enough, the aggressive probe resulted in a strong pint of dark and dirty. A condom, filled with rum, had been tied off and placed in the canteen. Now we had a mixed drink!

I had a brainstorm and decided to use the same technique to our advantage. The medical inspection room provided us with ten condoms per man. Every time one of us took a drink of water during a scheduled break, he would insert the condom through the neck of the canteen, inflate it enough to take up the empty space, tie it off, replace the cap and presto—no gurgling as we marched.

When the day of the competition arrived, we mounted four three-quarter-ton trucks and reported to a location about thirty-five miles to the west. On arriving at 1500 hours, it seemed every senior officer in the brigade was there, including all the commanding officers of the units with platoons in the competition. I was directed into a large marquee tent set up in the woods. My platoon was told to relax outside. Three of the tent's walls were covered with air photos. On rare earlier occasions, I had seen single air photos when they were dropped to us by an L-19 reconnaissance aircraft. What I now faced was a mosaic of, at a rough guess, one-hundred-plus photos, carefully spliced together and extending some thirty-five yards along the tent walls.

I took my seat in front of a six-foot folding table and pulled out my message pad. A staff officer from brigade read me my orders. They were a bit long, presumably for effect, but hidden inside the mandatory order's subheadings was the mission: "Proceed to Grid Reference 87143621 and destroy the enemy missile launcher located there by not later than 1200 hours Zulu tomorrow the 26 of September." I was told I could have thirty minutes by myself to study the photos and my map, select our patrol route and prepare my orders. Following that, Sergeant Graham and our three corporal section commanders would be allowed into the tent so that we could study the air photos together for a maximum of fifteen minutes. For security reasons we wouldn't be provided with our own copies of any air photos, so we would have to rely on our maps.

The first thing that struck me was the distance involved. The objective was a good twenty miles away, of which at least fifteen were behind "enemy lines." With less than twenty-four hours to get there, stealth would be a challenge. With a large enemy force provided by an entire eight-hundred-man battalion from the brigade, each and every one of them keen to capture us en route, we could move only during hours of darkness. We needed to reach an assault position by first light the following day, where we hoped to be able to observe the missile location and wait for the best time to attack the site before the deadline.

Thanks to Germany's enviable obsession with maintaining its forests (well before the Green movement was popular), there was a good deal of cover for most of the twenty miles. I assumed that the enemy force looking for us would have infiltrated through our forward positions, so we would have to be as invisible as possible for the entire patrol. The four of us studied the air photos, picked a route that would take us to the south side of the missile location and marked it on our maps in pencil. We picked out rally points in case we were ambushed along the way, and then selected a location close to the objective where we would take up a defensive position while I and two others went forward to confirm the best route to attack the site and destroy the missile. We spent the next few hours inspecting our kit for anything that would make the slightest noise as we moved through the woods.

The Canadian army had no proper rain gear in those days, and most soldiers purchased their own, usually at a U.S. Army surplus store. Unfortunately, some of these coats had a waterproof exterior that "sang" as the wearer brushed against branches while he sneaked through the woods. I decided that even though it was beginning to rain, we would leave our pathetic collection of international rain gear behind. As soldiers are wont to say, "God gave us the ultimate waterproof rain gear and called it skin."

The weather was turning in our favour. It was now raining harder, and a breeze was accompanying the front as it moved into our area. Windy, rainy weather is ideal for patrolling because enemy solders, particularly in a static position like a missile site, frequently bundle up to keep warm and turn their backs to the wind, thus increasing their chances of being caught by surprise. After an hour of rehearsing the way we as a group would move across the country, through the woods and around obstacles to finally assault the objective and get back to our lines, we were almost ready. After a final noise test, in which all of us jumped up and down like a bunch of drowned rats without making any sound except for the squishing of our boots in the mud, we were on our way.

The air photos we had studied earlier were a great help. They showed individual treelines rather than the green glob on our maps that represented a forest. The penciled route we had inscribed on our maps proved to be extremely accurate. We would stop every five minutes or so, depending on the cover, and listen for about thirty seconds while holding our breath and listening for any strange noises. We spotted a few enemy groups in the open that were obviously given the task to find and capture us. This was not a competition for them, however, so they were not as keen, and the noise they made gave them away.

The rain continued and got even heavier, so we made good time. My calculations suggested that we might not make our final patrol base less than a mile from the objective during the hours of darkness. Nevertheless, it was no good trying to move faster, because that would probably guarantee our detection and capture—read failure.

Fortunately my timings were a bit off, as forty-five minutes before first light we arrived at our penultimate destination, the patrol base. By this time, everyone was saturated from head to toe and dog-tired. No one spoke, and hand signals were the language of the day. Three of us left the other thirty-one with Sergeant Graham in charge and started the agonizingly slow move forward to get as close to the missile site as possible. It took over an hour to get within a hundred yards of the site. We could see a lot of activity as breakfast was being prepared by the defenders. Since we had the wind to our backs, we couldn't smell the eggs and bacon frying over an open flame, but we could imagine the heat from the fire—which, considering our condition, seemed even more desirable than the food. Fortunately there were quite a few Jeeps and trucks making their way to and from the site. When a vehicle arrived, there was a good deal of activity as numerous soldiers appeared to help with the offloading. If we could coordinate our attack with the arrival of a convoy, it would add to the element of surprise.

At first we couldn't detect the missile, but after cleaning the condensation from the eyepieces of my binoculars I spotted it under a poorly draped camouflage net, smack in the middle of the site. Thinking the competition organizers might have placed a dummy there to attract our attention and embarrass us when we blew up an elaborate piece of wood, we scanned the site for a few minutes more but could detect nothing suggesting that the missile we could see was not the real thing. We headed back to our patrol base.

On the way in to the objective, the three of us had noticed a large area in a dense forest where a large culling operation was under way. A number of trees had been cut down, but most of the effort to date involved cutting about forty per cent of the limbs from very tall spruce trees. The limbs were in good shape, thick with needles, and some of the larger ones were about six feet long. As we passed through the area on the way back to our patrol, an idea came to mind. As soon as we arrived at the base we gathered in a tight group, leaving two sentries on our perimeter, and I whispered, "Our plan is confirmed: proceed as we rehearsed, with one change. On the way from here, in about

97

three hundred yards you'll see hundreds of spruce tree limbs on the forest floor. Pick one your own size, one that would cover your entire body if you were lying down, and bring it with you. We will carry on to where we said our assault position was to be. If we are not detected by then, we'll get down on our stomachs, pull the tree limbs over us and slowly crawl forward. As soon as we are detected we will assault, or if you hear me fire a shot because vehicles are arriving at the site, we start the assault. Any questions?" It was hard for me to tell the difference between those who were shaking from the cold and those whose head shaking meant no questions, so I assumed it was the latter. We moved off.

Twenty minutes later we were in our assault position, a mere hundred yards from the edge of the site and another fifty from the missile. The defenders of the site, appearing to be about twenty strong, were going about their business as usual—but I suspected that it might be a trap. Nevertheless, deciding that we might as well get as close as possible, I got down on my stomach, pulled a branch over my head and started to crawl forward. Looking around as best I could, I saw the entire forest floor for thirty yards on each side of me undulating in the same direction, as if some underground monster were emerging. I kept waiting for the enemy to detect our presence; some of them were less than ten yards away, but they were busy washing up after breakfast and receiving orders for their day's routine.

At that perfectly timed moment (luck), two three-quarter-ton trucks drove down the track we were straddling. They were completly unaware of our presence and stopped about twenty yards in front of us. Perhaps ten of the defenders rushed up to greet them, and the stars were aligned. I fired my rifle as we stood up in unison, and we rushed forward towards a bewildered platoon of defenders, of whom at least half were separated from their weapons, having left them behind when to greet the vehicles. The last thing we needed was prisoners to slow us down, so we gathered up their weapons and indicated to the neutral umpire on the site that we were destroying them. Meanwhile, our demolition team placed the explosives around and on the missile. When we were less than a minute away from the site, the time-delay fuse went off and the missile crumpled to the ground.

Right then we were the most vulnerable. It was daylight, it had stopped raining and we had hundreds of enemy soldiers between us and our friendly lines. We opted for speed over stealth, and in hindsight I think the organizers decided to reward our success on the objective by giving us a free run as we trekked the twenty miles back to the safety of our own lines.

The following day, wearing full kit, we completed the last part of the competition, a forced march of ten miles over rough terrain in less than two hours. The guys made it look easy, and we waited on tenterhooks for the following week until it was announced that we had won the competition by a convincing margin.

You see what I mean about luck—even the weather can influence a career. With no wind, no rain, no high-quality German forestry maintenance, no timely arrival of two trucks and no outstanding Sergeant Huey Graham and thirty-two of the finest Canadian soldiers, those twenty-four hours could have been an unmitigated disaster. My career might never have recovered.

8: Libyan Desert Dust-up

*"A three-day exercise in the desert was terminated
after a few hours and the 'enemy' was victorious,
thanks to 'low Canadian cunning.'"*

LIEUTENANT-GENERAL SIR PATRICK HOWARD-DOBSON

IN EARLY 1967, seven years after my commissioning, I was
still a lieutenant.* I had just completed a two-month staff course
and was preparing to return to Cyprus for a second tour, when
somewhere just east of Fort William (now part of Thunder
Bay), on my way to Calgary, my car radio crackled: "Lieutenant
Lewis MacKenzie should report to the nearest police station at
his earliest opportunity." I assumed the worst and decided that
either my mother or father, or both, had met an untimely end.
Thirty minutes later I was handed a single sheet of paper by the

---

* In the years before the unification of the Canadian Armed Forces under Defence Minister
Paul Hellyer in 1969, an army officer who was not a university graduate served two years
as a second lieutenant and five years as a lieutenant before being eligible for promotion to
captain. As a sop to that "next generation of leaders," Hellyer dramatically reduced the officer's qualifying time for promotion to captain. The unfortunate effect of his action was to
diminish the prestige of the rank: now a captain would be asked, "Are you a real captain or a
Hellyer captain?" The despised common green uniform with gold rank insignia issued to all
the personnel of the navy, army and air force was the most visible sign of unification.

night-shift duty policeman at a detachment in Fort William. The teletype read, "Posting to 2nd Battalion Queen's Own Rifles of Canada for Cyprus tour of duty cancelled. Report ASP to Army Personnel Directorate, Ottawa, for processing prior to proceeding to Germany for two-year exchange posting with the Royal Sussex Regiment, 10th Armoured Brigade, British Army on the Rhine, stationed in Lemgo, West Germany."

Two weeks later I was in Lemgo, joining a battalion that was still arriving from its tour of duty in strife-torn Aden, at that time the capital of the People's Democratic Republic of Yemen. I was assigned to C Company as second-in-command, despite my lowly rank.

In 1967, before Colonel Muammar Gaddafi had seized power, King Idris ruled Libya and Britain had an agreement to assist with the security of Libya's borders if they were threatened from outside, Egypt being the prime suspect. As a result, the British Army regularly rotated its battalions of infantry and armoured regiments through a month's desert-warfare training in the Libyan desert a few hours west of Tobruk and south of the Mediterranean coastal town of Timimi. As the threat of an Egyptian incursion heightened, my new battalion was moved up the deployment schedule, thanks to their recent tour in the hot climate of Aden.

Early on in our deployment procedures, I was advised that army HQ had denied me permission to proceed to Libya with my British Army company. Presumably they were concerned that if Egypt attacked Libya and my battalion was required to respond, the Canadian government would be less than happy that a Canadian officer had been involved in the battle. I was devastated. In the short time I had been with the battalion, I had integrated well with my British colleagues and got along with my company commander, Major Charles Tarver, and the company sergeant major, "Chippy" Wood. Now I was supposed to wave farewell as they departed for North Africa and sit around waiting until they came home, regaling me with the usual "Man, you should have been there!" I had to do something.

I drove the sixty miles to Soest, the home of the headquarters of the 4th Canadian Brigade Group, and visited the brigade major, the second-most-influential appointment in the entire Canadian army in Germany next to the commander. Major Charlie Belzile was the incumbent, and in spite of the significant difference in our ranks we were good friends. I had served as the reconnaissance platoon commander attached to his rifle company during a major amphibious exercise on the west coast of Vancouver Island some three years earlier, and we had taken the parachute-qualifying course together a year earlier. Charlie, immediately seeing a loophole in the crisis, sent me on thirty days' special leave and didn't ask where I was going. (Risk-aversion was not something Charlie understood, which probably explains why he ended up commanding our army for five years, retiring as a lieutenant-general with the respect of all who worked for him.)

Huddled in the back of British Army trucks, we made the two-hour journey from the airport at Tobruk to Timimi. Then, turning our backs on the azure-blue Mediterranean, we turned south for the thirty-mile drive to the British camp. We all waited for our mental image of the desert to materialize. Having served in the Gaza Strip for two years, I thought I knew what to expect: magnificent sand dunes and endless expanses of flat, sandy nothing. The desert in north Libya, however, is misnamed. It is cement-hard clay, topped with rocks of all sizes, maxing out with boulders the size of Jeeps strewn about the terrain. Since the desert floor can't absorb the moisture of the occasional rains, the rushing surface water cuts ditches, which harden when the water evaporates, leaving scars that make cross-country movement by vehicles bone-jarring and creating ankle-breaking obstacles for foot soldiers like us, particularly at night.

Thirty miles later, we spotted the austere British camp in the distance. Hundreds of sun-bleached tents in a massive circle surrounding a flagpole was the extent of the "construction." As we got closer, I could make out the vehicle park and the vehicles we would be taking over from the Parachute Regiment, which was on its way back to the United Kingdom. Every one of them had a large white cross on the windshield, or on their sides if they were armoured personnel carriers (APCs). I assumed the cross was intended to identify neutral umpires who would be assessing the success or failure of our exercises. Then I heard one of the soldiers say, "Look at all those PCC'd vehicles!" I asked, "What does PCC mean?" His response was not encouraging. "I don't know what the initials stand for, but I do know that it means a vehicle has been written off and is only good for cannibalizing or, I guess, training in the desert!" His guess was right.

The heat was oppressive but bearable, averaging around 45°C at midday. Our company routine started with us working hard for the first two hours after sunrise and the last two hours before dark. Each day we added two hours of work to the beginning and end of daylight. After four days of this, we were acclimatized and conducting training throughout the day. Moving across the desert on foot with fifty-pound packs, ammunition and weapons, we were consuming water at a rate of "a water bottle per man per mile."

After two weeks on the ground it was announced that our 10th Armoured Brigade commander, Brigadier Patrick Howard-Dobson, would be flying in from Germany to visit us in about three days. Our commanding officer had been planning an ambitious exercise for his battalion, starting the next day, so the timing was perfect: the brigadier would see our entire battalion well into the exercise and under more stressful conditions.

We were delighted when the exercise orders were issued. The entire battalion, except for our C Company, would deploy to a ridge line (in Libya, a feature perhaps ten to fifteen yards above the surrounding desert) and take up a fully prepared defensive position in anticipation of an attack by the Fantasians from the south. C Company would be the enemy force. Everyone was to deploy to their start exercise positions by last light that day; however, no vehicle traffic would be permitted forward of our positions prior to two hours before first light two days from that time. Presumably the commanding officer wanted to give his battalion a full forty-eight hours to prepare an elaborate defensive position. We would use that time to prepare our company for the attack. Unfortunately, we would start our advance some twenty miles south of the battalion's defensive position, so we would have a long "advance to contact" in some very unreliable vehicles, particularly the APCs.

With the sun blocked out by the dust created by over one hundred vehicles moving in two different directions deep into the Libyan desert, we set off on a slow thirty-mile move to our "enemy" start position, arriving just after last light. As our role was to be an aggressive enemy in about thirty-six hours, we had lots of time for vehicle maintenance, rehearsals and even rest. Once battle was joined, there would be precious little sleep for at least seventy-two hours, so putting a few hours of shut-eye in the bank would prove useful.

It was around midday, sixteen hours after we had arrived in our position, that the penny dropped. I recalled that during the orders launching the exercise, the commanding officer had said, "There will be no vehicle traffic forward of the main and enemy forces before two hours prior to first light two days from now."

That "now" meant none prior to two hours before first light the following day, when we were scheduled to begin our advance.

I rushed over to see Major Tarver and blurted out, "I know the idea was that there would be no contact between us and our objective, the battalion's defensive position, until tomorrow, but the colonel only restricted vehicle traffic! Why don't I take a small foot patrol, say five plus myself, and we'll cover the twenty miles tonight? If we have the time, we'll get as close as possible to their defensive position, watch their final preparations and identify their layout. You and the rest of the company can pick us up just before your attack, and we can guide you to the weak points in their defence." If I remember correctly, all Major Tarver said was "Go!"

I asked for volunteers and was impressed that I soon had more than I needed. There was the attraction of perhaps outwitting the soldiers in the rest of the battalion, and earning some bragging rights. I picked five lance corporals, the rank indicating soldiers who did not have all the formal qualifications to be corporals but who had been identified as future leaders in the battalion. As a rule they were all extremely fit, keen and confident.

The rehearsal was short and sweet. We broke ourselves into two groups of three, lightened our load to nothing but personal weapons, ammunition and all the water we could reasonably carry, plus two radios and two compasses. According to the map, we would be proceeding almost due north. When I took a bearing I was delighted to see that we would be heading one finger to the west of the North Star, which made navigation pretty simple. Our objective would be a fairly long, prominent rocky outcrop at least fifteen yards high, less than three hundred yards directly south of the battalion position. We would aim for the centre of it, so if we were off by a hundred yards after a twenty-mile march we would still bump into it, or at least see it.

We didn't strike off until dark in case the battalion had realized the loophole in the restriction on vehicle traffic and had sent a foot patrol south to watch us. The going was difficult, primarily because our move south had taken us to the edge of Libya's Sand Sea. We were now marching over a combination of a real sandy desert and rocky outcrops.

About two hours into our patrol I could hear firing off to our left, perhaps a little less than a half-mile away. As it got closer, I noticed tracer fire disappearing to our right. I recognized the characteristic sound of the coaxial machine gun on the British Chieftain tank. The coaxial machine gun helps the main 120 mm gun strike its target, so if there was a lot of coaxial fire the main-gun shells would not be far behind. We went to ground and hugged the sand like only infanteers under fire can, staying in that position for at least a half an hour while a British armoured regiment, the Scots Greys, conducted a live-fire exercise with my small band of brothers in the target area!

It was then I realized why our exercise vehicle traffic had been restricted until first light the following day. The exercise organizers who coordinated the allocation of training areas had placed the restriction to ensure that no one would be in the target area for the live-fire exercise conducted that night by the Scots Greys. Unfortunately for us, they hadn't anticipated that anyone would be foolish enough to march the twenty miles between our battalion's two positions.

Regrettably, when we went to ground, the leader of our other group of three twisted his ankle and broke the glass face of his compass. Once the firing stopped, we decided he was in no condition to continue. I knew that the rest of the company would pass this exact point in about eight hours on the way to our first-light attack. I said, "The three of you stay here; you have lots of water and the frequencies of the company radios, so as they approach you in the dark around 0500 hours—and you'll hear them miles away—make radio contact and use the red filter on your flashlight to get their attention. The three of us will carry on. With any luck, we'll see you early tomorrow on the objective!"

It wasn't easy leaving half our patrol behind, but there was no way I was going to leave the injured corporal by himself, and I was confident they would be easily spotted by the hundred-man company and the twenty armoured vehicles as they made their way to our objective early the next morning.

The march became a boring, routine grind, which everyone in the infantry is used to. One foot in front of the other, two steps forward and one back in deep sand, and ankle-twisting pain on the rocky outcrops. The further north we got, the harder the desert floor became, which was a blessing. With the North Star to guide us, it was easy to doze off while marching (yet another infantry "skill"), but within seconds, tripping over a stone or stepping into a soft sandy area would jar us awake again. We carried on that way for another eight hours, when we calculated by the number of paces we'd covered that we were a mile or so from our objective. Two of us had carried fifteen small stones in our pocket, and the third corporal carried ten. At every thousand paces, one of us would throw away a stone. I was the last to throw away his stones; when I had only two left, we knew we were close to our little ridge line in front of the enemy position. (Today's soldiers use Global Positioning Systems, or GPS; any of them who are reading this, stop laughing now!)

In about ten minutes we could make out a jagged, rocky ridge line silhouetted in the bright moonlight to our immediate front. I was amazed that we were within a hundred yards of the centre of our objective after twenty miles on the march. The ease of navigation, thanks to having the static North Star as a beacon, obviously helped.

When we reached the base of the ridge we found it relatively easy to scale its nearly vertical wall because it had stony projections that stuck out like steps and that were easy to grab. I was concerned that when we reached the top we too would be silhouetted, and that with the bright moonlight we would be easy to detect from the battalion defensive position, which was supposed to be a mere few hundred yards to our front. I went first, and as I reached the top I eased my head over the top next to a boulder so that I wouldn't be so visible and looked around. Less than five yards to my right was proof that there is a patron saint for soldiers. There, waiting for its new occupants, was a perfectly constructed circular stone wall protecting a depression that had been chipped in the lava. Its appearance suggested that it had probably been constructed as an observation post during the Second World War's North African campaign. The three of us moved to the right and slithered into our new home from the rear.

As we peered through the gaps between the stones, we couldn't believe our good fortune. There on the horizon, a few hundred yards to the front, were at least two hundred soldiers constructing fire positions by piling stones around depressions in the rock. They had obviously found it impossible to dig in, so they were using the same techniques used by generations of soldiers before them in this inhospitable landscape. If those soldiers were from two of the unit's three rifle companies, the remaining one had to be somewhere. It didn't take us long to find it; it was right below us on the desert floor, laying a massive minefield. The defenders had obviously decided that the minefield would cause our company to attack them from a flank, which determined the way the two rifle companies on the ridge line were facing, east and west.

An hour later the sun inched its way from behind the horizon and a sand-induced, bright-orange glow illuminated the area to our front. The minefield had been completed, and we watched with satisfaction as the soldiers withdrew through the ten-yard gap they had left in the minefield, the last one through connecting the wire from each side of the gap and on the wire hanging a number of triangular signs that read "MINES." To anyone coming upon the minefield from the south, like our attacking company, it would appear to be a solid minefield in front of the entire battalion, and thus any attack would have to be mounted from a flank.

While we were intently watching the preparations to our front, I heard a noise directly behind us. I turned around, and there was our other three-man team. "What the hell!" I whispered.

The corporal with the twisted ankle replied, "Well, Sir, ten minutes after you left I decided I could limp the rest of the way, heading just left of the North Star. We got here half an hour ago and hit the far end of this ridge and, like you, found a prepared trench. Did you notice the big gap they left in the minefield?"

"Yes," I said. "Stay right where you are for now; our company should be here any minute. Well done for disobeying my direct order to stay put!"

I got on the radio and broke radio silence. In a crude code, I asked Major Tarver how long it would be before the company arrived for the attack. He responded, "Twenty minutes," and I could already see the dust rising from the vehicles to our south. I said, "You'll recall the ridge line—that was my objective. It's two hundred yards directly south of the battalion position. We are all on the east end. There is a massive minefield directly in front of us and in front of the battalion. They want us to attack from the flank, which is well protected. We know where the gap is, in the centre of the minefield. If you head towards our position, the battalion will think you have made a mistake and that you are attacking the wrong ridge line. We'll run down to you from our position and guide you through the minefield gap straight up the centre of the battalion position, which is very lightly defended."

Major Tarver responded, "Wilko, out" (heard, understood and agreed).

Then I noticed someone on the ridge line to our left. He was silhouetted and was giving our position away. I cancelled the whispering mode and yelled, "For fuck's sake get off the skyline and report here!"

A minute later, the beret of Brigadier Howard-Dobson, our brigade commander and destined to be Lieutenant-General Sir Patrick Howard-Dobson, appeared just below the rear of our position.

"Sorry, Sir, I didn't know it was you," I whispered.

He graciously responded, "Quite right, what you said. I should have been more careful. Tell me what is going on."

I briefed him on the plan, and a few minutes later our company "attacked." We ran to the vehicles, and less than a minute later we were driving straight through the gap in the minefield, splitting the battalion position and attacking the two forward companies from the rear. The planned three-day exercise was over by 0900 hours on the first day.

The brigadier suggested to our commanding officer that we start again the next day. In his comments on my annual personnel efficiency report that was sent to army HQ in Ottawa, he generously wrote: "A three-day exercise in the desert was terminated after a few hours, and the 'enemy' was victorious, thanks to 'low Canadian cunning.' "

More luck and good fortune, in concert with excellent soldiers.

9: The Wainwright Swamp

*"A soldier's morale is directly proportional to what
he can be proud of and brag about in the canteen ."*

AN OBSERVATION FROM LIFE

THE "ENEMY" POSITION was on the forward slope of a knoll,
facing southeast. From the air photo I could detect at least forty
soldiers, well dug in with an elaborate trench system duplicat-
ing the layout favoured by the Soviets. The area immediately to
the front of the position was pretty well open, but there was a
good chance that the enemy had deployed small groups of two
or three soldiers well forward, in well-concealed trenches, to
detect and interfere with anyone foolish enough to try a frontal
assault. To the north of the position was a heavily forested area
with a treeline that ran southeast for at least a mile. The terrain
inside the treeline was broken, with many gullies and depressions. Although it was undoubtedly mined and booby-trapped,
it offered an ideal covered approach to the enemy position.

To the south was another wooded area, which at first glance
seemed equally inviting as an approach. The treeline extended

for over a mile to the southeast and almost reached the point where I was now observing the objective through my binoculars. The approach seemed too good to be true, until I checked my map and discovered a large swamp measuring at least a half a mile in diameter midway between the place where my 120-man company was preparing for battle and the treeline leading up to and beyond the enemy position.

It was 1972, and I was a brand-new major commanding B Company in the 1st Battalion, Princess Patricia's Canadian Light Infantry (1 PPCLI). Our unit had served in Cyprus with the United Nations Force during the summer of 1971, so we had missed that year's annual training concentration, conducted for the five thousand soldiers of the 1st Canadian Brigade Group in Wainwright, Alberta.

Since our brigade's units were spread from Victoria to Winnipeg, it was an expensive undertaking to bring them together; however, with the Cold War alive and well, funds were normally found to underwrite one training concentration per year in the summer and one in the winter. The training usually lasted about six weeks, during which each tactical building block, from a ten-man infantry section to a thirty-man platoon to a one-hundred-man company to an eight-hundred-man battalion to the five-thousand-man brigade itself, would have an opportunity to practise its skills before being exercised by the next commander up the chain of command. Formal evaluation was a contentious issue. The majority of senior folks were of the opinion that if a tactical group, say a platoon, performed well on an exercise, it should be considered operationally proficient and no further assessment was needed. Others, albeit in the minority, disagreed and felt the group should break down its key combat tasks into a series of activities, be formally evaluated and then scored, resulting in a rating from "failed" to "outstanding." As a rule, army officers were leery of such evaluations. Whereas their counterparts in the air and at sea could quantify a good number of their activities to assess success or failure, for army units this was deemed to be a much more subjective undertaking. In addition, the risk of being graded by an inexperienced evaluator was considerable. A poor rating could spell the end to a promising career, and occasionally it did just that.

Our brigade commander at the time was Brigadier-General G. (George) G. Brown. G.G. was a tough s.o.b.; he played hard and expected his subordinates to do the same. As a young officer in the PPCLI, he had fought in the Italian campaign with the regiment, and in the late 1950s, as a lieutenant-colonel, had commanded the 1st Battalion of the PPCLI as part of Canada's NATO contribution in Germany. At times, when he was drinking, he could be a bit of a bully, but he rarely held a grudge and usually conveniently forgot any serious encounters by the next morning. No one would ever accuse him of being the shy, retiring type, and love him or revile him, depending on the time of day we all respected him. G.G. had decided that every infantry company in his brigade would undergo a "test" exercise that summer. The word test was ultimately replaced by "evaluation," but we all knew that the former term was more accurate. Twelve infantry company commanders felt a chill go down their spines.

As luck would have it, my company's name was the first one drawn from the hat. I'd only just been promoted to major, and as the battalion's operations officer in my previous rank I knew B Company's morale to be the worst in the unit by a long shot. The previous company's commander was a nice guy and meant well, but the soldiers had a hard time relating to him and it showed. They needed a boost and something to feel good about, and over the years I've noticed that a soldier's morale is directly proportional to what he can be proud of and brag about in the canteen.

The open-centre and mined-right approaches to the enemy position were problematic unless someone had a death wish, so that left the woods and swamp to the left. The way the enemy position was laid out, it appeared their commander considered such an approach highly unlikely if not impossible.

It wasn't until we were about a hundred yards from the swamp that I began to question my decision-making ability. It had been impossible to conduct a reconnaissance of the swamp because of the time constraints. What if we couldn't make it through the obstacle? To use a soldier's favourite term, I would have one major "jug-fuck" on my hands and nowhere to go but to the rear, as the first company failure of the day.

As soon as our scouts and guides entered the swamp, they sank to their chests in the ooze. But to their credit they kept moving forward at a snail's pace. More than a hundred of us were strung out behind them for some three hundred yards just inside the treeline, waiting to join them. We inched forward and I stepped into the muck. Touching bottom and getting relatively firm footing, I was about to exhale for the first time in what seemed like ten minutes when the sergeant, carrying a .30 calibre machine gun only a few steps in front of me, disappeared under the slime. Everyone stopped while those in the immediate area of the missing officer groped around in the muck, which was made even thicker by our frantic efforts.

In short order, the unwilling diver was hauled to the surface, his machine gun still firmly planted on his left shoulder (another investigation thwarted). It seemed pretty obvious that the bottom of the swamp could sustain only so much weight—a pound over that limit, and you broke through into the pudding-like substance. The word quickly went out, and everyone evened out their loads with their fellow soldiers on either side. Explosives, spare ammunition, mortars and mortar bombs—anything that added to a soldier's normal load—was shared, with the lightest soldiers assuming the heaviest load. Well over an hour later, we were safely on the other side and I gave a silent prayer of thanks.

By now we were about five hundred yards short of the objective and well concealed deep inside the treeline to the enemy's right. I had sent a small diversionary section of eight soldiers along a gully leading to the centre of the clearing, about four hundred yards directly in front of the objective. They had made their way there without being detected, and now, on a pre-arranged signal, they opened up with everything they had. The noise from six semi-automatic rifles and two machine guns, plus a variety of training explosives designed to represent anti-tank weapons and mortar fire, was more than enough to capture the enemy's attention. Our scouts reported by radio that the entire enemy force was redeploying to face our diversionary group and returning fire. The ruse was working, so we continued to work our way inside the treeline, well out of sight of the objective. Ten minutes later we were beyond the enemy position and approaching it from the rear. I was with the lead platoon. As we crested the hill we saw a magnificent sight. There, laid out in front of us, were at least fifteen slit trenches dug into the hillside manned by at least thirty-five soldiers in Soviet-style uniforms—and facing in the wrong direction! They were so mesmerized by the continuing antics of our diversionary group and so confident that no one would approach their position through the swamp that they had ignored the back-door approach.

I walked up to their rearmost trench, manned by two soldiers, bent over and tapped the taller of the two on the shoulder. He stopped firing to his front, turned and looked up—probably expecting to see his own platoon commander or his section commander—only to observe a Canadian army major with a twisted grin on his camouflaged face. Within a second or so the putrid odour of rotting swamp gas infiltrated his gaping mouth, and seeing at least thirty other equally undesirable characters to my rear he dropped his weapon and raised his hands in surrender. He was soon joined by his trenchmate. Fortunately, the rest of the enemy force was still concentrating on returning fire in the direction of our friends to their front. They failed to notice that they were slowly being given an enema by a superior force. I knew that our good fortune and the element of surprise would end the moment the first enemy soldier noticed us, before we had a chance to disarm him, so using hand signals only I deployed the leading platoon I was with to the crest of the hill. There they assumed firing positions dominating the enemy position to our front. We were able to reach two more trenches and disarm the occupants before we were spotted. The moment we were brought under fire, all hell broke loose and our covering platoon shot up the entire position from the rear. The umpires adjudicating the encounter blew their whistles and declared the enemy position defeated. No casualties were assessed to us, the "good" guys.

We reorganized on and around the objective, and soon we were called together for a debriefing by our commanding officer, Lieutenant-Colonel Bill Hewson, and the officer responsible for operational readiness from HQ, Lieutenant-Colonel "Bud" Taylor, a veteran of the Korean War. Colonel Taylor was good enough to say that ours was the best company-sized operation he had seen since assuming his appointment. The hundred-plus soldiers of B Company let out a cheer, and for the first time in the last hour we started to notice how filthy and putrid we all were.

At first glance, it would be reasonable to assume that the boost to the company's morale was primarily due to the success of the attack and the complimentary remarks from someone who had done it for real in Canada's last shooting war. But I think there's more to it than that. As important as success and recognition may be, they are secondary to the fact that we did something both difficult and dangerous together. We excelled thanks to the contributions of every member of the company. If we had taken the easier approach to the right, using the treeline and the broken terrain to achieve a lesser result, the feeling of satisfaction and pride would not have been close to the one we enjoyed as a team of drowned rats that morning, on a barren hillside in eastern Alberta.

Thank God for the luck of that swamp's bottom supporting a soldier's weight. Otherwise...

10: Mutiny at Battle River

"Sir, I have to speak with you, and it's pretty important...
The lads have just found out that the seventh game with
the Soviets is scheduled for the twenty-sixth."

B COMPANY SERGEANT MAJOR JACK MURRAY

DURING THE 1972 training concentration in Wainwright that started with the company "test" competition, our commanding officer, Lieutenant-Colonel Bill Hewson, had to get his battalion ready for the final five-day brigade-level exercise. He gave his three company commanders two weeks to train their company up to a standard at which he could exercise the entire battalion as a whole in all phases of war.

My borderline obsession with patrolling and its ultimate test of a small unit's operational readiness had not diminished with age or rank. Rather than having all our company's nine sections (of ten men each) or three platoons (of thirty men each) practise independently and then bringing them together for the final few days, I opted to create a rare, very large fighting patrol that involved every man in the company. We would spend at least four days rehearsing for the patrol, which would involve the infiltration of individual platoons through the enemy's front lines (as played by one of the other companies practising defensive drills), the crossing of a river obstacle and the rendezvous of all three platoons and my headquarters near a position where we would ambush a large enemy convoy on its main resupply route.

Che Guevara, one of Fidel Castro's key commandantes during the Cuban Revolution of 1959, wrote extensively on the principles of war as he saw them. He included a new one: patience. He opined that ambushes, in particular, were usually sprung too early and that as a result the enemy escaped. Wanting to test that principle, I planned an ambush in which we would arrive at our rendezvous position around 11 PM on September 24, thus being forced to lay back behind the enemy's front lines for almost forty-eight hours without being detected before launching our ambush at last light on the 26th. If we were successful, we would be evacuated by helicopters immediately after completing the ambush.

Meanwhile, rumours had morphed into fact regarding the much-anticipated Canada–U.S.S.R. hockey series. We all knew that if Canada would send its best pros to represent the nation rather than an all-star amateur team or the Allan Cup–winning team, there would be a slaughter, with the Soviets on the receiving end. Too often, Canada's amateur teams had come up short at the World Championships and the Olympics, so if the Soviets wanted a series with the best, Canada would be only too happy to accommodate them. No precise dates or locations had been set for the games yet, but it looked like the match would occur in September.

To my surprise and satisfaction, our request for helicopter support on September 26, in three months' time, was approved. The squadron commander, Lieutenant-Colonel Paul Argue, had been one of my instructors when I'd attended the Army Staff College in 1969–70, and we had played together on the college's rep volleyball team, which probably helped. The few helicopters were much in demand, so it was essential that I didn't try to change the date we needed them. If I did, our approval would be cancelled and we would have to exfiltrate on foot when the ambush was over.

We arrived in Wainwright on September 10. Every one of us in the company, and most of the nation, was in a state of shock. After kicking Soviet butt for the first few minutes of game one of the hockey series in Montreal, the momentum had slipped away from Canada. Now into the two-week hiatus before playing the last four games in Russia, the Canadian team was behind with only a single win and a tie. Unless you were in a coma you had to be aware that our national pride was in considerable danger of a meltdown. To make matters worse, the dates had been finalized for the last four games.

Jack Murray, my company sergeant major (CSM), sidled up beside me after a day of patrol rehearsals and whispered, "Sir, I have to speak with you and it's pretty important."

The CSM is the company commander's primary link with the company's soldiers, and vice versa. When the troops are bothered about something, they approach the CSM. Nine times out of ten he sends them on their way due to the frivolous nature of the requests, so I assumed that this time it must be important. We walked behind my Jeep, and I said, "Shoot."

"Sir, the lads have just found out that the seventh game with the Soviets is scheduled for the twenty-sixth, and that's the final day of our patrol exercise." The CSM was looking worried. "The game is in the morning, so we will definitely miss it. The men want to know if there is any way we can reschedule by a day or two."

I replied, "I'm sorry, but an essential part of the exercise is the helicopter extraction the night of the twenty-sixth. That can't be changed, so I can't change the exercise. We'll just have to suck it up and accept that we will miss the game. The way things are going, it probably won't matter much anyway."

During the next two weeks, we didn't just train for my pet patrol exercise. In order to be ready for the colonel's exercise, we marched, dug, fired our weapons, attacked, withdrew and practised the defence—all good infantry training, and all the more so if done in wet, miserable conditions and with a minimum of sleep. The relationship between me and the soldiers of my company became frosty, to say the least. I could tell that they were well and truly pissed off at me for scheduling an exercise during game seven of the series.

On Friday, September 22, the nation received another stake through its heart. We lost 5–4 to the Soviets, putting us down three games to one with a tie. We would have to win the remaining three games to win the series, which seemed about as likely as my soldiers dropping their grudge against me. We were scheduled to depart our patrol assembly base at last light on Sunday. That meant that we were able to watch game six earlier in the day. Down 1–0 early in the second period and knowing that a loss would give the series win to the Soviets, our spirits were rock-bottom. Then, magically, in the space of two minutes Canada scored three quick goals, the first two by Dennis Hall and Yvon Cournoyer separated by a mere five seconds, and Paul Henderson's coming less than a minute later. The entire country erupted with joy at the realization that our team had dodged the bullet of elimination and still had a chance to win the series if it won the next two games. But every eye in the company turned on me as if to say, "You son of a bitch. We'll be on your stupid patrol exercise, flat on our face on the ground in the middle of nowhere, when game seven is played." The phrase "If looks could kill" was never closer to the truth.

I had briefed the patrol that the tough part of the exercise would start when we reached the far side of the Battle River and took up our position on the bluffs overlooking the road where we would spring our ambush. We would have to remain undetected for about forty hours. That meant absolutely no noise whatsoever, including no talking. We would send simple signals via the wires connecting each of us by the wrist. If someone had to defecate he would advise his buddy on each side of him, release the wire, crawl backward twenty yards to the rear in the forest and, without standing up at any time, do his business. Urination would be done in place. For many soldiers, in those simpler times, the restriction on smoking was the major challenge. Many of them had never gone even a few hours without a nicotine hit, let alone abstaining over two days. We would carry no food other than a loaf of bread with peanut butter between each slice. We would place the prepared loaf in the bottom part of our mess tin, place the cover on top of the loaf, stand on it, compressing the bread to the thickness of a book, and, presto, we would have a survival ration, which along with a container of water would keep us going for two days.

We left our base camp at last light, and our infiltration was uneventful. The Battle River's water level was low for that time of year and we were able to cross on foot, with water only up to our waist. On reaching the river bank, half of each platoon, covered by the other half, took off their boots and socks and kept them out of the water during the crossing. This was not to accommodate comfort but to avoid making the squishing noise of ninety-plus pairs of boots, which would be easily heard by the enemy force as we attempted to sneak through the woods on the far side.

By midnight we had reached our layback position. It was ideally suited for our task. We took up a position on the edge of a thickly wooded area. We were facing north towards an open area with few bushes for cover, so it would be hard for anyone to surprise us from that direction. It would also be an ideal place for the helicopters to land at night in two days. To our sides and rear was thick forest, which would keep us well hidden. A dirt track ran from right to left across our front, neatly dividing the open area, and off to our far right, about one hundred yards away was the main north-south road, probably the enemy's main supply route. That would be the site for our ambush in about forty hours.

As the clouds cleared, the temperature dropped drastically overnight. Everyone was chilled to the bone, being soaking wet from the waist down. We travelled light and so did not have the luxury of a sleeping bag or a blanket. During the hours of darkness, we rotated sentry duty so that at least twenty-five per cent of our force was alert at any one time. The following day, the Alberta autumn sun was pleasantly hot and we lay still on our stomachs, keeping an eye on the open area to our front. A few sentries watched our flanks and rear. Occasionally I saw someone crawling back to relieve himself. We could hear and see the dust of vehicle traffic on the main road to our right, but the track to our front remained deserted. We nibbled on our peanut butter patties at our own pace, and they were not in fact too bad.

The problem with lying absolutely still in one position for hours on end is that when you have to move quickly to, say, deal with a surprise encounter with the enemy, your body can become boardlike and just won't move—no matter how young and fit you are. It's possible to minimize the negative effects by flexing as many body joints and muscles as possible at least three or four times per hour. Fingers, wrists, shoulders, back, hips, knees, ankles and feet can all be exercised without much body movement, which might give your position away. So when it came time for me to defecate, the crawl to the rear was actually a relief for my stiff joints. On the other hand, completing the requirement while lying on my side made me thankful that I was alone.

Spending the second night on our stomachs was a real endurance contest, made all the more so by the knowledge that every one of my soldiers was thinking about having to miss the seventh game against the Russians. Face-off was scheduled for 9 AM the next morning, and just about every Canadian, except for an underprivileged company commanded by a bull-headed individual and hiding in a forest west of the Battle River valley, would be watching.

The day dawned dark and dreary, matching the mood around me. The compressed loaf of bread, now the size of a deck of cards, gave itself up to the demands of breakfast. After a few stretching exercises, we all settled down to another silent, boring day on our stomachs, testing Che Guevara's patience principle.

At 8:55 AM, we were startled to see a two-and-a-half-ton truck enter the clearing to our front on the track leading from the main road. It stopped about a hundred yards directly in front of us and started to back up. It continued to reverse until it was only fifteen yards in front of me. I had prearranged that four quick tugs on the wire connecting each soldier to his buddies on each side was a signal that they should crawl to my position. I gave the signal, and five minutes later every man in the company was silently huddled around me in a blob of ninety-plus soldiers.

The truck's engine stopped. The driver and the co-driver dismounted, and then, in a scene like the one in the film *The Bridge on the River Kwai,* the tarp covering the back of the vehicle was rolled up to expose not a threatening machine gun, as had happened in the movie, but a twenty-six-inch Zenith colour TV. It was 8:58 AM, so my timing wasn't bad.

The rest, as they say, is history. Boris Mikhailov kicked

124

Canadian defenceman Gary Bergman during a fight when Bergman drove Mikhailov's head into the chicken wire above the boards (no Lexan panels in Moscow in those days), and the teams squared off sans gloves. The nation cheered—silence from our company. With minutes to go in a tie game, Paul Henderson beat four Russian players, slipped the puck through the legs of one defenceman, picked it up on the other side, fell forward and flicked the puck over Soviet goalie Vladislav Tretiak's shoulder for the 4–3 win. All of Canada went wild, except for the forced and eerie silence from our company—the only people in Canada who couldn't join the cheering. Mind you, I did see about a hundred shit-eating grins. Two tugs on the wire and some hand signals, and everyone crawled back to their positions.

That night, we launched the ambush in a driving rainstorm. Paul Argue led his helicopters into our pick-up zone under cover of darkness and flew us back to our base camp. The wash-up/ debrief took place in the welcoming warmth of a large, heated marquee tent. The first thing that happened was that two of the smokers who had gone without a cigarette for more than forty-eight hours fainted from their first puff. A few beers later, the stories got better. It was only two days to the final eighth game, and we'd be able to watch it in the comfort of a heated building. We cheered louder than anyone when Henderson did it again, scoring the winning goal in the final seconds of the game, more than making up for our forced silence in game seven.

I haven't recounted this potentially defining career moment because it had a positive impact on my bosses. It showed both me and my soldiers that they were the most important factor in any success I might have, then or in the future. Without their support, I'd have no career. They might have doubted my commitment to them in those few weeks, but hopefully, they wouldn't doubt it in the future.

11: Segue

"Canada's first female general, L. MacKenzie,

to head up combat trials for women."

THE *OTTAWA CITIZEN*, AUGUST 1997

THE STORIES TOLD in the previous chapters, of the "luck" that probably had a positive influence on my military career, occurred between 1960 and 1973. Many of the events that took place between that time and my post-military career are related in my first book, *Peacekeeper: The Road to Sarajevo*, and I will not retell those stories here. It may, however, be useful to describe the thirteen appointments I held between 1973 and 1993, to relate a few incidents not mentioned in *Peacekeeper* and to make some clarifications that benefit from hindsight.

In May 1973, a helicopter carrying Canadian Captain Charles Laviolette, a member of the International Commission of Control and Supervision (ICCS) monitoring the 1972 Paris Peace Accord's ceasefire, was shot down over Vietnam. The captain's death sparked outrage in Canada, and many people, including veterans, called for Canada's withdrawal from the ICCS. I wrote a letter to the *Calgary Herald* indicating that if the mission was proper, we should stay—after all, accepting risk is what soldiers get paid for—and I indicated that I would be prepared to go to Vietnam "tomorrow." I was sent there a week later. Just a coincidence? I had, in fact, volunteered months earlier.

On returning to Calgary from Vietnam, I found that things were heating up in the Middle East. On October 6, 1973, Egypt attacked Israel across the Suez Canal, and the Yom Kippur War was underway. Shortly after the ceasefire on October 26, the United Nations deployed a peacekeeping force to the Sinai. Its logistic support, provided by Canada and Poland, was based at the Cairo horse-racing track, next to the airport. A month later there was some very negative publicity in Canada regarding the leadership and living conditions at the Canadian base, and I was assigned to our contingent in Cairo to report directly back to National Defence HQ in Ottawa and do what I could to improve morale.

I returned from Cairo in April 1974, having been warned that I would take over as the brigade major for Canada's western-based army brigade. The brigade major's position was the most-sought-after appointment for any major, as it had proven to be a launching pad for the careers of many senior officers. A month before I was to assume the position, the army reorganized the rank structure of its four brigade headquarters, and the brigade major's positions, now renamed "Senior Staff Officers Operations" (eeech!), would be occupied by lieutenant-colonels. As a consolation prize, I was posted to the Canadian Forces HQ located in Lahr, West Germany, as the executive assistant to the commander, Major-General Jim Quinn, a veteran of the Italian Campaign in the Second World War. I remained there for two years, working in my second year for Major General Duncan A. MacAlpine, who had been our Canadian commander in Vietnam a few years earlier.

As I neared the end of my executive assistant duties, I was told I would be promoted and would take command of 3rd Mechanized Commando, an infantry battalion just up the road from Lahr, near Baden-Baden. It too was a much-sought-after posting, and I was delighted. About two months before I was to take command, the Chief of Defence Staff, General Jimmy Dextraze (the same officer who was commandant of the Infantry School in 1959 when I was in officer training) arrived from Canada. With no warning, he announced that 3rd Mechanized Commando would be disbanded as part of the downsizing of the Canadian commitment to NATO. Wow! With two prime postings in a row self-destructing within months of my scheduled arrival, I was feeling somewhat vulnerable.

This time the consolation prize was a posting to Rome and six months attending the NATO Defence College. Not too bad, I hear you say. Following that, it got even better, as I returned to Calgary to take command of 1 PPCLI, the battalion I had served with as operations officer and company commander. The battalion served in Cyprus during the summer of 1978—my third tour on the island.

Until the 1990s, anyone who had commanded a battalion-sized unit as a lieutenant-colonel entered an extensive period that did not offer much opportunity to lead soldiers. There was only one command appointment for an army colonel, and that was the Airborne Regiment. I had volunteered every year for a decade to serve with the regiment but had never made it. As a result, it was unlikely that I would be considered as its commander—even if I did, in the future, make the rank of full colonel. I was posted to the Canadian Forces Command and Staff College in Toronto as a member of the faculty for the one-year course preparing young majors for more senior rank. It was the longest posting of my career, ending after three full years. By that time I had been married for twelve years, and my daughter, Kimm, was eleven. My wife, Dora, and I felt so much at home that we bought our first home then.

The year 1982–83 was spent at the United States Army War College in Carlisle, Pennsylvania. The close to three hundred students were the top two per cent of lieutenant colonels in the U.S. Army; sixteen of us were full colonels from abroad, referred to as "international fellows." It was an enjoyable and productive year. We dealt with strategic planning at the highest level and stayed fit with everyday sports periods. I made many valuable contacts that I would turn to over the next ten years.

My first warning of a posting after Carlisle was as the director of infantry at National Defence Headquarters (NDHQ). This would be my first posting to Ottawa, as far away from soldiers as it was possible to get, and I wasn't looking forward to it. Dora and I went to Ottawa before my War College course was completed and bought our second house, having made a few bucks on the first one. Then, not for the first time, my posting was changed. The commander of the army, with its headquarters in St. Hubert, Quebec, was none other than Lieutenant-General Charlie Belzile, who, sixteen years earlier when he was Major Belzile, had helped me get to Libya with my British army battalion. General Charlie thought that my relationship with my future boss in Ottawa would be like oil and water, so he had me reassigned to his headquarters and put me in charge of army training, which would include organizing Rendezvous 85 in Wainwright, Alberta, the biggest army exercise in Canada since the Second World War.

Two years later, once again with General Charlie's input, I was posted to NDHQ as the colonel in charge of the career management of all officers in the Canadian Armed Forces up to and including the rank of major. It was to be a two-year posting, but early into the second year, while waiting for a military plane to return me to Canada from a meeting in the United Kingdom, I was called to the phone in the waiting lounge. It was Perrin Beatty, the minister of national defence. "Colonel, I have good news for you and other news," he started. "The good news is that you are promoted to brigadier-general, effective now, and the other news is that I'm putting you in charge of conducting trials to determine if we should permit women to serve in the combat occupations of the Canadian Armed Forces."

I arrived home in Ottawa that Friday evening. There was a brown envelope in my mailbox. It held two brigadier-general's rank badges but no general officer's hat badge. The media had got wind of the story regarding women being considered for the Forces' combat trades: navy—both surface and sub-surface; air force—pilot; army—artillery, armour, infantry and combat engineers. Concurrent with the announcement of my promotion was that of Canada's first female to make general officer rank— Sheila Hellstrom. The *Ottawa Citizen* assumed that a female would be put in charge of the combat trials for women and titled a front-page article in its Monday edition, "Canada's first female general, L. MacKenzie, to head up combat trials for women"! As I arrived at work, a few of my friends started to call me "Louise." (A few of them still do.) To make matters worse, I assumed the erroneous sexual designation had gone national in the media. When my mother phoned from Nova Scotia later in the day, she said, "I just saw the paper. Why didn't you call and tell me you had made general?"

I couldn't resist; I replied, "I was waiting for news of the sex change to die down."

There was a *very* long pause at the other end of the line. I waited to hear something other than heavy breathing before blurting out, "Didn't the article say I was Canada's first female general officer?"

"No," she whispered, now totally confused. It took me a while to reassure her that everything was still in place. (I discovered later that only the *Citizen* had made the mistake.)

I spent only part of 1987 preparing for the women-in-combat trials, before the Canadian Human Rights Commission blessedly rescued me from the job and made the idea of a trial redundant when it declared: Thou shalt not discriminate by sex regarding employment opportunities in the Canadian Forces—except in submarines. I thought the caveat was ridiculous; soldiers are much closer together in a slit trench than they are in a submarine, but even that restriction was lifted a few years later. The trials never would have happened anyway, as we had nowhere near enough female volunteers to create a cohort to qualify for a scientific trial.

In late 1987, following the illness of a general officer serving at NDHQ, the ripple effect sent me to Canadian Forces Base (CFB) Gagetown to command the largest military base (by area) in the Commonwealth, and the Combat Training Centre, where the junior leaders, both commissioned and non-commissioned, for the Artillery, Armour and Infantry Corps are trained. The following two years were about as pleasant as could be, since I was surrounded by soldiers learning their profession.

In late 1989, UN Secretary-General Javier Pérez de Cuéllar expressed frustration that most of the money spent on peace-keeping was directed to the Middle East or Africa. There was a major conflict going on in Central America as the U.S.-supported Contras fought with Daniel Ortega's Sandinista government forces back and forth over the Honduras-Nicaraguan border. An agreement was reached whereby troops from Central American countries would not conduct cross-border operations, and foreign militaries (that is, those of the United States) would depart. The Contras would be demobilized by a UN peacekeeping force.

In the summer of 1990, I was posted to Central America as the deputy commander of the UN mission, and a few months later took over as the commander. During the summer of 1991 I returned to Toronto as deputy commander of Land Forces Central Area, affectionately known as the "Army of Ontario," which comprised all regular and reserve soldiers in the province.

Things were now heating up in Yugoslavia, as Slovenia and Croatia declared their independence. Cyrus Vance, representing the UN secretary-general, brokered a ceasefire in November 1991, and the UN, moving at its usual glacial pace, did not start to put the force together until four months later, in March 1992. The force's five general officers had never served with the UN, so they needed an experienced officer as chief of staff. I had volunteered and was selected; I reported to UNHQ in early March. A few months into my tour in Sarajevo, in June 1992, I was able to talk my way out of the chief of staff's job and became the first commander of Sector Sarajevo. By September of that year I had been promoted to the rank of major-general but was declared *persona non grata* by the Bosnian government because I blamed it for breaking the majority of the many ceasefires we arranged. My outspoken comments to the media, accusing both the Bosnian Muslims and the Serbs of orchestrating events to make the other side look bad, along with the Bosnian government's complaint that I was not favouring its side, was making the UN in New York "uncomfortable." When my soldiers, including my Russian deputy, were detained by Bosnian Muslim soldiers and threatened with death because "you work for that fucking MacKenzie," I resigned—probably less than twenty-four hours before the UN was set to fire me. I returned to Canada as the commander of the Army of Ontario that year.

The war in Bosnia was the world's top news story, so not surprisingly I was constantly being interviewed by the media, and the government was regularly sending me to Europe, NATO, Her Majesty, the U.S. Congress and other venues to discuss the war. I was ignoring my day job. I submitted my resignation, requesting an early retirement in March 1993. Marcel Masse, the minister of national defence and soon to be a member of Quebec's provincial separatist party, the Parti Québécois, accepted it.

My father, Eugene Murdock "Connie" MacKenzie, as a new recruit in Halifax, N.S., around 1939.

This is me at six years of age, with my mother, Shirley, and sister, Katheryn, in Truro, N.S., 1946.

Katheryn and I pose with some of our best friends in Princeport,
N.S., around 1949.

Wearing my soccer uniform in Cultus Lake, B.C., around 1955.

That's me standing on the far left, as a fifteen-year-old corporal in the Air Cadets in Abbotsford, B.C., about 1955. Shortly after this photo was taken, I was relieved of my appointment as the NCO in charge of the B.C. contingent for misinforming the recruiters about my age when I joined the cadets two years earlier.

I and my Sydney, N.S., basketball teammates take on a visiting U.S. "All Star" team in 1958. Gerry "Hotrod" MacNeil is on the right; I'm in the centre, attempting to break a visiting team member's leg.

My father had just retired, and I was a newly commissioned second lieutenant ready to leave home in December 1960.

Company sergeant major and friend Jack Murray points me in the right direction. Jack alerted me to the pending "mutiny" in the company over my decision to deploy on exercise during the Canada-Russia hockey series in 1972. (Canadian Forces photograph)

PART TWO

ROADS FROM SARAJEVO

12: Naked on Civvy Street

*"General MacKenzie, why don't you come to
Belgrade and we'll talk about it?"*

RADOVAN KARADZIC, LEADER OF THE REBEL BOSNIAN SERBS

IT WASN'T UNTIL the corporal behind the counter at the personnel section took my identification card and cut it in half that the life-sustaining umbilical cord that connected me with the Canadian Forces was truly severed. A minute earlier, I had been responsible for 15,000 soldiers; now, one snip of the scissors later, I was in charge of nothing but myself. I would always be a loyal and outspoken supporter of the men and women who had made me look good for over thirty-five years, but the way in which I demonstrated that support would change.

The biggest immediate shock came when I made my first telephone call. For years when I called someone and said, "Hello, this is General MacKenzie," there was usually both recognition and a certain degree of respect evident at the other end, deserved or otherwise. Post-retirement, when I said, "Hello, this is Lew MacKenzie," the response was along the lines of "Yeah, and what do you want?"

A few days after my release I received a call from Douglas Bassett, head of Baton Broadcast System (BBS), who suggested I drop over to his office at the company's CFTO affiliate in Toronto for a chat. At the meeting, Douglas suggested I come on board as a commentator on defence and foreign policy issues for CTV. I thought that was a grand idea, particularly if BBS sponsored what had now become my motor racing habit. We shook hands, and my flirtation with the media began.

Within weeks it was decided that Tom Clark, one of CTV's best-known and most respected personalities, and I would visit Somalia in April. We were to report on the activities of the Canadian Airborne Regiment (CAR), which was operating in the area of Belet Huen as part of the UN-mandated and U.S.-led peace-making mission. The CTV staff were already referring to our pending visit as "the Lewis and Clark expedition."

In February, before retiring, I had asked that I be permitted to visit the CAR in Somalia. The unit, stationed in Petawawa, was part of my new command when I returned from Sarajevo to take command of the Army of Ontario. During their preparation for a UN peacekeeping mission in the months preceding Christmas 1992, it became obvious that "keeping the peace" was not going to be possible. Somalia was deteriorating. I gave instructions that the unit should drop a number of "nice to have" positions, such as cooks, from their nominal role and replace them with "bayonets"—soldiers trained and ready to fight. I wanted to see how the unit was doing, but my request was denied because my retirement was only a month away and my bosses thought my visit might well become a media circus. My decision to increase the number of fighters was vindicated just before the unit deployed in December, when the United States was given a mandate by the UN Security Council to lead a "Chapter Seven" peacemaking intervention mission, one that would be authorized to use deadly force to "establish law and order thereby permitting the safe delivery of humanitarian aid." Canada agreed to be part of that force, and the CAR's blue berets (UN peacekeepers) were withdrawn and replaced by helmets. Their vehicles, painted peacekeeping white, with black UN markings, were already en route to Somalia, and unfortunately they would have to stay that colour after they arrived on the Horn of Africa. As a result, both the Canadian public and the media erroneously referred to the CAR's task as a peacekeeping mission during its entire six-month tour.

Our CTV crew arrived in Belet Huen on April 19, 1993. Both the commanding officer, Lieutenant-Colonel Carol Mathieu, and his regimental sergeant major were away on a week's leave. We went on patrol with both the CAR's soldiers and the armoured unit attached to the CAR. They were well received by the local population, including the thousands of internally displaced persons who were huddled around the town as a result of the fighting and drought. At the conclusion of our visit we filmed the only parachute drop the regiment did during its six-month tour. I envied the jumpers as I watched the hot updrafts gently deposit even the heaviest of them like a feather on the desert floor. We beamed out good-news stories with the help of the CNN satellite in Mogadishu and started for home with Nairobi, Kenya, as our first stop.

We were in our Nairobi hotel for only a couple of hours when Tom received a call from CTV in Toronto. He hung up and said, "The CAR's doctor in Belet Huen has sent a letter to his wife in Petawawa indicating that a Somali boy by the name of Shidane Arone was beaten to death by soldiers of the CAR. The letter has been made public, and they want us to go back in and get the story. I told them it was 45 degrees back there and they said it was 40 degrees in Toronto and I said, Celsius? and that was the end of the conversation."

It wasn't easy finding a flight back to Mogadishu, but begging works and two days later we were in Belet Huen. The unit was locked up tighter than a drum, and no one was allowed to speak with us. The Military Police Investigation folks arrived at the same time, so people were even more gun-shy.

We decided to attack the problem from the other end, and so we tracked down the dead Somali boy's father. With a crowd of at least one hundred locals tightly packed around us, Tom asked the father through an interpreter: "What is it you want from the Canadian government?" Mr. Arone hesitated and then uttered a short sentence. The entire crowd murmured, and a few even groaned. The interpreter whispered something to the father, and he replied with a longer statement. The interpreter turned to Tom and said, "Mr. Arone asks for fifty camels, which is normal for such an act." Everyone in the crowd nodded in agreement. When we got back to Toronto and checked the tape with our own interpreter, we were told that Mr. Arone's first request was for five camels but that during the crowd's commentary he was urged to up the ante. In the end the Canadian government paid the family $5,000, much closer to the price of fifty camels than five.

Back in Nairobi, we turned to CNN to see what had happened in the world during the past week. The lead international story involved the approximately one hundred Canadian soldiers deployed in the UN "safe haven" of Srebrenica in Bosnia. They had been sent there by the UN commander in Bosnia following the decision of the UN Security Council to declare six safe havens throughout Bosnia for trapped Bosnian Muslims, now more commonly known as Bosniaks.*

The safe havens would have been a good idea if the UN had provided the manpower to protect the sanctuaries, but they didn't even come close. Appearing in front of a U.S. Congressional committee, I opined that over 135,000 additional UN troops would be required. The UN commander in Bosnia at the time, General Francis Briquemont, from Belgium, said he agreed but was prepared to try with 65,000. Secretary-General Boutros Boutros-Ghali requested the Security Council to approve 27,500. The Security Council approved 12,000, and six months later fewer than 2,000 had shown up in Bosnia. The remainder never arrived. As a result, the Bosnian government infiltrated fighters into Srebrenica to do the job the UN was mandated to do. These fighters subsequently became brazen and started attacking Serbian villages around Srebrenica, killing the occupants and burning the villages to the ground. The Serbs retaliated, and the Canadians found themselves smack-dab in the middle of another UN-generated mess.

As part of the retaliation, the Serbs had blockaded Srebrenica and refused to let resupply units and reinforcements through to the isolated Canadian company in the town. They also denied access to any convoys bringing food to the trapped Bosniaks. Our hotel television showed the leader of the breakaway Bosnian Serbs, Radovan Karadzic, telling a CNN reporter that because the Bosniaks were attacking his people he wouldn't let the Canadians be resupplied until the Muslims stopped the attacks.

---

* During the time I served in Sarajevo in 1992, we referred to the three sides in the conflict as Bosnian Muslims, Bosnian Serbs and Bosnian Croats. All three sides agreed to these terms. "Bosnian Muslims" was, however, somewhat misleading, because it included a number of non-Muslims who nevertheless had remained loyal to Alija Izetbegovic, the president of Bosnia-Herzegovina, which was recognized as an independent country by most nations on April 6, 1992. The term currently used when referring to the community led by the Bosnian Muslims, and the one I use from this point on in this book, is Bosniak.

This was ridiculous. Our guys were less than one hundred strong; there was no way they could deal with more than ten thousand combatants on both sides of this conflict in that location. I picked up the phone and asked the hotel operator to get the number for the Hotel Yugoslavia in Belgrade. I knew from meetings I'd attended the previous year that Karadzic had a room there, and the background in the live interview looked like the hotel. A minute later I was speaking with the front desk and asked for Karadzic's room. "Not possible," was the response. I tried: "It's General MacKenzie" and I was relieved to hear, "I'll put you right through."

Surprisingly, Karadzic answered the phone. I knew how sensitive he was to all the bad international publicity he was incapable of countering. Early in the war the Bosniak government had hired a North American public relations firm to spin its case, but the Bosnian Serbs thought they could do their own PR and had failed miserably. I played the media card. "Mr. Karadzic, what you are doing around Srebrenica is a PR disaster. You're gaining absolutely nothing from your actions. The Canadians in Srebrenica need to be reinforced so that they can do their job better. For God's sake, why keep food from the Bosniaks trapped there?" Karadzic caught me off guard by replying, "General MacKenzie, why don't you come to Belgrade and we'll talk about it?" The best I could think of was "I'm in Nairobi, but I'll check out the possibilities and get back to you."

Within an hour, Tom had confirmed that CTV would pick up the tab if we could get to Belgrade. They were delighted at the opportunity to get a live face-to-face interview with Karadzic. I called National Defence HQ and explained that there was at least the possibility that I might be able to do something about the current blockade of Srebrenica. They supported the attempt; however, I indicated that I wouldn't arrange the trip unless Foreign Affairs endorsed the idea. NDHQ called back within the hour indicating that Foreign Affairs was on side and wished us luck.

Tom had been working with CTV in Toronto on flight timings and determined that we could be in Budapest late the next day, which would allow us to drive to Belgrade for a meeting with Karadzic the following morning. I got back to Karadzic, who agreed to meet us at Bosnia House in Belgrade at 9 AM in two days' time.

Our trip to Belgrade was uneventful except for the delay at the border between Hungary and Serbia, where we were held up for a couple of hours—not because there was a problem, but because the customs guards and their bosses insisted on sharing their slivovica (a well-known and dangerous plum brandy) with us. Fortunately we had a hired driver and made it to the Hotel Yugoslavia before midnight.

The next morning we left our rooms and took the elevator to the lobby on our way to the 9 o'clock meeting. When the elevator doors opened, we were confronted by a swarm of media newshounds. Most of the major TV networks were there with their lights blazing and their mikes in our faces. Obviously, word of our meeting had been leaked, presumably by Karadzic's folks. I tap-danced around their questions, saying that we would have a statement following the meeting with Karadzic.

Arriving at Bosnia House, we agreed that I would meet privately with Karadzic and then engage in a discussion filmed by the CTV team. Finally, Tom would have a one-on-one interview with Karadzic.

Once Karadzic and I were alone, I continued to play the PR card. "You are really failing miserably with the media," I started. "But, you know, the situation in Srebrenica offers you a chance to make a positive move which should get you some credit. I recommend you do three things. First, allow the Canadian company to be reinforced and resupplied. Second, let the food convoys through to the Bosniaks in the town. Third, ask the UN to place their observers with your mortar and artillery positions in the hills surrounding Srebrenica so that you can prove that you are not shelling the town—like you say you are not." I knew I was giving advice to someone who would be indicted as a war criminal in the near future, but if I could help lift the blockade of both the Canadians and the Muslims in the town, I didn't really care. With only a little discussion, Karadzic agreed. He left the room and told the waiting international media what had been decided.

Back home, it was two in the morning in central Canada and therefore time to rewrite the day's editorial. We returned to Canada later the same day. I was amazed to read the criticisms of my discussions with Karadzic: "Who does he think he is?"—"Operating way beyond his ability"—"Interfering in delicate negotiations"—"Karadzic will never live up to his promises, and Canadian lives have been endangered."

Within twenty-four hours the blockade around Srebrenica had been lifted, the Canadians were reinforced, food convoys were permitted into the town and the UN dispatched a few observers—though not enough—to the Serbian gun positions. No one from NDHQ or Foreign Affairs indicated that they had supported the negotiation, and the papers that had vilified the undertaking were silent as the blockade was lifted.

As the world knows, the situation in Srebrenica deteriorated over the next two years. Attacks launched from the UN safe haven and led by a Bosniak, Naser Oric, resulted in the deaths of between 500 and 3,000 Serbs in the surrounding villages. In July 1995, Bosnian Serb forces, led by General Ratko Mladic, retaliated by capturing the safe haven, evacuating the women and children to the safety of the Bosniak-controlled town of Tuzla and then systematically slaughtering the male population of the town. (There is much debate regarding the number of people killed, with estimates ranging from 3,000 to 8,000.) Oric and the majority of his force had abandoned Tuzla two months before the Serb attack.

Naser Oric was indicted by the International Criminal Tribunal for the former Yugoslavia (ICTY) in The Hague and served two years in prison for his role as the Muslim commander in Srebrenica. General Ratko Mladic has also been indicted by the ICTY, but he has yet to be captured and turned over to the tribunal.

13: Rapist

"Allegations against Major General Lewis MacKenzie are unfounded."

KOFI ANNAN, QUOTING A UN COMMISSION'S CONCLUSION

ON THE EVENING of December 1, 1992, while I was still in uniform, I received a phone call from Canadian journalist John Burns, a Pulitzer Prize–winning reporter with the *New York Times*. John, the newspaper's senior reporter in Sarajevo, was calling from London, England, where he had just flown to see his son. He and I had got to know each other in Sarajevo, and he said he wanted to give me a heads-up regarding the firestorm of accusations that he thought might soon surface: I had been branded a rapist and war criminal. Neither of us had any idea that these accusations would continue to circulate for the next fifteen years or, indeed, that they would continue to this day.

In late 1992, the Bosnian-Serb soldier Borislav Herak was arrested by the Bosnian police in Sarajevo and charged with the murder of multiple citizens. He had allegedly described how he practised cutting the throats of pigs in preparation for doing the same to his Bosniak victims. The trial received worldwide coverage, and John Burns was permitted to do a one-on-one interview with Herak, with a Bosnian government "minder" present.

John explained to me that during the interview Herak recounted how he had worked at the Sonja Café, which had been converted to a prisoner camp in northern Sarajevo. He said that I had come by in a Jeep and had taken away four young Muslim girl prisoners, who I then presumably raped and murdered, since their bodies were found later. Herak insisted all this had happened sometime in mid-August 1992. John knew that I had departed Sarajevo in July, so he asked Herak how he knew it was me. Herak replied that he had seen me often on TV. When he was asked to describe my uniform and rank badges, he described something similar to that worn by a junior officer from a Scandinavian country. All of that, combined with the fact that I never moved about in a Jeep, caused John to turn to the Bosnian government's keeper and advise him that his government should not go public with the accusations against me because they would destroy the credibility of the rest of the story he was writing on Herak. John described Herak as "a Charles Manson type" and didn't think Herak's accusations regarding me would be released to the media, but he wanted me to be prepared if they did.

Within thirty-six hours, the accusations made headlines in the Arab world, just at the time Bosnian President Alija Izetbegovic was arriving at the Islamic conference in Saudi Arabia. The North American press showed better taste and, considering the source—a prisoner of war accused of multiple murders—declined to carry the story. This was not the case in Germany, Italy and Croatia, where the accusations were repeated.

Within weeks, those accusations were officially discredited: it was determined that a number of the people whom Herak had allegedly murdered were alive and well and that many of his other "achievements" as a soldier were fabrications. It was generally accepted that Herak had been coached before his interview with Burns—but not particularly well, it would seem. Nevertheless, the damage had been done. Most people, particularly those in the Muslim world, who based their opinion of me on Herak's evidence, were not going to change their mind overnight. With my encouragement, the UN carried out an extensive, two-month formal investigation of the accusations by the Bosnian authorities. It was followed by a personal letter to me from Kofi Annan, under secretary of the UN at the time, in which he repeated the commission's conclusion that "Allegations against Major General Lewis MacKenzie are unfounded." He went on to say, "May I say again how appalled I am to hear of the difficulties with which you have had to deal and take this oppourtunity to thank you for your service to UNPROFOR."[1] My critics, however, were far from convinced, and the slander gained momentum in Germany, Italy and the Muslim world.

Six months later, I inadvertently contributed to the volume of the criticisms against me when I accepted a contract to speak to the Heritage Foundation in Washington, D.C. I was doing one or two speeches a day in Canada, and this one didn't seem out of the ordinary. It was arranged by a serving U.S. congresswoman, Helen Bentley, whom I had met in Belgrade during my time in Yugoslavia when she was attempting to locate and return an American citizen's children who had been spirited there by the father. During the speech I indicated that the Bosnian Serbs certainly bore the majority of the responsibility for the fighting that was going on at the time but that there was a good deal of responsibility left to be shared by the Bosniaks and the Croatians.

I returned to Washington two weeks later to fulfill the second half of the contract. This time I gave no speech, but I did appear as a witness before a U.S. congressional committee and did a number of media interviews, including spots on CSPAN and *Larry King Live*.

That evening I received a phone call in my Washington hotel room from Roy Gutman, another Pulitzer Prize–winning journalist who had covered the Balkan conflict. He asked, "Did you know that your speaking fee when you spoke to the Heritage Foundation was paid by Serbnet?"

I drew a blank and could only respond, "What's Serbnet?"

Gutman replied, "It's a Serbian-American group that monitors the media and tries to put their own spin on all the bad press the Serbs are getting."

The best I could come up with at the time was: "I suppose I'll have to check it out."

The next day the story was all over the front pages of most newspapers, particularly in Europe and the Muslim world. I was branded everything from a "hero with feet of pay" to a Serblobbyist who was on the Serbs' payroll during my entire time in Sarajevo and the months that followed. So I contacted Congresswoman Bentley for some clarification. Then I got the bad news: Serbnet had indeed paid part of my fee for the single speech. Although I donated the entire amount to CANFAR, the Canadian Foundation for AIDS Research, the damage had been done. Accusations of "MacKenzie's pro-Serb, cross-America speaking tour," paid for by the Serbs, became the story.

Shortly thereafter I was visited by the RCMP, who explained to me that reliable intelligence sources had advised them that three "hit teams" had left Sarajevo. Their three targets were the UN Secretary-General Boutros Boutros-Ghali, Prime Minister Brian Mulroney and yours truly. Boutros Boutros-Ghali was marked presumably because he was insensitive and ignorant enough to go to Sarajevo and tell its citizens, who were under fire at the time: "I can list ten other cities in the world where the situation is worse than Sarajevo!" And Brian Mulroney was on the list because his wife, Mila, was born a Serb in Sarajevo.*

I was the only one of the three who had no security other than my own military background, so it was decided that RCMP Corporal Dave Hartley would keep an eye on me and coordinate a modest level of security, particularly during my frequent travels. I was spending a lot of time on the road fulfilling the many professional speaking engagements that were being requested at an alarming rate. I had signed on with David Lavin and his Lavin Agency, headquartered in Toronto and with an office in Boston, and as a result I was crossing the U.S. border frequently. Dave arranged for the FBI to monitor me when I made presentations in the United States.

My first concern in this situation was for my family. I was spending a lot of time away from home. Dora and I hadn't made up our minds yet about where we would settle. At the time, we were renting an unfurnished penthouse apartment close to the Lester Pearson International airport in Etobicoke while we considered our options. It was a relatively easy building to monitor, and I was pretty confident that Dora was well protected. Our daughter, Kimm, who was living in Ottawa, also needed protection, so arrangements were made by the police to enhance her security.†

I was also authorized to carry a handgun. I didn't feel I needed it, but the weapon stayed with Dora in the apartment when I was away. To ensure she was comfortable with it, we ventured into the backwoods of Muskoka, where she proved to be a quick learner with the 9 mm pistol. A senior police chief

---

* Mila, née Pivnicki, and her family left Yugoslavia for Canada when she was five years old.

† Kimm is finding this out only now as she reads this!

and friend mentioned to me that it might be a better idea to have Dora get comfortable with a pump-action shotgun, as it would be "more accurate" in a high-pressure situation and that even the "clack-clack" of it being cocked would be enough to dissuade most potential troublemakers. I took the advice and then advised all my male friends: "For God's sake, don't get into the booze and decide to pay me a surprise visit on a Friday night unless you're sure I'm home!"

Corporal Hartley became a close friend to our family. It was a terrible shock when, on the first day back at work following a few weeks' holiday, he suffered a heart attack and died during his daily exercise routine. I never asked, but I doubt if this young, dedicated policeman was a day over forty.

Shortly thereafter, the threat level was reduced and we were back on our own. But I still wouldn't recommend that you try to sneak into our house when I'm away!

14: On the Road Again

*"Are you out of your bloody mind? You stole the
pistol of an indicted war criminal!"*

DAVID KIRK, DIRECTOR OF *A SOLDIER'S PEACE*

LARGELY THANKS TO the free publicity provided by the
international media during my relatively short tour of duty in
Sarajevo, my first attempt at writing ended up being a best seller
in 1993–94. I was flattered when I learned that American and
Canadian networks were discussing the wisdom of producing a
movie based on the book. I was apprehensive, though, because
I knew it wouldn't have a substantial budget, and the previous attempt at turning a book about the Canadian military into
a Monday night TV movie was a disaster. Robert Mason Lee's
insightful book, *Death and Deliverance,* concerning the heroics
associated with the 1991 crash of a Canadian Forces Hercules
resupply aircraft en route to the Canadian Forces' Station Alert,
close to the North Pole, deserved much better than it got in the
movie *Ordeal in the Arctic.* Fifty-seven-year-old actor Richard
Chamberlain, who had become famous as TV's Doctor Kildare
three decades earlier, played the young Canadian captain John

Coach. Most of the movie was filmed in an aircraft hangar in Edmonton, where—at a simulated 20 to 30 degrees below zero— no one's breath was visible throughout the entire movie.

Literary agent Linda McKnight, who had taken me by the hand and led me through the process of writing my first book and getting it published, came to the rescue. Linda explained that documentary filmmaker extraordinaire Michael Maclear was considering making a documentary based on my book. That really piqued my interest because Michael is one of the very best in the documentary business. He was well known internationally as a combat reporter during his younger days, but his groundbreaking documentary, *Vietnam: The* 10,000 *Day War,* which looked at the conflict in Vietnam from both sides, including unique interviews with top North Vietnamese and Viet Cong leaders, set him apart.

Michael decided he would buy the movie rights to my book on the understanding that he would not make a movie, but would instead produce a serious documentary on the United Nations. He put together an outstanding team. David Kirk would direct the effort; with his CBC experience directing superior mini-documentaries for *The Journal,* his qualifications were unequalled. Mike Grippo, who had extensive experience in operational theatres including Bosnia when I was there, would be the cameraman; and Alistair Bell, one of the great characters in the sound game, would round out our team. Back at Michael's Toronto headquarters, Tom Gould, a well-known Canadian TV personality and journalist, would research and write the documentary's narrative.

It was decided that we would film in locations where I had served or where a UN mission was struggling to achieve its mandate. Croatia, Bosnia, Macedonia, Cyprus and Somalia would be our major stops, with side trips to interview well-known leaders and personalities, including President François Mitterrand of France, President Kiro Gligorov of Macedonia, Brent Scowcroft from President George Bush's administration, Radovan Karadzic and President Alija Izetbegovic of Bosnia, Cypriot President Glafcos Clerides and his Turkish Cypriot opposite number Rauf Denktash and our own prime minister, Jean Chrétien. We would travel light, carry our own kit and bum rides with military aircraft where and when we could.

At the end of January 1994 we flew to Cyprus, where I had served in 1965, 1971 and 1978 with the UN force monitoring the separation of the Greek and Turkish Cypriot communities. Since the force had been there since the intercommunal troubles of 1964 (and remains there to this day!), we wanted to make the point that the presence of a UN peacekeeping force often stands in the way of a negotiated settlement between the belligerents. Both sides in a conflict frequently remain intractable when they know that fighting is unlikely to break out again due to the presence of the "blue berets." To make the point, I interviewed Greek Cypriot President Clerides, following which I walked a relatively short distance across the Green Line to the office of Turkish Cypriot President Denktash. They were the leaders of the two communities on the island and, although they had gone to school together, they had not spoken to each other in an official capacity since the Turkish intervention in 1974. Furthermore, the international community had not forced them to do so in spite of the cost of maintaining a UN force on the island.

While looking for another example of the UN being exploited by a festering conflict, we discovered an outstanding case to make the point. The commander of the UN's Austrian contingent that was patrolling the Green Line on the south of the island had been on Cyprus thirty years earlier when he was five years old and visiting his father, who was commanding the Austrian contingent at the time. Here was a commanding officer walking the same patrol routes and observing from the same observation posts that his father had established three decades earlier. If that didn't make the point that the UN can get sucked into staying around much too long when the belligerents refuse to negotiate, nothing would.

From Cyprus we flew to London for an interview with Lord Carrington, the European Community's special representative for Bosnia during my time in Sarajevo. I recalled with him his comment to me as he boarded a plane at the Sarajevo airport during the summer of 1992, after talks with the Bosnian President Izetbegovic and Radovan Karadzic. He stopped on the top step of the ramp to his aircraft, turned, looked me in the eye and said, "Lew, I leave them to you. They are all mad!"

Two days later we were in Paris and very appreciative that President Mitterrand had agreed to an extensive interview. This was quite a coup, for two reasons. First, the president was terminally ill with cancer, and second, he rarely granted interviews to foreigners, particularly unilingual anglophones. We set up simultaneous interpreters in adjacent rooms to a grand ballroom in the Élysée Palace and waited for the president to arrive. An aide appeared at the door and beckoned me to join him. I followed him to a small room where the president was having makeup applied. I was shocked at his appearance. I could see the bone structure of his face quite clearly because his skin was translucent. He was obviously suffering from both the cancer and the treatment, and I felt guilty about taking up his time but enormously grateful for his co-operation. We chatted in English, recalling his surprise visit to Sarajevo, which helped kickstart the humanitarian airlift to the city in July 1992.

The interview lasted an hour and provided us with the soundbites we wanted regarding the laborious decision-making process at the UN Security Council. I could see the president was getting tired, so I attempted to bring the interview to a close. As I started to rise, he extended his arm, palm down, and moved his fingers gently up and down, motioning to me to sit down again. He then spoke softly for a few minutes. The gist of his message was: "General, I had no hesitation in sending my soldiers to Sarajevo under your command. I was confident they would be well led and safe with you. And you exceeded my expectations." I was dumbfounded, and before he departed I managed only to thank him for sending me such fine French soldiers, including the four bodyguards he had directed to be assigned to me during my last month in Sarajevo.

A three-week filming hiatus followed during which I fulfilled a contractual obligation with Price Waterhouse. I was to head up a small team, of my own choosing, to study the structure of the Irish Defence Force and make recommendations for its reorganization. I chose two old friends to work on the project: retired Lieutenant-General Charlie Belzile, who had commanded the Canadian army for five years and had been a mentor to me, and retired Colonel Don Ethell, who had been a sergeant patrol commander in my platoon during our first tour of duty in Cyprus in 1965, and whose rapid rise through the officer ranks reflected his outstanding abilities. Together we produced a plan that was well received, and many of its recommendations were implemented to the letter. Unfortunately, the plan also generated one of my most serious and embarrassing cock-ups.

Our plan was submitted to the Irish government by Price Waterhouse. It was confidential and highly sensitive, and it was not to be discussed until it was released by the government. A few months later, I received a call from an Irish journalist who told me that the government had released the report and that he had been given a copy. He read from the report and asked me for some clarifications, which I obligingly provided. Twenty-four hours later, all hell broke loose in Ireland. It soon made its way to my end of the telephone line in Canada. Apparently, the report had not been released by the government after all; the reporter had obtained a bootleg copy via questionable channels and had duped me into giving him an interview. For someone who was pretty familiar with the media, I had been naive in the extreme. I was mortified. Price Waterhouse, too, was less than pleased, and it was easy to understand why.

Still reeling from my humiliation, our documentary team went on the road again, this time flying with the U.S. Air Force into Mogadishu, Somalia, via Cairo. It was important to highlight the UN's failure in Somalia in our documentary because of the general public ignorance about the mission. Most outsiders assumed that the United States was in charge because the intervention devolved into a disaster culminating in the Black Hawk Down incident, in which the stripped cadaver of an American helicopter crewman was dragged through the streets of the capital.

In fact, the UN Security Council–authorized, U.S.-led intervention in Somalia in December 1992 to rescue a floundering UN-led mission was the most successful in the history of the organization. A measure of security was quickly established, and humanitarian aid was delivered throughout the country. Six months later, the United States started to withdraw its troops and the UN took over command of the mission. The UN convinced the U.S. to leave a small contingent of combat troops in Somalia because other nations were not lining up to take over the major combat role. The U.S. reluctantly left behind a small force to work under a UN mandate and control. On October 3, 1993, two U.S. Black Hawk helicopters were shot down during a misguided UN attempt to capture or kill warlord Mohammed Farah Adid. Once again the UN had proved itself incapable of commanding and controlling combat operations. President Bill Clinton ordered all remaining U.S. soldiers out of Somalia by March 1994, and the UN abandoned the country a year later, leaving it in worse shape than it found it. Unfortunately, we had yet another good example for our documentary of what was wrong with the UN.

While filming in Mogadishu, we decided to visit the site of one of the downed Black Hawk helicopters. We were guided through a rabbit's warren of back alleys no more than two metres wide, defined on both sides by crumbling adobe walls linked with similarly constructed homes facing the alley. As an infantry soldier I couldn't imagine a more difficult place to fight an enemy who would be familiar with the complicated and haphazard network of tiny passages. After a kilometre we came to an open clearing the size of half a football field. A Black Hawk rested on top of a collapsed adobe shack. It had been stripped clean of everything of value and was a mere aluminum and magnesium skeleton. We started to film, as Mike with his camera and Alistair with his sound equipment took up their positions a metre in front of me.

We had hired two "technicals" for our protection. They were much in demand and as a result expensive, around $500 a day, thanks to the inflated fees paid by the major U.S. television networks. Ours were armed with AK-47s. They stood off to the side during the filming.

A minute into my script, I could see a crowd forming as I looked over Mike's shoulder and directly in front of me. The crowd was rapidly growing and moving in our direction. I decided to stop my commentary and turned to look at our protectors. They looked very ill at ease. One raised his AK-47 and cocked it to put a round in the chamber. As he pulled the cocking handle to the rear, the bottom fell off his magazine, the spring followed and a single 7.63 mm steel-jacketed round fell

to the ground! That was the limit of his arsenal—a single bullet. So it looked like it was time to negotiate. By now the crowd
had surrounded us and was chanting and making threatening
gestures. More than once I heard, "Americans, Americans." The
light came on just as the second of our protectors started yelling,
"Canada, Canada!" To my considerable amazement, the crowd
calmed down as our guard explained what we were doing. The
mood of the crowd shifted to one of pride in having a U.S. helicopter "trophy" in their midst. One elderly woman, though,
remained aggressive towards us. It turned out that the helicopter had crashed on top of her house, killing some members of her
family. She wanted to be compensated and presumably thought
we looked and acted enough like Americans to qualify as potential compensators. Much as we empathized with her plight, we
agreed that it was time to get out of the area—before the mood
changed again.

Our crew's next stop was the Balkans. It became a bit complicated when Bosnian President Izetbegovic refused to grant us
an interview. There was a warrant out for my arrest in Bosnia, so
we decided to fly on a UN flight to Sarajevo from Zagreb, Croatia.
We would spend only a few hours on the ground in the UN-con-
trolled area, say hello to the UN commander, Sir Michael Rose,
shoot some footage at my old headquarters and then return to
Zagreb on what the UN now called "Maybe Airlines."

Since I was not welcome on the Bosniak side of the frontline
separating the Bosniak and Serb forces, it was not possible for us
to drive the short distance over the mountain to Pale for another
interview with the leader of the breakaway Bosnian Serbs,
Radovan Karadzic. The odds were that I would be identified
and arrested (or worse) as I left or returned to the government-
controlled area. We flew back to Zagreb, rented a car and, with
a few sets of dummy plates that we changed as we crossed each

national border, drove from Zagreb to Budapest to Belgrade. Three days later, we took the back route through the Serb-controlled area of Bosnia into Pale.

Karadzic always enjoyed the opportunity to plead his case with the West and immediately arranged for the interview to take place in his office. It was beginning to snow. There was some concern that if we waited too long, we might not be able to make it to our overnight accommodation farther up the mountain at one of the hotels close to the 1984 Olympics down-hill ski course.

During the interview, Karadzic sounded more like a real estate agent than the leader of a warring faction in a three-sided civil war. He took me to the map of Bosnia and explained the colour codes, indicating that some areas of Bosnia were more valuable than others—sort of a play on the three priorities when buying a house: "location, location, location." He explained that the Bosnian Serbs would be prepared to trade land with the country's Muslims; he always called them Turks, a pejorative reference harking back to the Ottoman invasion and their victory in the Balkans in the fourteenth century. The size of the present-day territorial exchanges would be determined by the assumed value of the property. Karadzic's aim was to carve out a contiguous area for his Bosnian Serb Republic within the borders of the existing Bosnia.

The interview over, we started to pack up our kit. Karadzic motioned to me to remain behind as David, Mike and Alistair moved outside to our rented Volkswagen van. He sat behind his desk, reached down and opened a drawer. He removed a small wooden box and said, "General MacKenzie, you will recall that when you left Sarajevo two years ago I tried to present you with this personally engraved 9 mm Yugoslavian military pistol. You explained that as a member of a UN mission you could not accept gifts from any side in the conflict. I understand that, but you are now here as a journalist and I want you to accept this pistol. It has your name on it." My mind was quickly going through the options, particularly the one that had me refusing the gift, upsetting Karadzic in the middle of "his" territory while being almost out of fuel for our vehicle. We would be walking the 290 kilometres back to Belgrade if we couldn't bum some fuel. I reached across the desk and accepted the pistol. I had to be careful here. I said, "I won't be able to take the pistol back to Canada with me but I will hand it over to our ambassador in Belgrade for shipment to the police in Canada. Once they contact me, I'll have it properly registered." We said our goodbyes, and I caught up with the team outside. Alistair was the only one standing outside the vehicle, so I passed him the pistol and said, "I'll explain later. Just slip this in one of your equipment bags when you have a chance."

With the snow now falling more heavily, the ride up the mountain to the site of the '84 Olympics downhill competition was treacherous enough. But without any treads on our tires and no limited-slip rear end on the van the climb turned into a comedy. Just as we were killing ourselves laughing while sliding backwards (contrary to our preferred direction), Alistair blurted out: "David, we have to go back to Pale!"

Our intrepid director, seated beside my driver's seat, yelled over the scream of the Volkswagen's boxer engine looking for traction, "For God's sake, why?"

Alistair, in the con of his life (and he has perpetrated many), explained: "David, do you remember when Karadzic took Lew up to the map on his office wall and started to talk about exchanging territory with the Bosnian Muslims?"

David nodded.

"Well, you and Mike were so intent listening to the two of them that I did something really stupid. I'd been admiring Karadzic's pistol, the one that was sitting on his desk, and when no one was looking I took it and put it in my sound bag." With this, Alistair reached into his bag and waved the pistol in the air. "I know it was the wrong thing to do, but it's probably best we go back and 'fess up."

Even in the dark (no headlights were allowed at night during the war), David's face was visibly alternating between the flush of rage and the drained look of panic. "Are you out of your bloody mind? You stole the pistol of an indicted war criminal! We'll never get out of here alive, even if we do go back. We are totally screwed! Is it loaded?"

At this point, the combination of us sliding backwards down one of the highest mountains in Yugoslavia, having no headlights, having consumed some plum brandy earlier and now listening to Alistair's imaginative con got the best of me. I burst out laughing, soon to be joined by Mike who, while not in on the con, was always up for an adventure. Finally Alistair admitted it was all a joke, and David started to breathe again.

A good thirty minutes later, we had climbed the kilometre to the Olympic hotel and settled down in our rooms—no heat, no lights, a thin blanket and no running water. It was like being back in the infantry.

The documentary that came out of this adventure, *A Soldier's Peace,* led off the CBC's *Witness* series in 1994 and was released at the same time on the BBC and the A&E networks. It has been shown in over sixty countries, and in 1996 won a New York Film Festival award. Its observations on the inability of the UN Security Council to deal with serious threats to international peace and security are clearly still relevant: it continues to be aired on history and documentary channels. I imagine David shudders and Alistair smiles whenever they catch a glimpse of it while channel surfing.

15: Hostage Release by Cellphone

"Tell the general I'm going back to the field."

CAPTAIN PAT RECHNER, HANDCUFFED TO A LIGHTNING ROD NEAR
AN AMMUNITION DEPOT IN PALE, BOSNIA

IT WAS THE spring of 1995, the conflict in Bosnia continued to dominate the media and I was about to be dragged back into the morass yet again.

The organizers of Nova Scotia's Annapolis Valley Apple Blossom Festival invited me to be their parade grand marshall on May 27, and then to help judge the Miss Apple Blossom contest at Acadia University that evening. Since the request had come from my home province and I had close relatives in the valley, I accepted. The organizers asked me to wear my uniform during the judging ceremonies, and I explained that I never wore my uniform when there was a chance that I might criticize government policy during my remarks (a principle I apply to this day), and thus I had not worn it since retiring twenty-six months earlier. I went on to admit that surely a beauty contest would not be controversial and that foreign policy would be the furthest thing from people's minds. So, yes, I would be happy to make an exception on this occasion and wear my scarlet mess kit.

During the previous week I had been outspoken in my interviews with the media, including spots on PBS's *McNeil-Lehrer News Hour* and *Larry King Live*. I criticized the UN's ridiculous plan to escalate the United Nations Protection Force (UNPROFOR) peacekeeping mission to a combat role involving NATO air strikes against the Bosnian Serb positions without first removing the UN's unarmed observers from their positions co-located with the Serbs. I predicted that the natural outcome of the action would be UN observers held as hostages and shields against further air attacks. On May 26, I boarded an Air Canada flight in Toronto for Halifax, intending to drive from the airport to Wolfville, arriving around noon.

Meanwhile, in Pale, west of Sarajevo and the site of the downhill skiing competitions in the 1984 Olympics, three unarmed UN observers were taken hostage by Bosnian Serbs as the NATO bombing continued. One of the hostages, Canadian Captain Pat Rechner, was destined to become the public face of yet another failed UN policy. Pat was a fellow member of my regiment, the PPCLI, and a few years earlier he had been my aide de camp (personal assistant) at CFB Gagetown. Early on in his ordeal at Pale, he was handcuffed to a tall and sturdy metal antenna located directly in front of a massive ammunition bunker. The threat was clear: if NATO bombed the bunker, Pat would be vaporized. His captors must have watched too many American police shows on television because they decided to undo his handcuffs for a few minutes and let him make one telephone call. He decided to call his parents.

Pat's family had left Czechoslovakia when he was a baby. They had emigrated first to Austria and then to Canada, settling in Vancouver, where his dad was head of Austrian Airlines in Canada. Pat was glad to get the chance to call home, but on his first attempt his parents' answering machine asked him to "leave a message." As his captors started to take him back to the antenna for handcuffing, Pat said: "Look, I didn't get through to my parents. Can I make one more call?"

"Who would you call?" was the skeptical response.

"General MacKenzie," Pat replied.

His captor was more than a little surprised, and fortunately he was impressed. A conversation ensued regarding how we knew each other and the fact that Pat had the number for our apartment in Etobicoke. He dialed it, presumably around the time I was passing over Montreal, about an hour from Halifax.

Dora picked up the phone and said, "Hello."

"Dora, is that you? It's Pat Rechner."

Dora hesitated and then blurted out, "Pat, what's going on? I was just watching you—in fact, I'm still watching a clip of you on CNN right now. Are you OK?"

"Yes, I'm OK. Would you please tell the general to let my parents know I'm fine and perhaps NDHQ also."

Dora asked, "What's happening to you now?"

What followed was a response that would not be clarified until new pictures flashed on the TV screens the following day. "I'm going back to the field," Pat said. Unfortunately, the response could be interpreted as "I'm going back to my duty as a UN observer" or, more ominously, as "I'm going back to be handcuffed to my antenna in front of the ammo dump!"

Coinciding with all the coverage of Captain Rechner and his ordeal, the news media started to phone our apartment in search of an interview. The first call was from CTV. Dora explained that I was en route to Annapolis Valley. The CTV rep explained that he wanted to talk to me about Captain Rechner. Dora said, "I expected that. In fact, I just spoke with him."

"Spoke with whom?" was the response.

"With Captain Rechner," she said.

A long pause followed as the caller absorbed what he had just been told. "Mrs. MacKenzie, Captain Rechner is the lead story on every network as we speak. What did he say, and why did he call you?"

For the next hour, Dora explained what had transpired and refused requests for on-camera interviews. Twenty minutes out of Halifax, the co-pilot came back to see me and said: "The folks at the airport have told us that there is a crush of media waiting to ambush you the moment you get off the plane. We thought you'd like to know."

"Thanks. Any idea what it's about?"

"Sorry, we haven't heard a thing," was all I heard just before the intercom announcement that we had started our descent into Halifax.

When we disembarked at the Halifax airport, a swarm of reporters appeared, reminiscent of the scrums in Sarajevo. They all wanted a comment about what I knew about Captain Rechner's situation. I had to admit to them that I only knew what I had seen along with everyone else who'd been following the saga on television. When they told me that Dora had been talking to Pat, I was more surprised than they were. I begged off any extensive interview, promising that I would be available later in the day at Acadia University and that I would then share with them anything I had discovered.

When I reached Dora, she described what had happened. I tried to get her interpretation of how Pat sounded when he said, "I'm going back to the field." I asked if he sounded anxious or relieved. Dora didn't recall anything specific, so exactly what he meant remained a mystery until we saw him handcuffed to the antenna the following day.

That evening at Acadia, I gave my first and last interviews in uniform since my retirement, including the ensuing thirteen years to today. Assuming that the media would have little interest in one of the judges at the Miss Apple Blossom pageant, I had been ambushed by events. My friends watching the television news that night must have wondered what I was doing, decked out in my formal mess kit while discussing such a sensitive subject.

There is a tradition in the PPCLI that if you don't make it to the mess dinner in honour of your retirement within two years of your retirement date, the invitation is cancelled. My schedule had prevented me from making it to Calgary on the dates suggested for the previous two years; however, in April we settled on June 17, and Dora and I flew from Toronto the day before. This was the twenty-first day of Captain Rechner's ordeal. To make matters worse, a dozen Canadian soldiers, members of the Royal 22nd Regiment (the Van Doos) had also been captured, in another location outside of Sarajevo, and were being held against their will as potential shields to thwart the NATO bombing of Bosnian Serb positions.

The night of the mess dinner, Dora and I were about to leave our hotel on MacLeod Trail. Just as we approached the elevator, my cellphone rang. Thinking I would lose the connection in the elevator, we let it go without us. "Hello," I answered.

"General MacKenzie, its Nicola Koljevic calling you from Pale." Three years earlier, at the beginning of the war, Vice-President Koljevic had been my primary point of contact with the Bosnian Serb breakaway leadership under Radovan Karadzic. He was a professor of Shakespearean literature who had taught at U.S. and

Canadian universities. I found him to be the most reasonable of Karadzic's entourage, and I noticed that Karadzic rarely made a decision without seeking Koljevic's advice.

By this time, Dora and I had returned to our hotel room. I knew this would be dicey. "Professor, thanks for calling," I said. "Perhaps we can discuss the hostage issue. You know, you're earning some really bad press, which you can do without."

"That's why I'm calling," he said. "I only just found out that Captain Rechner worked for you and that he spoke to your wife a few weeks ago. I want you to know that we will be releasing him and his two colleagues tomorrow."

I replied, over a bad connection, "That's good news, Professor, but there is still the issue of the Canadian soldiers you are holding."

"We would like to release them too, but there is no way to get them over the mountain here to Pale to join up with Rechner for the trip to Belgrade," he explained.

There appeared to be an opening, so I continued: "Come on, Nicola, that's just not true. I know you bulldozed a dirt road around the mountain just after I left in '92. You can use that route to move the Van Doos soldiers." Professor Koljevic, not known for his map reading, immediately came back with: "I'll check it out, General. If it's possible, we will do it. I'll get back to you in a couple of hours."

Having been burnt before—when I got involved with the Canadians blockaded in Srebrenica—I knew what to do. I called NDHQ and asked if the leadership wanted me to proceed. I was advised that the French general commanding UNPROFOR was continuously negotiating to have our and others' soldiers released, but so far to no avail. I then called Foreign Affairs and confirmed that their duty personnel wanted me to proceed. Now a good forty-five minutes behind schedule and a couple of hundred dollars poorer, thanks to cellphone connections with Bosnia, Dora and I jumped in the waiting car and drove to the PPCLI Officers' Mess in southwest Calgary.

The reception before the formalities lasted about forty-five minutes before the bugle sounded to announce dinner. As cellphones were not permitted in the mess, I put mine on vibrate and slipped it into my inside breast pocket. Sometime around the end of the soup course the pleasant sensation over my left breast suggested that Professor Koljevic was calling back. I turned to the commanding officer and, in a serious breach of military protocol, feigned cramps and excused myself from the table. Just outside the front door of the mess, I opened the phone. It was Nicola: "General, you were right. We can bring the soldiers to Pale. They will be released tomorrow."

"That's good news, Professor. I'll pass the details on to our people. Say hello to Captain Rechner for me."

I passed on the news to NDHQ. The next day, CNN showed the bus holding the Canadians off-loading them outside of Belgrade. The professor was the first off the bus. He said to the reporter, "Thanks to General MacKenzie we were able..." and then the film clip ended. No one called from Foreign Affairs, but at least I wasn't vilified in the press. Dora wanted me to submit my cellphone bill to Ottawa.

I never spoke with Professor Koljevic again. Eight months later, he placed a pistol to his head and committed suicide. In 1992, whenever I had taken him to meetings with the Bosniaks, there would be embraces and tears as his former students at the University of Sarajevo, now Bosniak officials caught up in a war, greeted him. I fear the reality of the stupid civil war swirling around him was just too much for this learned professor of Shakespearean literature.

A final thought about the hostage taking: I have never understood why Captain Patrick Rechner was not decorated for the example he set during his weeks in captivity, under hazardous circumstances and in the glare of the international media. He was the face of a failed and naive UN policy that tried to combine peacekeeping and war fighting. Nevertheless, throughout his ordeal as the most high-profile victim of the UN's failure, he maintained his composure under great strain and in the view of millions. A lesser individual would have succumbed to understandable fear and agreed to read from scripts provided by his captors for the benefit of the international media. There are all too many examples of the latter, and Captain Rechner's performance deserved more credit than the less-than-warm welcome he received on his return to Canada.

16: Political Waters

"What's a membership?"

A ROOKIE PROGRESSIVE CONSERVATIVE PARTY CANDIDATE

THE NIGHT OF October 30, 1995, turned out to be the worst night of my life. I'll never forgive the CBC for superimposing that bar graph at the bottom of its television transmission that moved back and forth as the "Yes" and "No" votes were received from the referendum on Quebec's sovereignty. They might as well have shown "My country's gone" and "My country's saved" at each end of the graph, rather than Yes and No. The No side's victory was so slim that I didn't really feel like celebrating. The Yes side was not going to go away, and the next referendum or a universal declaration of independence was probably somewhere around the corner. It made me think back to a decision I'd made two years earlier.

Back in 1993, two days before my release from the Canadian Forces, I had been approached by both the Progressive Conservative and the Liberal parties to run for them in the upcoming October federal election. A soon-to-be friend, Hugh Segal, made the pitch for the Tories over breakfast on Bank Street in Ottawa, and the leader of the opposition, Jean Chrétien, had invited me to Stornoway for a similar conversation. It was not a hard decision to make, since I'd never thought I was cut out to be a politician. I had more or less followed the government's line while in uniform for thirty-six years, so it didn't seem like a good idea to immediately subordinate my personal opinions and priorities to those of any political party.

By 1997, however, with the near-death experience of the Quebec referendum still weighing heavily on my mind, the upcoming election looked like an opportunity to make a contribution to the debate. The exposure would give me an opportunity to address the issue of national unity. However, I had to decide which party to join. I had been approached yet again by both the Conservatives and the Liberals, as well as the Reform Party, and Paul Hellyer too had visited me at my home, trying to convince me to run for his new Action Party.

Most military personnel are small-c conservatives. There are a lot of exceptions, but the combination of conservative values and Pierre Trudeau's badly hidden contempt for the military in general has been and is a real handicap when the Liberals come courting the soldier's support at the polls. What really irked me as I tried to make up my mind was recalling the chronic habit of just about every party, once elected, to abandon its platform and promises at the Ottawa city limits on its way to Parliament. The NDP was an occasional exception, but the fact that they would probably never be elected to lead the country in my lifetime provided them with the luxury of being the conscience of Parliament without assuming the usual political risk of leadership.

If I couldn't decide on a party on the basis of ideology, I would have to decide on leadership—and that made the decision easy. During the run-up to the referendum, the leader of the

Progressive Conservative Party, Jean Charest, had taken a leading role in speaking out in support of the No campaign while his
fellow Quebecer and leader of the Liberal Party, Prime Minister
Jean Chrétien, had chosen a much more passive, almost invisible
role. Charest's stand was not popular with a significant portion
of Quebec's population and posed a considerable risk for his
political future. But he stood his ground, and then some, in support of a united Canada: Charest was the leader I would support.

Charest opined that I should run in the Toronto area. The
party would put together an impressive team to take me by the
hand through the nomination process and, if successful, the election campaign. But I had spent most of my life moving every one
or two years, and now, having settled in Bracebridge, close to
my wife Dora's hometown of Baysville in the Muskoka region of
Ontario, I wasn't about to move again. Charest didn't have what
you would call a large team to go on the road during the upcoming campaign. Elsie Wayne, the dynamic former mayor of Saint
John, New Brunswick, who I knew from my days of commanding CFB Gagetown, was the only other Conservative member of
Parliament at that time. We agreed that I would run where I lived,
in the riding of Parry Sound–Muskoka, and that I would go on
the road to support other Conservative candidates and speak out
on the issue of national unity. The fact that the Reform Party was
well represented and organized in the riding meant that we would
probably split the conservative vote and let the Liberal incumbent, Andy Mitchell, motor up the middle. That didn't bother me;
I would have a platform during the campaign to address the most
important issue, the future of a united Canada.

The team put together to take me through the process of running as a candidate was certainly not impressed—indeed, they
were depressed—at our first meeting at my home on February
2, 1997. Early on in the meeting someone said, "We really have

to get busy selling memberships if we are going to get Lew the party's nomination!" I unwisely asked, "What's a membership?" There was a very pregnant pause as everyone, including me, realized that their candidate had a very steep learning curve ahead of him. To complete a less-than-perfect day, I was "reminded" by Dora after the meeting broke up at 11 PM that this day marked our thirtieth wedding anniversary.

In the end, during a really miserable winter in one of the largest ridings in Canada, in which my friend and campaign manager, Don Smith, led the way with a dedicated team of volunteers, we travelled enough miles and sold enough party memberships to win the nomination. It was evident at the nomination meeting that I would probably have my desired platform to address national unity during the campaign. All three national television networks and the CPAC cable network were there to cover what would normally be a low-key event in the political process.

The campaign was rough on my team. The Progressive Conservative Party kept asking me to speak at numerous events coast to coast, and I didn't resist: each venue provided me with an opportunity to deliver my thoughts on national unity to a wider audience. Don Smith was frustrated because his role was to get me elected, and here I was, spending too much time out of the riding. My opponents wisely zeroed in on that fact and suggested that if elected I would focus on national and international issues at the expense of the local interests of the people of Parry Sound–Muskoka. The fact that national unity was critical to every riding in Canada was a moot point during the cut and thrust of a political campaign.

During my presentations on national unity I shamelessly recalled a particularly nasty event that had occurred in Sarajevo in July 1992, at the height of the Bosnian civil war. The UN had brokered a deal with the Bosnian Serbs to use the Sarajevo airport for the delivery of humanitarian aid to all sides in the conflict. We couldn't wait the month or so for the UN to find the additional troops to defend the airport, so the Canadian government generously agreed that we could "borrow" the Canadian battle group serving in Croatia for thirty days to take on the task. They reported to me as the commander in Sarajevo on July 2, just missing Canada Day. The battle group was based on the 1st Battalion of the Royal 22nd Regiment, the Van Doos. Attached to the battle group for its six-month tour of duty in the former Yugoslavia was a large company from the Royal Canadian Regiment. By sheer happenstance, the battle group's composition was the reverse of Canada's national representation group (NRG): two-thirds francophone—the Van Doos, and one-third anglophone—the Royal Canadian Regiment (RCR).

Shortly after their arrival I tasked the commanding officer, Lieutenant Colonel Michel Jones, to get some food and medicine to an isolated Bosnian Serb neighbourhood on the south side of the city. Most of the up to three hundred tonnes of humanitarian aid arriving daily was delivered to the primarily Muslim citizens of Sarajevo; however, in keeping with the peacekeeping principle of impartiality, it was important to get aid to those Bosnian Serbs who were also suffering. It was also a fact that with tens of thousands of Bosnian Serb soldiers, tanks and artillery surrounding six hundred Canadians, the humanitarian aid would only flow if the Serbs permitted it. The Bosniak population in Sarajevo and their leadership were not in the mood to accept the principle of UN impartiality and were furious with me for even thinking of sending any aid to isolated Serb locations.

Anglophone soldiers from the RCR loaded up a number of our armoured personnel carriers with food and medicine and headed through the city before turning south towards the Serb enclaves. Just after crossing the Miljacka River, and still in

Bosniak-controlled territory, they were blocked at gunpoint and surrounded by a large number of Muslim soldiers. The soldiers searched the vehicles and claimed the Canadians were smuggling ammunition to the Serbs. They threatened to kill every Canadian in the convoy. The area was completely dominated by high-rise apartments occupied and fortified by the Bosniak soldiers. There was absolutely no way out, and any rescue attempt would be borderline suicidal.

I called the UN peacekeeping department in New York to try and get the UN to have the Bosnian ambassador call the Bosnian president and have him release my soldiers. The official I dealt with had no idea who I was and didn't even know that UNPROFOR was in the former Yugoslavia. I hung up in disgust and proceeded down Sniper Alley to see the president himself. He and his defence minister were too scared to accompany me to the scene of the standoff, so I decided that a rescue mission by the Canadian battle group, no matter how risky, was my only alternative.

As we weaved our way back to my headquarters, I realized this would be the most difficult order I would ever give. I would have to be honest with the soldiers who'd been tasked to conduct the operation. They would have to be told that their chance of success was slim and that many of them would not survive. They would be subjected to deadly fire from 360 degrees, and from above, due to the fortified highrises. The alternative was to let the RCR soldiers be slaughtered, and there was no way I would even contemplate permitting such a result without a fight. I thought that after we arrived at headquarters and I gave instructions it would take at least an hour for the rescue group to get themselves organized, prepare their equipment and vehicles, give their own orders and move out.

A mad dash by my French marine commando driver brought our vehicle to my headquarters in less than five minutes. As we turned into the parking area behind the headquarters building, I was dumbfounded by what I saw. The entire expanse was occupied by armoured personnel carriers packed with soldiers and pointing in the direction of the confrontation that was less than three minutes away. I was advised that orders had been given, ammunition had been issued, a route had been determined and an assault plan briefed to the lowest level. All that was needed to launch the Van Doos rescue mission was one word from me: "Go!" A largely francophone rifle company was prepared to lay it on the line for a largely anglophone rifle company.

That, I told audiences in Victoria, Vancouver, Calgary, Edmonton, Toronto, Ottawa, Montreal, Saint John, Halifax, Wolfville, Sydney and other stops along the campaign trail, was my Canada. Not a country defined by a Constitution, a Charter of Rights or any other document, but rather by the synergy of two of the founding nations, French and English working together to create a country, not perfect, but better than any other in the history of the world when it comes to tolerance, accommodation and support for those less fortunate than ourselves. The fact that francophones would die to rescue their anglophone fellow soldiers said it all.

Sure, I knew there were bragging rights involved, as the Van Doos would never let the RCR forget that on July 20, 1992, they saved their butts, but that's soldiers' black humour. The more important message for me was that my country was more than the sum of its parts: it was a unique success story of two quite different cultures imposing themselves through conflict on a third culture and ultimately, with all the warts, actually getting along and making it work while the rest of the world looked on with envy. Were we prepared to stand idly by and let Quebec vote that unity out of existence? No way. That was my message.

The entire effort of running in a federal election campaign was worth it when I saw tears well up in the eyes of Canadians who, when they heard what our soldiers were prepared to sacrifice for each other, realized—perhaps for the first time—what a gift we Canadians had been given.

The night of the election, we Progressive Conservatives gathered at the Riverside Inn in Bracebridge. At one point I was slightly ahead, and Dora, who had so far moved twenty-four times in our thirty-year marriage, turned to me and said, "I hope you like Ottawa—by yourself!" Fortunately I didn't have to endure that arrangement. The excellent Reform Party candidate, Peter Spedinski, received 10,909 votes; yours truly, 11,435 and the incumbent Liberal, Andy Mitchell, 17,752. I wasn't disappointed: I had convinced at least a few Canadians that this country was worth fighting for.

Unfortunately, my running in the 1997 campaign gave the false impression that I wanted to serve as a member of Parliament. The many subsequent requests that I run for the leadership of the Progressive Conservative Party, and subsequently the Conservative Party, were good for my ego, but I was smart enough to take on a subordinate and much safer role, the one made famous by Robert Stanfield (also from Truro, Nova Scotia): the best prime minister we never had.

I knew in my heart that if I was ever successful in obtaining any political office, the reaction twenty-four hours later would be, "Oh my God, what have we done?"

17: Back to the Balkans

"Five hundred U.S. Marines pre-positioned in Macedonia deserted today, refusing the order to invade Yugoslavia."

SERBIAN STATE TELEVISION, BROADCASTING FROM BELGRADE

DURING THE BALKAN wars that commenced with the declarations of independence by Slovenia and Croatia in 1991 and Bosnia-Herzegovina in 1992, conditions in the Serbian province of Kosovo continued to deteriorate. The ninety per cent Albanian majority were treated as less than equals by the Serbian minority. Appointments in the civil service, universities, police and military all favoured the Serbs. However, although the Albanians in many areas were treated as second-class citizens, there was little if any violence between the two communities. There were also growing cries for independence from the Kosovo Albanians, and an armed resistance group calling itself the Kosovo Liberation Army (KLA) looked north to Bosnia and saw the United Nations manoeuvred into assisting that country in maintaining its recent independence from Serbia.

The KLA decided to jump on the independence bandwagon and commenced its terrorist campaign against the Serbian minority in

Kosovo. Serbian police, the KLA's favourite targets, were regularly ambushed, captured or killed. The CIA added the KLA to its list of terrorist organizations. As is the habit when an authoritarian government is challenged, particularly under communist rule, the reaction by those in power was heavy-handed. Under the leadership of President Slobodan Milosevic, the Serbian security forces in Kosovo were reinforced, and a campaign to track down and eliminate the KLA was launched. Following the Bosnian government's example, the KLA hired a respected U.S.-based public relations firm to represent its cause, and the propaganda war was on. International sympathy started to swing in the KLA's favour; international calls for Milosevic to moderate his campaign to eliminate the KLA started to dominate the news.

In 1999, NATO marked its fiftieth birthday as the most successful military alliance in history. It had never been forced to fire a shot in anger, and at the end of the Cold War it was still intact as a powerful military force. But it faced a dilemma: there was no consensus regarding what NATO's new role should be. Every option, from disbanding to becoming the world's policeman, was on the table.

Early in 1999, the eyes of the international community were focused on Kosovo. On January 15, the media had repeated ad nauseam film clips of more than forty cadavers in a ditch near the town of Račak in Kosovo. The site was visited by William Walker, the U.S. representative of the Organization for Security and Co-operation in Europe (OSCE) in Serbia. For all to hear, including the television audience, Walker said that this was a massacre of civilians carried out by the Serbs. Subsequent forensic investigations concluded that there was no massacre and that this was a staged event: KLA cadavers, the result of earlier fighting, had been deposited in the ditch, and some of them had had their uniforms replaced with civilian clothes before being shot

again for effect. It was a brilliant propaganda victory for the
KLA and became known as Kosovo's "Gulf of Tonkin incident."

NATO, sensing a role for itself and therefore its survival, went
into overdrive. When the emergency conference dealing with the
crisis in Kosovo, held in Rambouillet, France, in February, with
a follow-up meeting in March, issued an ultimatum to Milosevic
that U.S. Secretary of State Madeleine Albright acknowledged he
could never accept, NATO finalized its plans to forcefully intervene in the internal matters of a sovereign state. For all intents
and purposes, NATO would serve as the KLA's air force. NATO's
bombing campaign against Serbian installations and security
forces in both Serbia and Kosovo began on March 24.

On March 31, U.S. Army Staff Sergeants Andrew Ramirez and
Christopher Stone and Specialist Steven Gonzales were captured
by Serbian forces in the area of the Macedonian-Kosovo border.
The three men were part of a NATO force that had recently been
deployed to the area to secure the border. The Serbs claimed they
had crossed the border into Serbian territory, whereas NATO
claimed they were in Macedonia when captured. The debate mat-
tered little; the three Americans were prisoners of war.

At the time, I was being kept busy responding to media
requests for interviews about the bombing campaign. I did not
support NATO's actions and its justification because I had my
suspicions about the "massacre" at Račak long before any forensic investigation confirmed my misgivings. I had seen the media
manipulated too many times in Bosnia to accept the initial
reports of any incident as gospel. The KLA was playing the West,
particularly Madeleine Albright, like a Stradivarius.

The three captured U.S. soldiers were causing a PR nightmare
for the Serbian authorities in Belgrade. I received a call from
the embassy of Yugoslavia in Ottawa suggesting that I might be
able to assist in releasing the soldiers. Coincidentally I had been

approached by CTV to join another "Lewis and Clark" expedition with my friend Tom Clark and travel to Belgrade to cover
the war. The two opportunities matched perfectly. I also agreed
to write an article a day for the *Ottawa Citizen* for as long as the
bombing campaign endured. This detail would ultimately prove
to be my undoing with President Milosevic.

We flew to Budapest on April 12 and then drove to Hungary's
border with Serbia to meet up with the car that had been arranged
to drive us to Belgrade. Serbian customs officials took us to a
small room beside the office of the senior customs officer and
asked us to wait. Tom and I feared that we would be detained for
hours, and perhaps days, as was the case for two CBS reporters
we had encountered a few minutes earlier sitting on the sidewalk
in no man's land. Within minutes the officer in charge arrived
with the majority of his staff brandishing two bottles of slivovica.
"Welcome back to Serbia, General MacKenzie!" the boss exclaimed
for all to hear. It seemed the fact that I didn't blame the Serbs for
everything that went wrong in the Balkans—even suggesting
that the Muslims in Sarajevo had staged some of the atrocities
blamed on the Serbs, combined with my articles accusing the KLA
of staging the Račak massacre—had convinced many Serbs that
I hadn't bought into the slick PR campaign being conducted
against them.

On arrival in Belgrade we checked into the Hyatt Regency,
the hotel where most of the foreign press corps were billeted.
Our first stop, thanks to the intervention of the Yugoslavian
ambassador to Canada, was the foreign ministry, much to the
envy of the other foreign journalists. We were told by Foreign
Affairs Minister Zivadin Jovanovic that we would have a car and
driver permanently assigned to our CTV team and that one of his
personal staff would be our contact with his office. We could go
where we wanted and speak to whomever we wished. I asked

about interviewing President Milosevic, hoping this would raise the issue of the three American POWs. The minister didn't bite, and we returned to the hotel.

During the next few days we visited and reported on the destruction of the refinery and petrochemical production capabilities in Pančevo, close to Belgrade, and Novi Sad in the north. The bombing at these two sites was unbelievably precise. At Novi Sad, the plant manager explained that he had been trained in Houston, Texas, and was in charge of the plant's subsequent construction. There was only one stack out of more than a hundred that was absolutely critical to the plant's operation, and a single NATO cruise missile had gone straight down the stack, destroying the control room. There was no other obvious damage, but the entire massive facility was shut down and there was no chance of starting up until after the war was over and the critical parts had been replaced. We also saw evidence of precise bombing the following day when we visited the headquarters of the special security service in Belgrade. The missile had gone straight through the front door before detonating and destroying the building and its few occupants; most of them, anticipating an attack, had left well before the missile struck. Unfortunately, the myth of NATO's "precision" bombing was shattered the following day.

In the evening, while watching CNN after our visit to the destroyed security service building, we heard that a town in the south of the country close to the border of Kosovo had just been bombed. We decided to drive there early the next morning. As we got close to the town, we could see smoke rising from its centre. Arriving at the impact area, we saw a number of low-rise apartment buildings, minus their exterior walls, facing us. They looked like doll houses—you could see the interiors of all the rooms.

An angry crowd began to form around us. Our handler was not having much luck in calming them down by explaining that we were there with the permission of their government. Then he mentioned my name: "This is General MacKenzie, from Canada." To our complete amazement, the mood of the crowd changed, and in the midst of this chaos they suddenly became friendly. It was then that I realized just how persecuted the entire nation felt. Although I had repeatedly apportioned the Serbs somewhere around sixty per cent of the blame for what went on in Bosnia, the fact that I had also exposed what the other sides were doing had earned me a reputation for being objective—at least, with the Serbs.

Then, coming from the right, through the rubble, an elderly lady was carrying something in her arms. When she reached me she held out the body of a three- or four-year-old child. The child had no head. It was her granddaughter. The woman screamed at me, asking why the Americans had done this to her family. I was at a loss for words. In the midst of this very emotional scene, her son ran back into the rubble, emerged with a dusty bottle of slivovica and insisted that I have a drink with him. I must say, not many innocent victims of an ill-founded bombing campaign would have been so understanding.

We left the devastated town centre and drove around look-ing for something, anything, that might have been the Serbian military target that NATO had missed. We found nothing. There was an abandoned army camp about fifteen kilometres outside of town, close to the main highway, but its state suggested that it hadn't been occupied for years. We returned to Belgrade.

The meeting with Slobodan Milosevic and discussions regarding the U.S. POWs was getting close, according to hints from the foreign minister. Unfortunately, my arrangement with the *Ottawa Citizen* to write an article a day was my downfall.

There had been increasing speculation in the press about the possibility of Kosovo gaining its independence. For all intents and purposes, the Rambouillet Accords immediately removed Serbia's sovereignty over Kosovo and stated that "Three years after the entry into force of this Agreement, an international meeting shall be convened to determine a mechanism for a final settlement for Kosovo, on the basis of *the will of the people*" (my emphasis).[2] Two weeks after arriving in Belgrade, I penned an article for the *Citizen* predicting that Milosevic might well "encourage" the hundreds of thousands of Serb refugees from Croatia to relocate in Kosovo in order to help the "No" side in any future referendum on sovereignty. The refugees had been ethnically cleansed from the Kyrenia region by the U.S.-inspired Croatian army's "Operation Storm" four years earlier. One paragraph of my article read: "If this is indeed the new Milosevic strategy, to see it unfold would be nothing less than another affront to humanity and a perverse exploitation of another group of innocent victims for political gain."[3]

I was writing the articles by hand and the hotel's front desk was faxing them to the *Citizen* in mid-afternoon. I assumed that each and every copy was being sent to the foreign ministry or Milosevic's office before it ever made contact with the hotel's fax machine, and I was right: within hours, our relationship with the foreign ministry cooled and the meeting with Milosevic was put on hold, never to be discussed again. Since any chance of influencing the fate of the U.S. POWs had evaporated, plans were made for my return to Canada. I was hesitant to leave because of my frustration with the propaganda being perpetrated by my old colleagues in NATO. The alliance's spokesman, Jamie Shea, stressed ad nauseam that the Serbs were not aware of what was really happening in Kosovo because they only had access to their state-controlled television. In fact, exactly the opposite was true:

in Belgrade, I had access to more news channels than I did back in Toronto. BBC1, BBC2, SKY, Channel 4, CNN (both domestic and international), CBC plus a number of others were all available, and there were satellite dishes on just about every building in the city and the surrounding areas. The propaganda on the state-run channel was so bad—"Five hundred Marines pre-positioned in Macedonia deserted today, refusing the order to invade Yugoslavia"—that the locals watched it only for entertainment.

Tom Clark stayed in Belgrade for a few more weeks. He was there when a NATO air strike destroyed the Belgrade TV studio building used by the international media. A number of the friends we had made during our reporting back to Canada were killed. The hands of the make-up girl who patted a bit of powder on our faces before we went on camera were found across the street from the bombed-out building. Nevertheless, every channel broadcasting from the building was up and running from other locations within hours. The NATO attack achieved nothing but needless carnage, much like the rest of the ill-founded campaign.

Fast forward to February 17, 2008—and contrary to UN Resolution 1244 of June 10, 1999, which recognized the continued existence of Kosovo as part of Serbia—the province's leadership declared Kosovo an "independent, sovereign and democratic state." In the celebrations that followed, ominously the most popular flag waved on the streets of the capital of Pristina was not that of Kosovo but rather of neighbouring Albania. The ultimate objective of a "Greater Albania" was on parade for all to see.

The Western media immediately announced the inevitability of comprehensive international recognition of an independent Kosovo. They failed, however, to point out that the leaders of the vast majority of the world's population did no such thing. China, Russia, India, Spain, Indonesia (the world's most populous Muslim nation), Greece, Argentina and Canada (at the time of writing) were among the majority of the UN's 192 nations that did not grant recognition. For Canadians who had served in the Balkans in the 1990s, the situation was particularly upsetting, considering the emerging leadership of the new "statelet."

The newly minted prime minister of Kosovo, Hashim Thaci, and his immediate predecessor, Agim Cheku, have less than heroic backgrounds—contrary to what has been argued by their Albanian supporters. Cheku was a commander in the Croatian army and was in charge when Croat units raped and murdered their way through the Medak Pocket, burning Serbian families alive in the basements of their homes before they were stopped by Canadian peacekeepers. He also had a leadership role in Operation Storm in 1995, when lightly armed Canadian peace-keeping positions were cowardly and intentionally shelled with heavy artillery and tank fire before being overrun by Croatian army units. Shortly thereafter, Cheku ventured to Kosovo and assumed a leadership role with the KLA along with its leader, Hashim Thachi.

At that time the KLA was recognized as a terrorist organiza-tion by the CIA. Under the leadership of Thaci and Cheku, the KLA decided to kill members of the Serbian security forces in Kosovo with the strategic objective of inviting a heavy-handed reaction from Serbia and thus resulting in Western intervention on the side of the KLA. NATO fell for the ruse, and once again the West was outsmarted by the complexities of Balkan politics. In this instance, it could be argued that we bombed the wrong side.

If a nation is to be judged by its democratically elected lead-ership, Kosovo's reputation is hanging by a very thin thread.

18: ICROSS Canada: Our Drop in the Bucket

"We will endeavour to ease the suffering,

and feed the victims of poverty on this battered

and bleeding planet."[4]

ICROSS CANADA PLEDGE

IT WAS 1998, and standing over the Kenyan graves of Canadian soldiers killed during the UN mission in the Congo during the 1960s, Billy Willbond felt compelled to find someone "qualified" to pray for their departed souls. He tracked down a Jesuit brother, Michael Meegan, and the rest of Billy's life took a sharp turn—much to the benefit of thousands of Africa's children.

Billy Willbond and I served with the 1st Battalion of the Queen's Own Rifles of Canada on UN duty in Cyprus during the summer of 1965. He was a corporal in a company headquarters and I a lieutenant commanding the battalion's reconnaissance platoon. We met but didn't really get to know each other. Billy went on to serve with the newly created Canadian Airborne Regiment in the mid-1960s and retired as operations sergeant of the Special Service Force in 1978. He then took up a position with the Central Saanich Police Department on Vancouver Island.

Twenty-eight years ago, Michael Meegan dropped out of his final phase of seminary training in Ireland and went to Africa. With the exception of trips around the world to lecture on AIDS and related subjects and to meet with supporters like Bill Clinton, Elton John and Elizabeth Taylor, he hasn't left. He founded the International Community for the Relief of Starvation and Suffering (ICROSS) and is an acknowledged leading expert on the AIDS pandemic devastating Africa. He has been criticized for allegedly misrepresenting his academic credentials, but his good works in Africa speak for themselves and reflect a unique and selfless dedication to the helpless victims of AIDS on the continent.

In a nutshell, ICROSS seeks not a cure for AIDS but rather dedicates itself to reducing the pain and suffering of those in the terminal stages of the disease. Michael lives in the field and organizes and trains Africans to look after Africans. He has little to spend on infrastructure and equipment—during a recent visit, we had get out and push to help our truck make it over a steep hill as brand-new SUVs from large NGOs roared past. All donations to ICROSS and all Michael's speaking fees go to easing the pain of the terminally ill.

Billy Willbond was so impressed with Michael's dedication that following his visit he returned to Victoria committed to assisting him with his humanitarian mission. Initially, Billy used the slow hours during his night shift at the Saanich police station and his modest military pension to solicit medications and equipment and ship them to Michael. The increasing use and popularity of e-mail by retired military personnel enabled Billy to put together a team of volunteers, primarily but not exclusively retired peacekeepers, and on October 1, 1998, he created ICROSS Canada. Since those early days, Billy and his national team of volunteers have begged, borrowed and "coerced" more than $3 million worth of medical equipment, medicines and medical supplies for those who need them in both east and central south Africa.

Seven years ago, Billy called me and said I was to be the national patron for ICROSS Canada. This was not a request, but an order from one old soldier to another, so I signed on. The first challenge was convincing the bureaucracy that we were a legitimate and useful charity, operating in the best interests of Canada. Following an extended and frustrating wait, we were successful in obtaining charitable status in 2002.

Initially, our focus was on AIDS victims in Kenya. This is where Michael operated from, so we assumed it would make sense to piggyback on his efforts. But Kenya turned out to be a frustrating experience. As we received more and more donated materials, beds, bicycles (absolutely critical for allowing caretakers to move between villages), wheelchairs, stretchers, medications and so on, we had to purchase large sea containers to ship the goods from Victoria, B.C., to Kenya's port of Mombasa. (A sea container is a good investment, because once emptied of its contents, it can be used as a permanent home for an austere medical clinic.)

Chronic Kenyan corruption reared its ugly head the moment the first container touched down on the dock in Mombasa. In spite of all the documentation being in order, the container was seized and customs duty was demanded for the contents— despite the fact that humanitarian shipments were supposed to be exempt. The container sat in quarantine for almost two weeks at a "storage" charge of hundreds of dollars per day. Ultimately, after less-than-energetic intervention on our behalf by the Kenyan ambassador to Canada and bureaucrats in Nairobi, ICROSS Canada was forced to pay all fees, including the storage charges at the port, in order to take possession of the contents. Once it had emptied, we were forced to sell the sea container to pay off the loan required to pay those fees.

Following the experience with the first container, we were assured by the Kenyan authorities that it would not happen again. So, over the next year we naively filled another container with $200,000 of critical supplies and sent it off to Mombasa. This time, Tom Clark and the CTV crew of W5 would be there along with me to film its arrival at Michael's location outside of Nairobi. But the container never made it. It too was seized and subjected to the same treatment as the one the year before.

It didn't take long to find a less bureaucratic, less corrupt and equally deserving recipient of our humanitarian aid. Billy met Dr. Chris Brooks, from Calgary, who had established a medical clinic near Ngodzi in the Salima district of Malawi. Chris had founded Lifeline Malawi (an independent medical relief and development organization), sold his worldly goods, including his golf clubs and a dear-to-his-heart white 1964 Mustang and, like Michael Meegan, had left for Africa.

Malawi is the fourth-poorest nation in the world. Its ninety-four doctors care for twelve million people. One million of its citizens are orphans of parents struck down by AIDS. Dr. Brooks treats around four hundred of them a year at a nearby orphanage (where Madonna adopted a boy), in addition to providing medical service to more than 35,000 people in the surrounding area. Before his arrival they had never heard of Aspirin, let alone seen or visited a medical clinic, which gets larger by the year as our containers are emptied of their goods and added to the complex. Currently, this "Schweitzer from Calgary" and his tiny team of Malawians see up to 250 patients a day. Following a 2006 complimentary article on ICROSS Canada and Dr. Brooks in the *Toronto Star,* we received a burst of donations that allowed us to purchase a CD4 (blood analysis) machine that greatly helps with the early identification and treatment of HIV.

To ship medical supplies, some of which are fragile, we need good packing material, which has been provided for several years by an unusual, or at least unexpected, source.

Brian and Carol Isfeld were a retired couple living in Courtenay, B.C. Brian, a flight sergeant, had retired from the Canadian Forces in 1989. Their son Mark, nicknamed Izzy, joined the Canadian Forces after typically troubled teenaged years and was trained as a combat engineer. His first operational deployment was to the first Gulf War, where he assisted with the thankless, dangerous and physically and mentally demanding job of clearing mines from the shifting sands of the Kuwaiti and Iraqi deserts. A mere one year later, Izzy was doing the same thing in Croatia as part of the UN mission there.

While on his daily patrols in the scarred Croatian countryside, he frequently saw small children running alongside his armoured vehicle. More often than not, they were filthy and their clothes were in tatters—no wonder, considering that they were surviving in a war zone where some areas changed hands daily. So Izzy wrote his mother about the destitute children, and Carol started to knit small woollen dolls, fifteen to twenty centimetres tall, and mail them to her son. Whenever Izzy saw a child—and it didn't matter to him that he couldn't distinguish between a Serb, a Croatian or a Muslim kid—he would stop, lean over the side and drop a small doll from his mom into the waiting hands of a grateful child.

On June 21, 1994, Izzy and his mine-clearing team returned to a road leading to a Croatian farmer's complex close to Kakma, Croatia. They had cleared half the route on the previous day. Izzy walked beside the vehicle as it moved forward to the remainder of the route to be cleared. The vehicle's track touched a near-invisible piano wire that had been stretched across the road.

This detonated an explosive only a few metres away, instantly killing Master Corporal Mark "Izzy" Isfeld.

Following her son's death, Carol Isfeld continued to make the dolls. The word soon got around about her personal commitment in support of her son's memory, and other mothers in and around Courtenay joined the knitting campaign. The mother of the province's lieutenant governor, Iona Campagnolo, joined the effort and then, thanks to the Isfelds' Web site,* the knitting campaign went national. Izzy dolls are now handed out by Canadian soldiers in war and peacekeeping zones all over the globe—in Afghanistan, Sudan, Haiti, Bosnia, the Congo, Sierra Leone and Nigeria. Altogether, ICROSS Canada has sent out more than 200,000 Izzy dolls to distressed areas.

The dolls have also served a very practical purpose of providing packing material for shipping medical supplies. ICROSS Canada doesn't use bubble wrap; it uses Izzy dolls, by the thousands. They are produced in all shades of brown and black, and when they reach their destination they are given to children with AIDS and orphans of victims of AIDS. Many of these children have absolutely no other worldly possessions, and many of them, when they succumb to the disease, are buried still clutching their little doll from a mother in Canada.

Izzy Isfeld's compassion for these children, so much less fortunate than ours, is chipped in stone, thanks to his mom. Carol Isfeld succumbed to cancer in August 2007, and Brian Isfeld died only five months later. Their son's legacy, however, lives on through the fingers of hundreds of moms across this country, who continue to knit ICROSS Canada's "packing material."

---

* Online at *www.isfeldbc.com*.

19: Accused Rapist, Again

"I wish to formally complain regarding the unprofessional and irresponsible conduct of Mr. Oleg Cavka."

AN IRATE LETTER-WRITER

I DOUBT THAT any of my retired military colleagues have an entire drawer in their filing cabinet labelled "Rape Allegations."

Following the orchestrated allegations against me in 1992 and '93, kickstarted by the evidence offered by the alleged war criminal Borislav Herak and subsequently discredited (as described in chapter 13), I assumed the issue of my complicity had been laid to rest. But once or twice a year, I would receive a call or an e-mail from a friend living abroad, usually in Germany or Italy, indicating that yet again they had heard or read about the same allegations but nothing more.

But the matter resurfaced with a vengeance in late 2006. The president of the Congress of North American Bosniaks, Emir Ramic, "representing the interests of the 350,000 Bosniaks who live in Canada and the United States," repeated the accusations from 1992 and '93 and inserted some new ones based on "eye-witness" accounts. He wrote to the following individuals and organizations: Her Excellency Michaëlle Jean; the Right Honourable Stephen Harper; the Canadian Research Institute for the Advancement of Women; the National Action Committee on the Status of Women; the Office of the High Commissioner for Human Rights; the Ontario Women's Action Coalition; and five other associations concerned with women's issues. In his covering letter to the accounts of new witnesses, Ramic asked that I be made available to the authorities in Sarajevo. Fortunately for me, his letter was riddled with factual errors, and empirical evidence was readily available to disprove his allegations.

The letter contends that I told Bosnian President Alija Izetbegovic: "If you don't sign this now, I will fry your ass on CNN tonight!"[5] Ramic goes on to say that my shameless display of arrogance was in relation to a massacre of citizens of Sarajevo at a local market. In fact, there was no attack and no massacre at any Sarajevo market during my service in Sarajevo. The record confirms that.

Mr. Ramic goes on to say that the so-called free world, especially Canada's establishment, "know that Gen. MacKenzie ate, drank and danced at the Karadzic's daughter's wedding." I didn't even know Karadzic had a daughter. Presumably I was in Canada or elsewhere if and when the event took place.

In the strongest indication that this is a letter based on rumour rather than on readily available facts, Ramic states that it "finally is the time to investigate why Mike Harris, former Premier of Ontario, wanted to install Gen. MacKenzie as his personal advisor on terrorism at the time. And also to find out why he did not do it, although he made public proclamation about that appointment. Was it because he received an email from a Bosniak who warned him about Gen. MacKenzie and his ultranationalist Serbian friends?"[6]

In fact, immediately following 9/11, I held the appointment, along with retired RCMP commissioner Norman Inkster, for the remaining term of Mike Harris and his successor, Ernie Eves. There was a fair degree of publicity surrounding our appointments and work in the public news media. I can only assume that Ramic wasn't paying attention to information available to everyone else at the time.

While the errors of fact were just bad propaganda, the "personal" accounts of witnesses to my alleged war crimes were infuriating. Some of them were ludicrous in their over-the-top descriptions of my actions; however, those who bought into the accuracy of earlier accusations were certainly reinforced in their hatred of me.

Remembering that we were in the middle of a war zone at the time, one witness recalls: "One afternoon, as I was cleaning up the garbage around the barracks, MacKenzie arrived in a transporter. They rolled out a red carpet, all the way to MacKenzie's transporter. He saw me bruised and bloodied, opened the door of his transporter and showed me in. He said, 'We must not give them Marija.' [Marija is presumably the witness's name.] He put his hand on his chest and said, 'I am now responsible.'"[7] This is a particularly ingenious accusation: it reads as though I did a good thing, but its more subtle and damaging message is that the Serbs found a red carpet and treated me like royalty when I arrived at their barracks. Where they would find a red carpet at that time and place is beyond me.

Other accusations were more direct. One elaborated on the accusation involving the return of a child to his mother: the "witness" described: "I was scared for myself and even more frightened about my baby. Shortly thereafter, an older officer entered, accompanied by two in his escort. I recognized General Lewis MacKenzie, who approached me with his hand straight out, and addressed me 'miss' (in English). In his right hand he held a red rosebud and he clumsily pressed it in my hands—I was terrified. As he was doing that, the two escort [sic] left the room and locked the door. General MacKenzie asked me what my name was, where I came from. I was silent and I pretended that I could not understand anything he was saying. I just pulled my shoulders together and retreated, as General MacKenzie was saying, in English: 'You can speak English very well and you understand everything. I am here to help you. That is in your interest as love, led by interest, is the strongest love.' I knew what situation I was in."[8]

One paragraph later, she continues: "With a trashy Serbian music emanating from that radio in the background, the General admitted to his passion and I defended my imprisoned infant boy. With my jaws clenched, with my heart shut. It lasted, with shorter intervals, some twenty minutes. The General visited me seven or eight more times. I asked him to intervene with the Chetniks to give me my baby back and to let us go."[9]

The sweet and sour genius of this accusation is that it describes me as a rapist and ends with the victim getting her baby returned to her, for which she is grateful.

The accounts of many other new "witnesses" were posted on the Congress of North American Bosniaks' Web site.

This new assault on my character followed on the heels of a press conference held by Oleg Cavka of the Sarajevo Canton prosecutor's office on October 12, 2006. During his statements to the media, he made public the dated and "untested" accusations that were contained in the file dealing with me, in spite of the fact that I had not been indicted.

This was the final straw. I sought and got advice from an old friend: my legal adviser during my last year as commander of the army in Ontario, Peter Tinsley. I decided to go on the offensive.

Since the war, Bosnia has established an Office of the Disciplinary Counsel, which accepts and deals with formal complaints regarding the conduct of the country's judges and prosecutors. Somewhat ironically for me, the office was established with significant funding from Canada, via the Canadian International Development Agency (CIDA). On October 23, 2006, I submitted my complaint to Judge Branko Peric:

Dear Sir,

Permit me to introduce myself. I am retired Major General Lewis MacKenzie and from March to end July 1992 I served with UNPROFOR, first as chief of staff and lastly as the first commander of Sector Sarajevo during which time the UN opened the Sarajevo airport for the delivery of humanitarian aid to the citizens of Sarajevo.

In July of 1992 I requested that I be replaced as the sector commander as my officers, including my deputy, a Russian colonel and some of my soldiers were frequently threatened with death by execution by members of the Bosnian Army primarily due to my personal unpopularity in the Bosniak community in Sarajevo at that time. Following my departure to Canada on the first of August 1992 and immediately thereafter following my appearance as a witness before a number of US Congressional committees I was subjected to a number of false allegations including rape and murder by the Bosnian authorities.

With my encouragement the UN Secretary General launched a thorough investigation of all the accusations against me and subsequently concluded in writing to me that all the allegations were unfounded. The investigation revealed that I had departed Bosnia, "approximately one month prior to any alleged incident."

It appears that the allegations originated from media interviews with the captured Bosnian Serb soldier, Borislav Herak who claimed to have murdered and raped Bosnian Muslim women. During an interview he indicated that I had frequently visited Sonya's Café in Sarajevo, selected captured Muslim girls, raped them and subsequently murdered them. It was subsequently revealed that Herak's evidence was a fabrication having been well coached and his descriptions of myself, my rank badges and vehicle bore no relationship with reality.

During the past decade as these libelous accusations reappear in the media it is frequently stated that I have been approached by the Bosnian authorities to be questioned and that I have refused. That sir is blatantly untrue. I have never been asked if I would agree to be questioned and frankly I would be happy to respond to questioning here in Canada. It is also stated that the UN and Canada have been approached to permit me to be interrogated and both have refused. To the best of my knowledge this has not happened as I assume that I would have been notified of such a request.

On the 12th of October 2006, Sarajevo county prosecutor Oleg Cavka repeated the unfounded allegations against me yet again to AFP and the comments received international attention. He again stressed my visitations to Sonja's Café, a location I have never seen let alone visited.

Friends who have served in Bosnia more recently tell me that the Bosnian judiciary has made giant strides in the past decade and has earned a reputation for fairness and honesty. It is with these facts in mind that the professional misconduct of Mr. Cavka is so troubling. I was shocked that Mr. Cavka would go to the media with the presumably confidential and "untested" contents of an investigation file and make public that information against myself while admitting that I have not been indicted. It is bad enough that I had no opportunity to defend myself; however, the clear inference of Mr. Cavka's statement that, "he has not been indicted because he has not been questioned" is that, but for the questioning, I would have been indicted. This conclusion on the part of Mr. Cavka demonstrates a clear absence of impartiality. Furthermore, he usurps the function of a court or judge in the indictment process, i.e. a prosecutor brings or files an indictment and a judge rejects or confirms and indicts.

I wish to formally complain regarding the unprofessional and irresponsible conduct of Mr. Oleg Cavka.

Respectfully, Lewis W MacKenzie, Major General (ret'd)[10]

On October 25, 2006, I was advised by the High Judicial and Prosecutorial Council of Bosnia and Herzegovina that I would have a response to my complaint *within two years*. To date, I have heard nothing.

20: Off's Fox

"Plumbing new depths in Canadian journalism."

J.L. GRANATSTEIN, IN A REVIEW OF
THE LION, THE FOX AND THE EAGLE

IN 1999 I RECEIVED a call from Carol Off, the award-winning CBC reporter whose documentary work I had much admired. She explained that she had been contracted to write a book about the Canadian judge Louise Arbour, soon to be appointed a Supreme Court justice and since 1996 the chief prosecutor for the UN war crimes tribunal in The Hague. The more Off researched the madness of Bosnia and Rwanda—the dual focus of Louise Arbour's efforts during her tenure at The Hague—the more she realized the critical involvement of General Roméo Dallaire in Rwanda and yours truly in Bosnia. She requested, and I agreed to, an interview.

Having read my book *Peacekeeper,* Off was well prepared for the interview and merely sought clarification and elaboration regarding some of the more interesting events that occurred during my six months in Sarajevo. Whenever there was a discrepancy between her research and my recollection of events, I offered her my daily diary and the names of non-Canadian members of UNPROFOR who had been witnesses to those events. I had served many years on peacekeeping duty in areas where not all the locals appreciated the UN's usually inadequate response to their crisis. They were therefore inclined to accuse the peacekeepers of bias and worse, so I always made sure that I was accompanied by some soldiers from other nations to serve as less-biased witnesses in dealing with any fabricated accusations. I explained to Off that she should not take my word where there were discrepancies in specific details, but rather that she should track down other, more unbiased witnesses. God knows there were enough of them.

At the end of the first interview, she was charming. She complimented my wife, Dora, on our home and promised to revisit when she had done more research. Months later, the second interview ventured into the sensitive subject of the allegations made against me by a prosecutor in Sarajevo.* In brief, the prosecutor claimed that I had regularly visited a café in the Serb-held area of Sarajevo where captured Muslim girls served Serbian officers; that I took away young Muslim women, presumably for sexual favours, and that they were subsequently found murdered. I methodically explained that I had never been to that area of Sarajevo because there was no reason for me to do so. I explained that if I had done so, many of the international media hovering around my headquarters—reporters who tagged on to my every move—would have followed me there and filmed the entire event. I also suggested to Off that she interview members of my staff from Egypt, Finland, Russia and the Palestine Authority for confirmation because I never went anywhere alone in the city. Once again, I offered my diary as evidence of my daily activities.

* These accusations and the fallout have been dealt with in chapters 13 and 19 of this book.

Just before her book was published, Carol Off came to visit me at my home in Bracebridge and thanked me for my candid response to her questions during the interviews. As she was entering her car to leave, she said, over her shoulder, "I think you were really on the wrong side of history." Little did I realize at the time how far on the wrong side she thought I was.

The Lion, the Fox and the Eagle hit the bookstores in November 2000. Of course I read the section focusing on me first. Riddled with disparaging innuendo, peppered with snide comments and a single-sided version of events, "The Fox" section read like it had been lifted from the professional propaganda that the Bosnian government had commissioned since the earliest days of the Bosnian war. I immediately considered suing for libel. I worked my way through the entire 112 pages of "The Fox," highlighting the factual errors, and took the result to a friend who held one of the most senior judicial appointments in the country.

His advice was succinct: "Lew, you can sue and probably win, but you will undoubtedly sell at least 30,000 books for her, which is probably exactly what her publisher wants." He went on to say, "You know, people who weren't keen on you before they read the book won't change their minds, and people who thought you were a pretty good guy—and I venture to say that they are the majority—won't change their minds either."

The last bit of advice turned out to be true. People would bring the book to my door and ask me to autograph it. I would say, "You know, I'm thinking of suing her." The usual response was "Oh, we didn't know it was negative, we bought it for our ———— (fill in the blank). He's a big fan." I always signed, "All the best—Lew MacKenzie, under protest!"

The most disturbing aspect of Carol Off's book was the naive notion that the war could have ended more quickly if only those of us representing the UN in Sarajevo, led by me, had acted differently. The fact that the UN Security Council had not adjusted to the post–Cold War world (and, in many ways, still hasn't) and that it continued to hold to the idea that the presence of lightly armed, impartial UN soldiers could keep the lid on a three-sided civil war was ignored by Off. She believed that if I had only condemned the Serbs as the aggressors and highlighted the Bosnian, primarily Muslim, population as the victims, the international community would have shown up like the U.S. 7th Calvary and ended the killing. I am tempted to add: "Just like they have in Darfur over the past four years?"

This miserable reality was even recognized by Bosnian President Alija Izetbegovic. After a few days of him accusing me of meeting too often with his enemy—the "Serb aggressors"—at their headquarters on the outskirts of Sarajevo, I replied in frustration: "OK, Mr. President, I'm the only one in your country meeting with the Bosnian Serb leadership, and I'm doing so with the same frequency as I'm meeting with you. I'm trying to arrange a lasting ceasefire, and so far it's usually your side that keeps breaking the agreement first. But I'll tell you what; I'll break off all contact with the Bosnian Serb leadership, stay in my headquarters down the road and only represent your case to the UN, OK?"

"No!" he said. "The Serb artillery will wipe us off the map if they have free rein!"

I replied, "That's my point, Mr. President. The international community is not going to come to the rescue of Bosnia. The international leaders that really matter have decided that the fourteen-thousand-man UN force currently in the entire former Yugoslavia is enough. You and I know it's not. Before the war, you asked for ten thousand, just here in Sarajevo, to stop the war from starting. I'm afraid the fewer than one thousand I have with me is all you are going to get, and that means I have to maintain a working relationship with the Serbs or they will wipe you and your people off the map."

Off seems to think that if I had used my "macho," "poster-boy," "media super-star" bully pulpit to condemn only the Serbs for their actions in a three-sided civil war, then President George Bush Sr., Prime Minister John Major, President François Mitterrand and the rest would have launched their forces in our direction, defeated the Serbs and pacified Bosnia. This is dreaming in Technicolor. When you are in charge and faced with both a moral and practical dilemma, you come up with the best plan possible to save the most lives. Taking sides in Bosnia in 1992 would have been an unmitigated disaster. It would have seen the withdrawal of the UN force under fire, the abandonment of Sarajevo and the elimination of Bosnia as a country after less then four months of existence.

Carol Off's ideas about what might have been done differently and better by those of us in Sarajevo during the summer of 1992 might have more credibility if her analysis was not riddled with a multitude of factual errors—some serious, others less so, but in total they revealed bias and superficial research.

A good example of the many serious errors of fact reflecting badly on both me and my soldiers is her comment about the aid that arrived daily at the Sarajevo airport once the airport was opened for the UN's humanitarian lift. She writes, "A high proportion of the goods entering Sarajevo went straight to the Bosnian Serb army, and there was nothing aid organizations could do about it. Once the supplies were inside the besieged city, it was the turn of the Bosnian army to pick through them for what they needed. Civilians came last."[11]

In fact—and this is not a secret—each and every aid flight was met and inspected by a team from my command consisting of UN officers, members of our UN civilian police, including members of the RCMP, UN High Commissioner for Refugees (UNHCR) personnel and, most importantly, officials from both the Bosniak and Bosnian Serb aid organizations. This was absolutely necessary to counter the inevitable accusations from both sides that their enemies were smuggling in weapons and ammunition on our UN aid flights. The aid was then loaded onto UN trucks, and the overwhelming majority of it—well over ninety per cent—was escorted by the Canadian battle group to food distribution points in the Bosniak area of downtown Sarajevo, where it was turned over to the appropriate local aid agency. *Absolutely none of the aid went to the Bosnian Serb army*. After it left our hands, most of the aid did not go to the Bosniak army either, as suggested by Off; it ended up on the black market, presumably lining the pockets of those local Bosnian officials in charge. This was a constant source of frustration to my soldiers, who had risked their lives to deliver the aid. When I approached UNHCR in Geneva, the lead UN agency responsible for the airlift, to complain about the corruption, I was told that if twenty per cent of the aid actually reached the civilian population that needed it on all sides, we were doing better than the norm! Off had bought into and repeated the Bosnian myth that somehow the Serbs ended up with most of the aid.

On a lighter note, but indicating a recurring acceptance of Bosnian propaganda as fact and without confirmation, Off relates an anecdote concerning my wearing of the UN blue beret. Referring to the UN Bosnian ambassador's displeasure with some of my speeches on my return to Canada, she wrote: "Ambassador Sacirbey tried to stop MacKenzie's speeches, but the UN's secretary-general declared that the retired Canadian soldier was free to say what he wanted. However, Sacirbey was able to persuade the UN to advise MacKenzie he couldn't wear a blue beret at his appearances. 'That blue hat is like a halo,' says Sacirbey.

'It represents truth and integrity, and it was being abused.' The UN agreed and the general was told not to wear the peacekeeping symbol..."[12]

Presumably Off was duped by Ambassador Sacirbey, because she quotes him. In fact, any member of a peacekeeping force removes the blue beret the moment he or she is taken off the strength of the UN force after returning to his or her home country. This happened to me thirty-six hours after landing in Ottawa. I never wore the blue beret again. The UN never contacted me or anyone else about the inappropriate wearing of the "blue hat." In any event it would have been impossible to wear the beret because within days of my return I donated it to a Heart and Stroke charity auction in Ottawa. Its sale raised just over $500.

Needless to say, the most disturbing part of "The Fox" is a gratuitous chapter entirely dedicated to repeating in vivid detail the allegations made by Bosniaks that I had raped and perhaps even murdered captive Muslim girls. Once again, there is disturbing evidence of superficial journalism. Off describes how a Bosnian prosecutor, Mustafa Bisic, and the Centre for Research and Documentation in Sarajevo had evidence from a Muslim woman who claimed that I forced her to have sex with me, following which I had her nine-month-old baby returned from captivity to her care. This was a particularly ingenious bit of character assassination by the Bosnians, since as I have mentioned before it had a "happy ending" for the alleged victim. The prosecutor was pursuing the case but would release the woman's name only if the International Criminal Tribunal for the Former Yugoslavia (ICTY) in The Hague agreed to his request that my immunity be lifted and that the tribunal pursue the case against me.

What Off didn't know was that I had often given evidence to the ICTY investigators as they were preparing their cases against

indicted Balkan war criminals. I developed a good working relationship with them, and during the last interview, years after
Off's book was published, I said to one of them: "I'm told that
there is a request from the authorities in Sarajevo that I be tried
for war crimes, including rape and murder. When you get back
to The Hague, would you check with the appropriate office to
see what the status is of the charges—including any request that
my 'immunity' be lifted?"

The investigator, a member of the RCMP, replied: "We don't
have to wait to return to The Hague. We are responsible for your
file, and I can assure you that there has been no request whatsoever from Sarajevo regarding you." I would have thought that an
investigative reporter from Canada, writing about criminal allegations against a fellow Canadian, would have discovered that
fact, or would at least have tried to discover it.

Whether it was bad note-taking or inaccurate recall by Off,
her repetitious misrepresentation of my opinion regarding a key
aspect of leadership was one of the reasons I decided to dedicate
the following chapter of this book to the subject in the context
of my professional disagreement with Roméo Dallaire regarding
a leader's priorities.

While discussing leadership with Carol Off, I said that in
war there is no debate about a commander's priorities. They
will always be mission, soldiers and self, in that order. I elaborated, however, that in poorly defined, poorly organized,
under-resourced missions that had been put together by a
dysfunctional committee (usually the UN Security Council),
there would be rare occasions when I would change my priorities to soldiers first, then mission and lastly self. If the task
assigned to me by the UN headquarters in downtown Manhattan was impossible, or if my mandate was no longer relevant as

the situation deteriorated, I would have no qualms about making the lives of my soldiers my first priority.

By error or design—and I suspect the latter—Off took that simple explanation to set up a false comparison between General Dallaire's leadership style and mine. She repeatedly indicated that I would *always* put the safety of my soldiers first, thereby ignoring or, at a minimum, subordinating any responsibility I had to the innocent victims in the conflict zone where I was serving. This erroneous misrepresentation of what I said is supremely insulting to my soldiers who risked their lives in support of the mission in Sarajevo.

Compounding her error, Off repeated her convenient misrepresentation of what I told her in 1999 in an essay she had published in the 2001 book *Warrior Chiefs: Perspectives on Senior Canadian Military Leaders*. She opined, "Lieutenant-General Dallaire contends that peacekeeping missions should follow the codes of other military operations—most obviously war—where the mission comes first, the soldiers second, and the commander last ... Major-General MacKenzie disputes it— not categorically—but principally in the area of peacekeeping. MacKenzie maintains his first priority is the safety of his soldiers, the second is the mission, and then, lastly, the well-being of the commander."[13] She goes on to say, "And yet, Major-General MacKenzie volunteered Canadian soldiers for—and then commanded them in—one of the most violent and questionable United Nations peacekeeping missions of the 1990s."[14] Off then argues that the daily delivery of three hundred tons of food and medicine to Sarajevo, facilitated by the Canadian battle group, was a bad idea. In hindsight, she makes some valid points; however, she concludes her assessment of my performance by writing, "What is clear is that Canadian peacekeepers found themselves wounded and even killed in the most dangerous city in the world on a mission that Lewis MacKenzie volunteered for on their behalf."[15] It's unfortunate that Off did not do a cursory check of what the Canadian soldiers achieved in Sarajevo in July 1992 and of the price they paid. Thousands of tons of humanitarian aid were delivered to the city in accordance with the will of the international community, and *no* Canadian soldiers—*no* Canadian soldiers—were killed in Sarajevo at any time during the Bosnian conflict. In fact, very few were seriously injured—though one fine soldier from Newfoundland, Master Corporal Dennis Reid, lost his foot to a land mine.

In a comment breathtaking in its hypocrisy and repeated to the media during her book tour, Carol Off reinforced the convenient representation of what I said by stating: "I think that if my son was going to war to be a peacekeeper someplace, I would want him to [be] there under Lewis MacKenzie, because I know that he would come back alive. But if I was in a distant village about to be ethnically cleansed, I would really hope it was Roméo Dallaire out there, because he'd have my interests in mind."[16]

The proverb says, "It's an ill wind that blows nobody any good," and in the case of *The Lion, the Fox and the Eagle* there was a dose of good—and some satisfaction for me—when the reviews were published. A few excerpts follow:

> Off even devotes a wholly gratuitous chapter to allegations made by the Bosnian Muslims that MacKenzie had a variety of sexual encounters with captive Muslim women. To say that there is not a shred of credible evidence in these pages is an understatement. In effect, Off uses biased Bosnian sources to smear MacKenzie, plumbing new depths in Canadian journalism...Thus we have a curate's egg of a book. The parts

that are good [Arbour, Dallaire] are very, very good; the part
that is bad [MacKenzie] is simply horrid and full of bile.—J.L.
Granatstein, *Southam News*[17]

The one-third of the book dealing with MacKenzie and Sarajevo is, in my view a travesty... Particularly upsetting is the
author's technique of innuendo. Off quotes an alleged war
criminal, Borislav Herak, saying he witnessed MacKenzie at
a Serb-run "rape camp" driving off with four Muslim women
"for the purpose of satisfaction of personal lust." After setting
the scene, Off then knocks down the allegations—Bosnia's
ambassador to the UN, Mohammed Sacirbey, rejected the
allegations, as did an investigative *Newsday* reporter, Roy
Gutman. A UN inquiry found MacKenzie had never been to
that site—and had left Sarajevo a month before the alleged
incident. It later turned out that Herak was tortured and had
told so many lies he was useless as any sort of war crimes
witness.—Peter Worthington, *Toronto Sun*[18]

Unfortunately for the credibility of the other passages, Off's
denigration of MacKenzie's tour of duty in Sarajevo is so rife
with factual errors that it reads like partisan propaganda for
the Bosnian Muslim cause.—Scott Taylor, *Globe and Mail*[19]

It's in the third segment devoted to the Fox, Maj.-Gen. Mac-
Kenzie, that Off's misguided thesis and venomous innuendo
come gushing out... In Sarajevo, Gen. MacKenzie bent the
rules, toughed it out and got the job done.—Bruce Garvey,
Ottawa Citizen[20]

In an unpublished portion of his review, Bruce Garvey made
an important point: "Ms. Off has conceded she is no historian,

a fact she ably demonstrates in her error-strewn account of the events in Bosnia. At times it is so skewed with Muslim propaganda that you begin to wonder if it wasn't written by President Alija Izetbegovic himself."[21]

There is no doubt that controversy sells, and I daresay I helped sell the book. I could even live with her accusations if Off had confronted me with them and asked for my response during our two eight-hour interviews. But to come into my home, make nice with me and my wife, warn me of accusations that might hit the media but that never do—until they appear in her book—was, to quote Jack Granatstein, "plumbing new depths in Canadian journalism." It was only the second time I had been duped in fifteen years of dealing with some of the best journalists in the world, and the fact that it was a fellow Canadian who was doing the "plumbing" was intensely disappointing.

21: Roméo Dallaire: A Leadership Disagreement

"If it was a Bagasora-led coup by the hard-

liners, aimed at derailing the Arusha accords,

I had no more mandate."

GENERAL ROMÉO DALLAIRE, IN *SHAKE HANDS WITH THE DEVIL*

IN 1997, LIEUTENANT-GENERAL Roméo Dallaire was invited to the Canadian Forces Command and Staff College in Toronto to speak to the students, mostly senior majors destined to be promoted to lieutenant-colonel in the near future, on the subject of leadership. During his presentation General Dallaire explained that a military leader frequently faces a dilemma associated with assigning priorities. He made it clear that it was his opinion that a leader's priorities should and must always be mission first, then soldiers and, lastly, self.

During the question period that followed the presentation, a student rose and commented along the lines of: "General Dallaire, General MacKenzie spoke to us a couple of weeks ago on the same subject, and while his priorities matched yours most of the time, he made the point that there will be occasions, albeit rare, when orders are received that make no sense whatsoever or are impossible to carry out because the resources to do so are not available, at which time his priorities changed to soldiers first then mission and self." The student's comment was somewhat unfair, because guest presentations at the Staff College are not for attribution, and to use one speaker's comments to put another speaker on the spot is considered inappropriate; however, a critical disagreement between Dallaire and me regarding leadership was now exposed to the very audience that would provide some of the Canadian Forces' general officers within the next ten years.

The jungle drums work extremely well within the Profession of Arms, and I was telephoned at my home within minutes of the completion of Dallaire's presentation and told that the general had not responded convincingly to the student's comment and that his response had gone off on a tangent bearing no relationship to the question he had been asked. In the next few months, after he had made additional presentations, I received many calls from mid-rank officers who believed that someone of equal or superior rank should try to convince the chief of defence staff to stop General Dallaire from making presentations on leadership that appeared to justify always making mission the number one priority for a leader. Since Dallaire was serving in the Canadian Forces at the time and I had been retired for four years, I decided to try to rescue both of us from future embarrassments. I made an appointment to see his boss and our mutual friend, Chief of Defence Staff Maurice Baril.

I explained to Maurice what had happened at the Staff College when Dallaire had made his presentation and related the gist of the calls I was receiving in the wake of his more recent presentations. I suggested it might be a good idea to advise his subordinate commanders that I should *not* be invited to speak to their personnel on the subject of leadership, and to consider limiting Dallaire's presentations to subjects *other than* leadership. The disagreement between Dallaire and me regarding priorities was obviously confusing for aspiring senior leaders in the Canadian Forces, and I felt that perhaps the best thing to do was eliminate the debate altogether. To his credit, Maurice thought otherwise. He viewed it as a healthy disagreement for future colonels and generals to hear.

Unfortunately the disagreement was far from healthy, and it was never resolved. As sides formed up on each side of the issue, my qualifier, "in rare circumstances," which was critical to my argument that loyalty to soldiers should occasionally come before mission, was conveniently ignored by some, particularly my critics. What resulted was a simplistic representation of the disagreement which indicated that I would always put soldiers first, no matter what the circumstances.

I hold to my opinion that in some circumstances, ill-conceived and impossible-to-execute orders must be evaluated by the leader, and if warranted, they should be ignored or disobeyed. During the early 1990s, as the United Nations in New York (UNNY) was experiencing great difficulty in adapting to the post–Cold War world, some of the orders issued to its commanders in the field were ludicrous. For example, early on during the humanitarian airlift into Sarajevo in 1992, we were held up for hours at various armed roadblocks as we attempted to deliver food and medicine. Without any discussion or analysis, UNNY directed us to "use such force as necessary to guarantee the safe delivery of humanitarian aid (medical supplies and food)." Being good soldiers, my staff were keen to issue instructions to our troops to fight their way through the multitude of armed roadblocks that interfered with our delivery of aid. At the time, we had fewer than 1,000 personnel, including headquarters staff and unarmed UN observers, in Sector Sarajevo. We were in a city of over 300,000 people, many of whom were less than sympathetic to our efforts to help them. We were surrounded by a heavily armed First World military force numbering in the tens of thousands who hated our guts because they saw a UN force that they knew had a mandate to be impartial in delivering humanitarian aid to their enemies. I realized that although we would be able to force our way through the first roadblock we encountered, there would nevertheless be about twenty more to deal with on the same route, and by that time our opponents would easily outnumber us one hundred to one. I placed my soldiers first in my priorities, ignored the mission order from the UN and continued to negotiate our freedom of movement, a tactic that proved to be successful even in the short term.

Considering the importance of our disagreement and being at a loss to understand General Dallaire's rationale for insisting on placing the mission first, no matter what the risk to his soldiers, I spent considerable time researching his only overseas command: the military component of the UN's ill-fated mission in Rwanda in 1993–94. Fortunately, the general's wildly successful, best-selling book, *Shake Hands with the Devil,* written in collaboration with his assistant, Major Brent Beardsley (who, in my opinion, received too little public credit for his extensive contributions although he is amply acknowledged in the book), proved to be an invaluable source of first-hand accounts. It was during this research that I unearthed some clues that might explain General Dallaire's inflexibility on such a critical issue and I learned some lessons that may be of value for future leaders who are faced with similar dilemmas.

Whether by choice or by chance, Roméo Dallaire never served on overseas operational duty with the UN before he achieved the rank of general. During the Cold War, it was generally accepted that volunteering for peacekeeping duty with the UN or certain other multinational organizations was not beneficial for your career. In fact, many senior decision makers in the military leadership regarded peacekeeping duty as "avoiding real work." Real work was deemed to be tours of duty at army headquarters in St. Hubert, Quebec, or at National Defence HQ in Ottawa, where you would be "exposed" to the minister and the senior military brass. I know this to be a fact, as I served in NDHQ for only sixteen months out of thirty-six years, and twelve of those months were as the director of personnel careers officers. As such, I witnessed up close the workings of various boards that decided which officers would be promoted in the following year. Reports of Canadian officers who performed outstandingly on peacekeeping missions were deemed to be chronically inflated, for two reasons. First, peacekeeping was considered to be pretty safe and routine stuff, so it really wasn't all that challenging. Although frequently this couldn't be further from the truth, perception trumped performance. Second, reports on Canadians were frequently written by senior foreign military officers who, according to the myth, always inflated their assessments. Many promotion board members actually admitted they believed that just about any Canadian would be rated highly by a foreigner.

Fortunately (particularly for me), the status of the operationally experienced officer, that chronic avoider of "real work," changed dramatically at the end of the Cold War, when such experience was all too rare and much in demand. The deployment of the United Nations Protection Force in the former Yugoslavia in 1992 was front-page news and the lead story on international television for most of two years. In spite of all the problems inherent in the ill-conceived mandate and its bizarre command and control arrangements, the media coverage of our soldiers' efforts and sacrifices was generally positive, particularly in Canada. This was dangerous work—soldiers were being killed and seriously injured—and Canada was playing a leading role on the international stage for the first time since the Korean War. Officers who aspired to the highest ranks of the Canadian Forces recognized the sea change and sought out a tour of operational duty with the UN, particularly in a command role if at all possible. Perhaps that is why, in spite of having no operational experience with the UN in earlier ranks, General Roméo Dallaire volunteered for overseas duty.

A long-overdue attempt by the international community in general and the UN in particular to resolve the conflict between the Hutu and Tutsi ethnic groups in both Rwanda and Uganda came to a head in June 1993. The UN Security Council authorized a modest mission of some one hundred military and civilian personnel, the United Nations Observer Mission in Uganda and Rwanda (UNOMUR), which would be deployed to the Ugandan side of the border with Rwanda. The UN force would be unarmed, and it would be responsible for monitoring the border and verifying that weapons, ammunition and Tutsi reinforcements did not make their way into Rwanda. Then, in spite of the availability of a large number of fluently bilingual, operationally experienced Canadian general officers, Brigadier-General Dallaire was offered to the UN as the chief military observer for UNOMUR—in civilian terms, the man in charge of the military component.

General Dallaire has been criticized by some for accepting the appointment even though he was aware of his inexperience. In his book, he admits that his first response to the notification of his UN appointment was: "Rwanda, that's somewhere in Africa, isn't it?"[22] It has to be mentioned in his defence, though, that the tiny mission was anticipated to be a quiet, safe and routine challenge, well out of the public eye and easily within his capability to command.

Three months later, the UN's Security Council found some backbone and authorized the creation of a much larger mission that would facilitate the implementation of the recently signed Arusha Accords. The new UN Assistance Mission in Rwanda (UNAMIR) would be responsible for helping with the security of the capital city of Kigali; monitoring the peace agreement, including supporting the transitional government; establishing an expanded demilitarized zone; developing demobilization procedures, and assisting with mine-clearance. UNOMUR personnel would be absorbed by UNAMIR, and the strength of the new mission was authorized at 2,548 souls.

Brigadier-General Dallaire was promoted to the rank of major-general and appointed force commander of UNAMIR, that is, commander of the military personnel in UNAMIR. Contrary to popular opinion, Dallaire was not in charge of the mission. As is the norm in most large UN operations, the UN secretary-general appoints a civilian to represent him—the special representative of the secretary-general (SRSG), who has the responsibility to oversee the mission and its mandate. In the case of UNAMIR, Boutros Boutros-Ghali's unfortunate choice was a Cameroon diplomat and personal friend, Jacques-Roger Booh-Booh.

The UN's member nations were characteristically slow to respond to the call for soldiers, and five months passed before the authorized strength was reached. Soldiers from Belgium and Bangladesh made up the majority of the UN force responsible for assisting with the security of the capital. Unresolved issues between the parties to the Arusha Accords and subsequent events meant that the inauguration of the Rwandan transitional government never took place, thereby eliminating one of UNAMIR's key responsibilities.

On April 6, 1994, at approximately 8 PM, the spark that led to the slaughter of some 800,000 Rwandans was observed by the unarmed UNAMIR observers at the Kigali airport. The plane carrying the presidents of Rwanda and Burundi, both of whom were returning from continuing peace talks in Tanzania, exploded into a ball of flame while attempting to land at the airport. The cause of the crash has never been determined; at the time, everyone had an opinion and the one that counted the most and that led to the genocide was the one held by the Hutu majority: the Tutsi minority would be held responsible for the crash. The killings started with the slaughter of Tutsis and moderate Hutu senior government officials.

Following the crash, General Dallaire had a series of meetings with the Hutu-dominated military led by Colonel Théoneste Bagosora. Dallaire discovered that they were making plans to assume control of the government following the death of their president. There was also a midnight meeting with the SRSG at his residence, during which Booh-Booh confirmed by phone with New York that the UN considered Prime Minister Madame Agathe Uwilingiyimana to be the legitimate head of government and that the Rwandan military leadership should consult with her. Bagosora scoffed at the idea.

Even though senior Rwandan government officials were being slaughtered throughout the capital city of Kigali, a senior official in the UN's peacekeeping department insisted by phone at 3 AM the following day that Dallaire's troops return fire only if fired upon—despite UNAMIR's rules of engagement allowing the use of deadly force "to prevent crimes against humanity." For a commander who had previous experience with the UN, this would be the time that he would indicate the telephone connection had gone bad and he couldn't understand what was being said at the other end—and then hang up. It is interesting to note that it was "timely" that the slaughter started during the night in Rwanda. If it had occurred during the day, when it was nighttime in New

York, the odds are that in 1994 no one would have been on duty at the UN to answer the phone.

Whenever I called the UN from Sarajevo in 1992, I got an answering machine. In fact, it was sometimes worse than that— there was no answer at all. During a speech I made shortly after I returned to Canada in late 1992, I said in frustration that "If you are a UN commander in the field, don't phone the UN after 5 PM New York time or on the weekends because there probably won't be anyone there to take your call!" I might have been exaggerating to make a point, but at least the comment woke up the UN. Two things happened following my speech: I was required to sign a "formal warning" by the acting chief of defence staff agreeing that I would stop saying things like that or be fired, and the UN established a twenty-four-hours-a-day, seven-days-a-week situation room at UNHQ in New York. It wasn't the operations centre that I would like to have seen and that the UN needs, but it manned the phones 24 hours a day—and now they knew who and where their UN commanders were in the field. When I visited the situation room soon after its creation, a handwritten sign on the entrance door read: "The General MacKenzie Memorial Situation Room—We work 24/7." That alone was worth the formal warning.

By mid-morning, Kigali was in chaos and movement was both difficult and dangerous. All local UN attempts at meetings with ambassadors and the Crisis Committee had failed. Elements of the presidential guard and the army were going from house to house with a list of names and were killing at will. UNAMIR's Belgian soldiers at the airport were being held prisoner, but UNHQ was still insisting that deadly force was not authorized unless UNAMIR was fired upon. Calls came to Dallaire's headquarters from senior Rwandan officials pleading for protection, and duty officers could hear the caller's family being killed before the caller himself was slaughtered. At this point, Dallaire states in his book that the possibilty of a moderate government was utterly lost: "If it was a Bagosora-led coup by the hard-liners, aimed at derailing the Arusha accords, I had no more mandate."[23] In fact, that's exactly what was unfolding.

Dallaire left his HQ with two of his staff, looking for an alleged meeting taking place between Bagosora and the gendarmerie. He had a handheld Motorola radio, another radio mounted in the vehicle and one pistol among the three of them. Soon their vehicle was refused passage at a roadblock, and Dallaire and one of his staff proceeded on foot. Their communication with Dallaire's HQ was now reduced to the handheld radio. After walking for a few kilometres they were picked up by a Rwandan major, who after some consultation at Rwandan army HQ determined the meeting they were looking for was being held at the École Supérieure Militaire.

The route to the meeting took them past an entrance gate to Camp Kigali. As they drove by, Dallaire saw two of his Belgian soldiers lying on the ground at the far end of the compound. He ordered the Rwandan major to stop the vehicle but was ignored, and the driver carried on to the grounds of the École. While it would have been possible to reach over and turn off the ignition in order to stop the vehicle, any venture into the camp alone and unarmed would probably have proven suicidal. As Dallaire approached the building where the meeting was taking place, an UNAMIR military observer from Ghana was momentarily released by the Rwandan soldiers who were forcefully detaining him. He explained to Dallaire that five of his soldiers were being held nearby and that a group of Belgian soldiers had been assaulted in Camp Kigali. Dallaire immediately proceeded to the École for the meeting. Surprisingly, it would appear from his own account, that he did so without advising his HQ of the fact that a number of his soldiers were detained and were being abused or worse. With over four hundred tough Belgian paracommandos dispersed around the city, the potential existed for a UN show of force that would have been more than a little intimidating to the unruly mobs doing the killing.

On entering the meeting, Bagosora was in full flight, fine-tuning the military's response to the ongoing violence, including the preparation of a communiqué designed to "calm the nation." He asked Dallaire to address the meeting, and when Dallaire agreed he stressed that his force would try to keep the Arusha peace process alive—even though earlier in the day he had indicated that he "had no more mandate" if Bagosora was taking over. He further called for calm within the army units, but he did not immediately raise the issue of his captured Belgian soldiers. This, in spite of the fact that he was meeting with the very Rwandan military leaders who commanded the troops that were capturing and abusing his soldiers as he spoke. He had hoped to raise the issue with Bagosora privately, but the opportunity never came, so he mentioned it to the chief of staff of the Gendarmerie, Major-General Augustin Ndindilyimana, who said he would look into it. Inexplicably setting the issue of his captured soldiers aside, Dallaire then assisted with the preparation of the communiqué.

An hour and a half after entering the meeting, Dallaire called his headquarters and was told that a number of Rwandan VIPs "protected" by UNAMIR (a bit hard to do, if you can't use deadly force) had been murdered, as had their families. Thirty-five of his military personnel had been captured, and anarchy reigned in the capital. His Bangladeshi troops refused to follow orders, except those originating from their capital that commanded them to not get involved or to take any risks. At around 1 PM, Dallaire proceeded to the location where Prime Minister "Madame Agathe" was supposed to be guarded by UNAMIR personnel, only to learn that she and her husband had been murdered. Still without mobile communications, Dallaire walked to the Ministry of Defence, hoping to find Bagosora, who didn't show up until 2 PM. Bagosora indicated that he could not get into Camp Kigali (which housed his own soldiers) because of the chaos, but that he would put a force together to restore calm in the camp.

At this stage, Dallaire phoned his HQ and was told that the Tutsi-led Rwandese Patriotic Army, primarily located in the north of the country, was preparing to move south to protect those Tutsis who had not already been slaughtered. Although the situation was completely out of control, Dallaire still held out hope that he could contribute to bringing the situation to some kind of resolution. This, in spite of the fact that two armies were squaring off with each other and that his modest force was spread over the entire country, in exposed locations, under his orders to return fire only if fired upon, and with some of them receiving directions from their capitals to "stay out of trouble." Dallaire spent the next two hours trying to get the two army leaders, Colonel Bagosora and Major-General Paul Kagame, to speak with each other on the phone. When at last the conversation took place between Bagosora and Kagame's representative in Kigali, nothing was achieved. It was two hours before dark. Dallaire brought up the subject of his detained solders with Bagosora, who conveniently ignored the issue.

At 4 PM, some six hours after he first saw his soldiers being held against their will, and after the murder of many political leaders and their families, after more of his soldiers were taken hostage, after a coup by the Hutu "leader" Bagosora was evident, after the Tutsi-led army was moving to intervene, after a number of his troops refused to intervene and after a ridiculous order from the UN not to use deadly force to protect anyone, Dallaire in a quiet moment acknowledged to himself that "the path to war and slaughter was now open."[24] He decided it was time to consolidate his troops in order to ensure their safety and then for him and his troops to do what they could to protect the innocents.

Nevertheless, there was still one more meeting to attend that day. At 6 PM, Dallaire drove to a meeting of the Crisis Committee at Camp Kigali. To his amazement, the camp displayed no evidence of the early morning chaos and was calm and orderly. Obviously someone, presumably Bagosora, was able to control the out-of-control mutineers when he wanted to. At the meeting, Dallaire was told that he should withdraw the Belgian contingent as soon as possible—anti-Belgium hate propaganda was being transmitted by RTLM, the local TV station. At long last, he blew his stack and insisted that the captive Belgian soldiers be turned over to him. Twenty minutes later, he was told that his soldiers had been found at the Kigali hospital.

The hospital was a mere two hundred metres away. On arriving there, Dallaire was directed to a small hut at the far end of a courtyard in front of the morgue. In the hut, he came upon a scene that would haunt any commander forever: the bodies of his Belgian soldiers were stacked on top of each other like "sacks of potatoes." Their intertwined, tattered uniforms and mutilated bloody flesh made it impossible to do an accurate body count. Initially Dallaire thought there were eleven bodies, but later it turned out to be ten.

The critical eight hours from the time General Dallaire observed his Belgian soldiers on the ground in Camp Kigali until the issue was forcefully raised with the Crisis Committee in the very same camp warranted a mere ninety seconds in the movie version of *Shake Hands with the Devil*. To say that the day's events and General Dallaire's priorities were glossed over would be an understatement.

The public has heaped much sympathetic praise on General Dallaire for his efforts as the force commander in Rwanda, but there has been much criticism of his leadership by members of the Profession of Arms, particularly in Canada. It is not my intention to pass judgement on the subject. This is, however, an opportunity to re-evaluate the events related to the loss of his Belgian soldiers in order to stress the importance of flexibility when determining one's priorities as a military commander.

Here is one way to understand military orders. Orders received by a commander in a war scenario that deal with immediate actions to be performed in the pursuit of victory are not debatable. Our nation's participation in any war occurs as a result of Canada's democratic process determining that it is in our national self-interest to do so. Orders received by a military commander, in the final analysis, emanate from the highest level of national decision making and must be obeyed. This interpretation will always put mission first in priority, before soldiers and self. It is worth noting that this interpretation and this determination of priorities was all that General Dallaire had ever experienced. Until his Rwandan tour of duty, he had spent his entire career training for conventional warfare on the Central Front, in West Germany, as part of the NATO forces squared off against the Soviet Union.

Orders received by commanders of multinational peace-keeping operations, most of them mandated by the UN Security Council, present a much more complex set of circumstances. Soldiers frequently and sarcastically remind themselves: "Just remember, all of our equipment was made by the lowest bidder!" There is a similar attitude regarding Security Council mandates: "Just remember, the wording of our UN mandate was the result of the Permanent Five agreeing to the lowest common denominator!" When China, France, Russia, the United Kingdom and the

United States look at a threat to international peace and security through the prism of their own country's national self-interests, they will never completely agree on everything. What follows in the pursuit of "doing something" is a mandate for the UN field commander that is laced with compromises and omissions, frequently to the point of defying interpretation. Field commanders familiar with the UN's flawed decision-making process learn to deal with the ambiguities and to rely on their own common sense. The unattractive and unworkable alternative is to regularly ask UN headquarters for advice or direction. Better to take the appropriate action, and ask for permission—or absolution—later.

General Dallaire, as a result of his inexperience in working with the UN, was not prepared to act on the fact that his mandate—by his own admission, and for all intents and purposes—had disintegrated by mid-morning on April 7, some thirteen hours after the president of Rwanda's aircraft exploded and kickstarted the slaughter. Dallaire had mused on the possibility of such a development a number of times that morning, but he took no action to shift his priorities, to concentrate his forces, particularly his Belgian paracommandos, and to place his soldiers' security first in the order of priorities. He opted for a futile attempt to perpetuate a mandate that had been overtaken by events and that was made even more implausible by the ridiculous direction from UNHQ not to use deadly force unless fired upon, no matter what the circumstances. If a Rwandan child is dragged off to be slaughtered under your very nose, so be it, the order implied.

Even with the benefit of fourteen years of hindsight, now Senator Dallaire steadfastly refuses to acknowledge that the mission does not always come first in a commander's priorities. There is perhaps an explanation for his inflexibility on this matter; it relates to the fate of the ten murdered Belgian soldiers. If

Dallaire is permanently wedded to the view that the mission must always come first, then his Belgian soldiers' sacrifice and the fact that he ordered no action be taken to assist them while they were being slaughtered could be both explained and justified. Acknowledging now that not immediately alerting his headquarters that he would be mounting a rescue operation was incorrect would be a heavy burden indeed. There are those who argue, as Dallaire has, that a rescue attempt would have been suicidal. But they should realize that macho bullies who beat, torture and murder defenceless women and children become cowards when they are faced with well-trained, professional combat soldiers. If they had been ordered to intervene, there was certainly a chance that the Belgian paratroopers standing by would have got the job done; by their own accounts, they certainly wanted to try. Future Canadian military leaders should be aware that they will probably face similar dilemmas, and they too should ponder what their priorities will be and where their responsibilities will lie when the time comes.

British General Jack Deverell, in a 2007 article titled "Can Disobedience Be a Military Virtue?" argues that in some circumstances disobedience has been not just a virtue but a necessity. General Deverell has ample qualifications to opine on the subject. He was the deputy commander of operations for Stabilization Force in Bosnia-Herzegovina and the commander-in-chief of NATO's Allied Forces North before retiring in 2004. He writes: "On balance, history indicates that disobedience by senior commanders was often justified and successful whereas disobedience by soldiers more often than not ended in catastrophe." He goes on to say, "Commanders must generate trust and confidence within their structures as conflicts today are increasingly complex and dangerous—and often politically ambiguous and culturally sensitive. Most important of all, everyone in the force must understand that at some stage, in the absence of clear instruction, or in spite of orders that have been issued in good faith but *overtaken by events, they may have to act independently and decisively*" (my emphasis).[25]

I will go to my grave arguing that there are times—important times, albeit rare—when a commander's responsibility for his or her soldiers comes before the mission. The trick is to recognize the times. Senator Dallaire, who has filled his life with good works both during his military service and since his retirement from the military, offers dangerously bad advice on this aspect of leadership when he argues to the contrary.

Dora MacKinnon and my mother in Sydney, N.S., 1966. Dora and I were married six months later.

Our daughter Kimm, on the left, joins Dora and me at the Grand Prix de Trois-Rivières in 1992. She refers to this photo, taken for *Maclean's* magazine, as our *Little House on the Prairie* picture. (Courtesy Peter Bregg)

Lew MacLenzie, A great soldier, with admiration, thanks, and best wishes
C.L. P___
CJCS

With General Colin Powell, CJCS, on my return from Bosnia in 1992.
(Office of the Chairman of the U.S. Joint Chiefs of Staff photo)

Negotiating the removal of the blockade of Canadian troops and humanitarian aid with Radovan Karadzic at Bosnia House in Belgrade, 1993. Left to right: Karadzic, Tom Clark (CTV), the author, Chris Elias (CTV).

In Belgrade with the CTV crew, fixer and security during our coverage of the NATO bombing against Serbia/Kosovo, 1999. Standing, left to right: Milicia Lanasi, security, the author, security, the driver. Kneeling, left to right: Scott Rothenberg, Geoff Richards, Tom Clark.

Master Corporal Mark "Izzy" Isfeld, in a photograph taken two months before he was killed while mine clearing in Croatia in 1994. Mark was the inspiration for the Izzy dolls handed out by soldiers and NGOs around the world on behalf of ICROSS. (Photo by Sgt. Grey James)

Meeting my old friend Leonard Fisher during a nostalgia visit to Chilliwack Secondary School in 1993, almost forty years after we attended school together.

A larger-than-life portrait of the author by artist Gertrude Kearns. This work is now held by the Canadian War Museum. (Gertrude Kearns, MacKenzie/Sarajevo/1992, 2004, 20070001-001, Beaverbrook Collection of War Art, © Canadian War Museum)

Receiving the Order of Canada from the Right Honourable Michaëlle Jean in 2007, thanks to the outstanding work of many people on the ICROSS team. (Courtesy Master Corporal Issa Pareq, Canadian Forces, Rideau Hall)

22: Leadership: What It Looks Like

"Getting people to do what they don't necessarily
want to do, and having them enjoy the experience."

ONE DEFINITION OF LEADERSHIP

SHORTLY AFTER MY retirement from the forces in March
1992, I fulfilled many public requests for presentations on what
was going on in the Balkans. My agent, David Lavin of the
Lavin Agency, took care of the logistics that required so much
time to organize.

It was close to the end of 1992 when a client of the agency
requested that I make a presentation to his management team
on the subject of leadership. I turned down the lucrative offer,
explaining to David that it would be too embarrassing to stand in
front of a civilian audience suggesting by my presence and topic:
"Hey, look at me, I'm a great leader and I'm going to tell you how
to be one too." I had heard others make presentations on the subject and usually got the impression that their offerings were much
too theoretical to be of real value. I'd had the same reaction when
the subject of leadership was addressed in our academic military
institutions. The lectures were dedicated to various leadership

styles, including authoritative, participatory, collegial and the like. Although they were interesting, they didn't really provide the listener with any practical leadership tools.

But the requests for leadership presentations started to pile up, and I began to think that perhaps I did have something to offer after all. I spent a good week coming up with ideas on how to make a presentation on the subject less arrogant and provide some practical and useful leadership advice.

Frist, I needed a definition, and it had to be short and simple. I came up with: "Leadership is getting people to do what they don't necessarily want to do, and having them enjoy the experience." It seemed to me that in the business world, where most of the requests were coming from, when sales were up, the stock market booming, budgets adequate and the workers happy, you could put a monkey in charge. Leadership was essential only when there were problems and challenges, and that was most of the time.

The example I would use to make the point regarding a leadership non-challenge for the monkey was based on a fictitious event, but one that almost happened to me in 1977. At that time, the rotation schedule for the six-hundred-man Canadian units serving on six-month tours of UN peacekeeping duty in Cyprus was less than rigid. Our battalion was scheduled to start its tour in late April of the following year; however, there were rumours in early December that we might have to deploy in a few weeks' time—over four months ahead of schedule—because of a diplomatic crisis for Canada on the island. I would "recall" for my leadership audience an imaginary talk I'd had with my soldiers as they gathered around me on the parade square in Calgary at −25°Celsius: "You have all heard the rumours, and I can confirm they are true. Cyprus is an idyllic island in the eastern Mediterranean. It is home to both Greek and Turkish Cypriots. They don't get along, and the Turkish Cypriots in the north and the Greek Cypriots in the south are separated by a demilitarized zone running between their two communities. We will man the section of that zone that runs through the middle of the capital, Nicosia. Now, I'm going to have to work your butts off 24/7, but only for twenty-eight days out of thirty. During the other two days, you can go anywhere you want on the island. Having done two previous tours in Cyprus, I can share with you that there is a large topless beach on the south coast of the island, occupied by large numbers of young Swedish female tourists during the winter months." This would not be a leadership challenge! In fact, the only challenge would be to get out of the way as the soldiers stampeded to the airport. The reader will appreciate that I've described this scenario only to make a point. Soldiers would never, well almost never, react this way in real life.

Having defined leadership, it would be important for me to describe what it looks like.

In 1982, when I was a foreign student (an "international fellow") at the one-year course conducted at the United States Army's War College in Carlisle, Pennsylvania, I spent the year studying the process designed to produce U.S. foreign and complementary defence policies.

Well into the course, and designed to give us an interesting break from the academic routine, there was a one-week elective. We could choose to visit just about anywhere or anything in the United States, providing it had some relevance to what we were studying—logistics, management, organizational experiments, decision making and so on. Some students decided to spend their days at Fort Knox, investigating how the nation's gold reserves were managed, while others joined the New York City Transit Authority to observe how an organization larger than the Canadian Forces operated.

One of my friends on the course was a U.S. colonel who said, "Let's spend our time with the New York police force at a precinct in Harlem. I've done a bit of research, and the one we should visit has had more murders within its precinct borders last year than all of your Canada put together. Only one of the murders involved a victim who actually lived in the area; all the rest happened within the drug community that came and went during the night."

Our time with the precinct was pretty depressing. Even the police officers saw themselves as part of a "revolving door" system. Users and pushers would be arrested, and since there were no rehabilitation programs for users, they would be back on the street the following day. Pushers could afford good legal support, so they were only a day or two behind the users in getting back on the street.

On the final day of our stay, the precinct held a smoker for us to say goodbye. In those days, "smoker" was an accurate description. The room where it was held was filled with plain-clothes undercover policemen whose cloud of cigarette smoke was the consistency of Bay of Fundy fog.

I was in the middle of a conversation with a fit, young, probably thirty-five-year-old detective when he started to recount a story that I vividly recall to this day: "When I was assigned to this precinct three years ago, I decided that unlike most of my colleagues I would move my family into the area. We rented a tenth-storey apartment just down the street from here. Just a week ago my wife and two children, one eight and the other twelve, were in the elevator with me on the way to our floor after we'd done some shopping. The elevator stopped, a scruffy individual got in, and when he saw me—perhaps recognized me, I'll never know—he pulled out a pistol and shot at me, and missed!"

"Missed you in the elevator?" was the best I could come up with.

"Yes," he continued. "And a split second later I shot him three times, and killed him in front of my family."

By this time I was searching for something bordering on intelligent to say but could only come up with: "Do you get extra pay serving with this unit?"

"No, I make the same as someone with my rank and seniority directing traffic in downtown Manhattan," he replied with a hint of frustration.

Digging my hole deeper, I asked, "Look, Detective, one of your colleagues told me less than five minutes ago that you'd just asked for a two-year extension with this precinct. In God's name, why?"

The detective smiled, rose up on his toes and scanned the room, peering through the smoky haze, looking for someone or something. His eyes rested on a man standing in a far corner and surrounded by four or five other officers in plainclothes. The man was short, overweight, balding, dishevelled and smoking a massive cigar, which I discovered later kept him permanently covered with ash.

"You see that short guy over there in the corner smoking that cigar?" he asked.

"Yes," I said.

"Well, sir, that's my boss, and I'll do anything to keep working for him, no matter where he goes and what he does. And he is going to be here for another two years."

Twenty-five years ago, that young police officer provided me with the best example I could ever have of what leadership looks like.

For the past two decades it has been satisfying to see the

subject of leadership regain importance. Starting in the 1960s, with the U.S. nuclear submarine project, large organizations—and that includes many militaries—genuflected at the altar of management. Program evaluation and review techniques (PERT) charts were everywhere as leaders (now calling themselves managers) joined U.S. Secretary of Defense Robert McNamara's management bandwagon, which produced the Polaris Class submarine and helped Neil Armstrong walk on the moon. Airport bookstores were filled with best sellers telling the reader how to be a better manager and do things more efficiently.

The problem, as I saw it, was that management techniques were only one piece of the puzzle for getting anything done. Management is "doing the thing right," whereas leadership is better described as "doing the right thing." There is a big difference between the two, and although they are complementary, leadership is the key contributor to success both in business and in the military, that is to say, in dealing with people. If I wanted to talk to groups about leadership, I would need to focus on interpersonal skills. I would also explain that studying and discussing leadership was a bit like studying first aid: you could spend an hour a day studying it, and if you used your skills to alleviate someone's suffering or even save a life just once in your lifetime, the many hours you had spent preparing for that moment were well worthwhile. So it is with leadership: no one ever masters the subject, so you can never spend too much time considering it. I decided to come up with ten practical leadership tips, with the thought that if at the end of a one-hour presentation each member of the audience found one or two of them to be useful, even if that time was far in the future, the hour wasn't wasted—particularly if I made the presentation entertaining.

It was also important to stress to the audience that I wasn't presenting myself at the podium as an outstanding leader—far from it, as many of those who worked with me over the years would probably attest. What I brought to the subject was practical experience that began at the age of twenty in commanding a platoon of thirty soldiers, including some Korean War veterans, and ending thirty-three years later in commanding the fourteen-thousand-strong Army of Ontario. In between those milestones I had the privilege of leading soldiers from more than forty countries and working for twenty-nine bosses, of whom six were not Canadian. I had ample opportunity to observe what worked and what didn't. Some of the ten tips I decided to present I learned the hard way and to my regret didn't always follow myself until later in my career.

Students of leadership will notice here many similarities to the opinions of other practitioners who write and speak on the subject. They will also notice some dissimilarities: in the following tips, there are neither pie charts nor references to the "vision thing." Many people who speak to me after listening to my presentations express some surprise that I focus almost exclusively on developing interpersonal relations. They anticipate that a general would explain how to give orders and how to discipline people who don't follow those orders. Fortunately, however, generals and other senior military officials do this less than one per cent of the time. The remaining ninety-nine per cent of their time is dedicated to motivating and, dare I say it, trying to inspire.

With an upfront apology to my navy and air force colleagues for this simplistic analogy as I try to make a point: consider the unique leadership challenges facing leaders in the army. On board a ship, when the captain turns the wheel starboard, everyone on the ship goes to the right. When the captain of an aircraft moves the joystick to the left, everyone behind the captain goes to the left. When an army leader says to the hundred soldiers behind him, "We are attacking that hill four hundred metres to our right—follow me!" he really should look over his shoulder before climbing that hill because he might just find himself alone. Motivation and inspiration—not orders—will take the hill.

Tip Number One—Be Yourself

The vast majority of the bosses I had and observed were excellent. A few, however, became real dorks on promotion and elevation to the rank of boss. They obviously bought into the idea that they were now the most important individuals in the organization. They actually thought that the perks—the car, the driver, the extra windows in the office, the additional staff and all the other trappings of increased responsibility—were for them. But they weren't. They were for the position, and when the boss moved on, the perks would pass to the new guy. The fact is, once you are out of diapers it's probably too late to change your personality. Don't even try. You have to work with who you are and what you are.

I get a kick out of the "loneliness of command" theory. It opines that the person at the top is going to be lonely because he or she has no peer group, since he or she is the only one wearing the senior rank in the organization. Over the years I have explained to a few individuals who have brought up the subject that it is impossible to be lonely in a military organization unless you intentionally isolate yourself. This isolation usually results from assuming that you are indispensable to the organization (see above). Once you accept that you are merely the conductor of the organization that employs a whole gaggle of experts to assist you in your leadership role, you can start to enjoy their company.

Above all, leadership—at all levels—should be an enjoyable and satisfying role. If it's not and you prefer to stay in your current role in your trade, job or profession, don't seek or aspire to a leadership position. Life is too short.

Tip Number Two—Lead by Wandering About

I know I'm showing my age by mentioning an in-box, but the observation still applies today, except it's now an e-mail in-box. The more senior you get, the more your in-box overflows. It's only natural. Crap follows the law of gravity and flows downhill, frequently arriving on your desk. Your job as the boss is to intercept it before it splashes onto your subordinates. All kinds of frivolous requests and demands will make their way to you as the boss. Here's an example: during a particularly heavy shelling of the area in and around our headquarters in Sarajevo, I received a fax from UN headquarters in New York. It complained that I had not yet submitted the design for the ribbon that would be worn with the UN medal to be presented for service with UNPROFOR. Similar idiotic demands will all too often make you feel like you are chained to your desk.

While all these frequently mundane requests are demanding your attention, it's important to remember your primary responsibility: the people who work for you. Sometimes it's necessary to appoint someone to remind you of that fact three or four times a day, particularly when you're in an operational theatre for military leaders. The appearance of the regimental sergeant major at the office door or the opening of the sandbagged bunker announcing "Sir, it's time to visit the troops!" provides an instant relief from the insanity of the mundane and severs the chain that ties you to less important matters.

Tip Number Three—Listen

It took me twenty years to learn how to listen. For the longest time, when I was talking to subordinates, peers or bosses, I was always thinking about what I was going to say in response to their comments. Not surprisingly, I missed a good deal of what they were really telling me. But when I started to listen, it was initially a bit disappointing. I discovered that a significant number, yes, even the majority of people who worked for me, were smarter than I was. I started to pay more attention and picked up on some really good ideas they had about our profession and about how we could do our jobs better. What really surprised me was that when I implemented a suggestion and publicly gave the individual or a group credit for the idea, the positive change was associated with me. The source of the idea got credit, I got credit and our organization got better—you can't do better than that.

Now, it's no good listening if no one is talking to you as you execute your leadership by wandering about. When I was a fifty-three-year-old major-general wandering about, visiting soldiers who averaged about twenty-two years of age in Sarajevo, the gaps in age and rank might have been a problem. Canadian soldiers haven't changed a lot over the years, and as a good friend, Lieutenant-General Charlie Belzile, said while commanding our brigade in Europe thirty-two years ago, "Only two things motivate a Canadian soldier: his car keys in one hand and his girlfriend in the other." I have yet to grow up, and I continue to race cars as a hobby. Frequently, soldiers would be the ones to break the ice with me by saying something like, "Hey, General, how's the racing going?" A few minutes later, they were sharing with me what they really thought about what was happening and how they felt about it.

The key to listening is to get people to open up and encourage them to be forthright and honest with their comments. Everyone is boring until you scratch their passion. That passion can be anything from gardening to freefall parachuting, but whatever it is most people have a favourite activity that either excites them or makes them feel relaxed, comfortable and happy.

It's important to find out and remember what that passion is because that's the door to discovering what people really think about their day job and what might be done better.

Tip Number Four—
Set Difficult but Achievable Objectives
No one ever brags about having accomplished something that was easy. The key to good morale is to give the people who work for you something to be justifiably proud of.

In early July 1992, I came back to my headquarters from the Sarajevo airport, which we had just secured for the delivery of humanitarian aid the previous day. As I entered the operations room, I noticed what looked like a United Way thermometer pinned to the wall. At the top, and presumably as an objective, was the number 23, and at the bottom, where the mercury was resting, was a 6. I asked Captain Jorge Reta, the operations officer on duty, "What the hell is that thermometer for?"

Jorge explained: "Sir, those yahoos (pretty good command of the English language for someone from Argentina) at the UN in New York will only allow six humanitarian aircraft a day to land at the Sarajevo airport. They say that we don't have any mechanical off-loading equipment, proper storage space and a bunch of other things, and that it's too dangerous. I think we can handle twenty-three."

I sat down with Jorge and went over his calculations—something the military calls a staff check. Sure enough, it looked like with extra effort we could handle twenty-three aircraft a day. We had soldiers from more than ten nations doing the unloading, and with the right amount of challenge and leadership each national group would end up competing with the others to unload the fastest. A few well-placed phone calls to UNHCR in

Geneva, the lead UN agency for the air flow, and we were accepting around twenty-three aircraft a day.

There is another component to this "enough to brag about" theory. After my discussions with Jorge I could have become a little too ambitious and said, "Jorge, I think we can do even more. Let's aim for thirty planes a day," and broken both the backs and the morale of our unloading teams at the airport. The trick for the leader is to determine how much is enough to be proud of, and how much is too much to ask.

Tip Number Five—Accept Responsibility,
Even When You Are Not Responsible
I know this sounds somewhat bizarre, but let me try to explain.

During the formal inquiry into the incidents involving the Canadian Airborne Regiment in Somalia, a number of senior officers, including the chief of defence staff, were called to give evidence. When they were asked about their responsibility for what had happened, a common response was something along the lines of "As a senior/general officer I was responsible—but . . ." There is no place for "but" after "I'm responsible" because that word is always followed by a long explanation devoted to outlining why the individual thinks he or she is really *not* responsible.

More often than not, it's the organization's denials and cover-ups following a mistake that most hurt the organization and its leadership. The best example of an individual accepting responsibility for the good of the whole in the not too distant past was the principle and practice of ministerial responsibility in the British parliamentary system. Sadly this is no longer the case, particularly in the Canadian model. As disasters unfold in a department, the minister in charge clings on to his or her appointment with a death grip—until overwhelming pressure from the public forces him or her to let go. At this point it's too late for the minister to gain any credit for the resignation, and the department remains under a cloud.

During my presentations to more than a million people on the subject of leadership, I have made only one common request of every group: "Put your hand up if you can think of anyone you thought less of when they said, 'I'm responsible.' " In fourteen years of asking I have yet to see one hand go up. The corollary to this observation is the deduction that accepting responsibility frequently makes the problem go away much more quickly, and thus the organization can get on with its real priorities sooner.

Tip Number Six—Think Outside the Box

For almost ten years, one of my ten tips was "touching." Particularly in an operational theatre, I found that placing an arm around someone's shoulder was completely natural and reassuring. A few CEOs, particularly in the United States, were uncomfortable with the concept in light of sexual harassment legislation, and they asked me to drop any reference to touching.

It was a while before I stumbled on a permanent replacement tip. I was never really comfortable with the overworked phrase "thinking outside the box." Then, in 2004, I was invited to speak at "Idea City," Moses Znaimer's annual speakfest in Toronto. I arrived early enough to hear a couple of the speakers who would present before me. One of them, Mers Kutt, the inventor of the personal computer, made sense of thinking outside the box.

His example drew on the Second World War and the Allied bombing of Nazi Germany. The Allies' bomber losses were extremely high, and commanders were frantic to discover how to decrease losses attributed to anti-aircraft flak and machine-gun and cannon fire from German fighter aircraft. It was decided to bring in an outsider to provide a fresh point of view. An eccentric professor from Cambridge was invited to one of the largest of the United Kingdom's Bomber Command bases, where there were hundreds of bombers.

At his initial briefing the professor was told by the air vice-marshall, "We have a serious problem, Sir. We can attach only so many armour plates to the bombers because they add so much weight. We tend to place them around the cockpit. If we added as many as we would like, we couldn't carry any bombs. Perhaps you could spend the next ten days or so with us and recommend where on the aircraft we should place the limited number of plates we can afford to mount."

The professor spent the next ten days at the base inspecting every bomber as it returned from its mission. He was never seen without a large roll of onionskin paper rolled up under his arm. Finally, he said he was ready to brief the senior officers on his findings and make his recommendation. As they gathered around, he unrolled his onionskin and spread it out on a long table. On the paper he had drawn rough outlines of the Lancaster bomber as viewed from its top and side. He had painstakingly marked, with a pencil dot, each and every hit from flak and ammunition sustained by every bomber during the past ten days. The two sketches of the bomber were almost black with dots, but there were a few spots that were totally blank, with no dots whatsoever.

He pointed to the blank spots (an undisclosed location) and said, "Gentlemen, this is where you should place your armour plates."

The assembled leadership of Bomber Command were aghast. One of the most senior commanders exclaimed, "That's madness, Professor! Look at the concentration of hits in other locations, as you yourself have marked them!"

The professor smiled and said, "Yes Sir, but those planes made it back. The ones that were hit in places where I couldn't record the strikes crashed somewhere in the German country-side or at the bottom of the English Channel."

The plates were attached at the places the professor rec-ommended, and bomber losses thereafter were considerably reduced.

The problems facing a leader are frequently simple. The chal-lenge, amidst the confusion and chaos of day-to-day activities, is to recognize that fact. This means making time available to step back and think about the problem, and not just to tinker with the status quo. Leaders should take time to close the door, put their feet up and think.

Tip Number Seven—
Strive for Ethical Decision Making

The next time you go through an airport, check out the book-store to see how many volumes are available on the subject of ethical decision making. They might be in upper case, double-spaced and cost thirty-five dollars, but they mirror an obsession with the alleged complexity of the subject. Don't waste your money or your time, because the issue is not that complicated.

We all face ethical dilemmas in our lives, regularly and often. Mind you, I've actually had people ask me, "When will I know that I'm facing one?" To which my response is always the same, "Don't worry, you'll know." The crux of the problem is that we often make bad ethical decisions when we are alone, literally and figuratively. The solution is to imagine someone you love—a parent, your spouse, a sibling or a best friend looking over your shoulder when making any decision involving an ethical issue. You will do the right thing—and you will have saved yourself thirty-five dollars.

Tip Number Eight—

Have the Courage to Disagree

When I mention courage, most people assume that since this advice comes from a soldier, I must be talking about physical courage under fire. Not so: I'm talking about having the courage to disagree and having the confidence to encourage people to disagree with you.

Soon after taking over a large command late in my career, I asked my assistant to have all the senior officers gather later that morning so that I could address them about a serious issue. Needless to say, there was a lot of speculation in the hours before the gathering as people tried to identify what the problem was. What sort of trouble were they in?

Standing in front of the assembled group, I cut to the chase: "Ladies and gentlemen, I've now been your boss for a week, and no one—and I mean no one—has disagreed with me yet. Sometimes I've been in the middle of a sentence when I see people in the back of the room rushing off to implement what they think I want done. Look, I'm not so smart that everything I say is gospel. There are a whole bunch of you sitting here who are experts in your areas of responsibility. It would be reassuring to occasionally hear you say, 'You know, General, we tried that idea of yours three years ago and the results were not good.' Having heard your advice, I might well decide to proceed anyway—but at least I would be doing so with some background or counter-opinion. I won't get that with the current reluctance to disagree with me on anything. I want you all to feel free to disagree with me—without being disagreeable!"

It's the leader's job to create an atmosphere in which honest disagreements are aired. Most of us have worked for a boss in situations where disagreements were reflected in a less than glowing personal evaluation report and were a potential career stopper. Fortunately, those bosses are in the minority. If you're not one of them, it's a good idea to be sure your subordinates know that early on in your leadership role.

Tip Number Nine—
Prepare and Train Your Subordinates

The most stable kind of business to lead is the one in which the boss has been away for a week and someone asks, "Has anyone seen the boss lately?" Yet everything is ticking along quite nicely. That can happen when the boss has taken the time to ensure that subordinates are well prepared to take over and execute the boss's responsibilities.

This requirement is second nature in the military. In fact, they take it one step further and train an individual soldier to take over from his or her boss and boss's boss. In other words, if the lieutenant platoon commander is killed or wounded and replaced by the platoon second-in-command, a warrant officer, and he or she is also killed or incapacitated, one of the sergeant section commanders is prepared to take over. To reinforce the point, this has in fact happened during Canada's current Afghanistan mission.

It takes time and effort to prepare subordinates in the business world. It doesn't happen by osmosis, so merely ensuring that people observe their boss at work is insufficient. They need to experience actually doing their boss's job, and not just while he or she is away on holidays. The real boss must be there to mentor and guide subordinates. It takes courage to implement such a program because your subordinate might get you in trouble if he or she screws things up, but it pays big dividends in the long term.

Tip Number Ten—Be an Actor

Good leadership demands consistency. If you have to go to the boss's assistant to ask, "What mood is she in today? Should I pass this to her now, or do you think I should wait until next week?" or "How did he do on the golf course yesterday? Do you think he's in the mood to see this controversial report?" you have an inconsistent leader. We all have bad days, but it's essential that on those days we *act* just as we do on our good days. Inconsistency and unpredictability in a leader destabilize the organization and detract from the very open and collegial atmosphere that many of the above tips strive for.

In the past decade I made presentations and conducted miniseminars on leadership to a number of large oil companies at the tar sands projects near Fort McMurray, Alberta. Since each attendee was at the sharp end as far as leadership was concerned, I always finished each session by asking: "If my ten tips on leadership were expanded to eleven, what new one would you add?" I was amazed at the consistency of the responses. The overwhelming majority of respondents wrote "Approachability" on the index card they dropped into the box.

I was pleased that six of my ten leadership tips—Be Yourself; Lead by Wandering About; Listen; Accept Responsibility; Have the Courage to Disagree; and Be an Actor—contribute to creating that most desirable leadership trait: approachability.

23: The Enduring Canadian Peacekeeping Myth

"Pearson's brilliance is diminished when he is
credited with merely inventing peacekeeping."

A FAN'S OPINION

CANADA FOUGHT WELL above its weight in the Second World War, when there was only a modest direct threat to our nation. In the 1950s, following demobilization, the military's top priorities were the defence of Canada, creating a modestly sized but significant special force to dispatch to the Korean War, some 11,000 kilometres away, and maintaining our land, sea and air commitments to NATO. Then our priorities changed.

In 1956 the president of Egypt, Gamal Abdel Nasser, nationalized the Suez Canal. The narrow ribbon of water that connected the Red Sea to the Mediterranean Sea was built, owned and operated by the Suez Canal Company, which belonged to England and France. The two countries, with the collaboration of Israel, decided to confront Egypt and re-establish their control of the canal to guarantee the uninterrupted passage of Middle Eastern oil to Western markets. On October 31, the Israelis invaded

Egypt, reaching the canal by nightfall. France and England conducted an airborne drop in the area of Port Said. The world held its breath as the United States and the Soviet Union squared off over the escalating situation.

We Canadians should remember that our geometry teachers lied to us in saying that "the shortest distance between two points is a straight line." In fact, on our earth's surface it's a curve, and that curve between Russia and the United States goes over Canada, and that's where the missiles would meet—over Edmonton, Winnipeg, Toronto, Halifax and points in between. It is therefore always in our national interests to temper any tensions between Russia and the United States.

When I and my peers got into a schoolyard fight during my high school days in Chilliwack, the five-foot-nothing female teacher would intervene and stop it. We could have beaten her to a pulp, but we didn't. She represented the authority of the school, and we knew there would be serious consequences if we defied that authority. Not to mention the fact that we were usually pleased to have an excuse to stop fighting.

Lester Pearson, Canada's foreign minister at the time of the Suez Crisis, applied that reasoning to the battlefield. Picking up on a British suggestion he'd overheard in an elevator at UN headquarters that some sort of neutral force should intervene in the unfolding crisis in the Sinai, Pearson grabbed the moment.

Pearson's brilliance is diminished when he is credited with merely *inventing* peacekeeping. There were plenty of ideas in the air regarding the use of an outside multinational military force to stop a conflict. Pearson's unique contribution to resolving a conflict that could have triggered another world war was taking an idea and convincing a fractious UN Security Council to *act* on it. If you don't think that was impressive, consider the Security Council's rigor mortis since 2004 in responding to the genocide in Darfur and the fact that this despicable inactivity is occurring while the veto-holding members of the council are actually getting along with each other. Not so in 1956.

Pearson was convinced that the presence of an impartial military force that was backed by the authority of the United Nations would convince the belligerents to agree to a ceasefire and break contact on the battlefield. This pause would allow the UN force to interpose itself between their front lines, thereby permitting diplomacy to begin in search of a lasting solution to the conflict.

Pearson declared that for a force to qualify as a peacekeeping force, three criteria would have to be met: it would have to be invited in by all sides in the conflict; it would have to be lightly armed, using deadly force for self-defence only; and it would have to be impartial.

Not auguring well for the future—and sowing the seed for many UN mission failures to come—the Security Council decided to ignore one of Pearson's three criteria and deploy the first UN peacekeeping force even though Israel refused to recognize its authority or permit it on Israeli soil. Eleven years later, when President Nasser ordered the UN force to leave his country at the beginning of the Six-Day War in 1967, the Security Council had no choice but to give in to his demand as his country was the only signatory to the UN agreement creating the force. Fifteen UN soldiers were killed and twenty-one were wounded during their withdrawal.

Canada was a major contributor to that first UN force. It provided a large logistics base, communications and an armoured reconnaissance squadron that, with a similar unit from Yugoslavia, shared the responsibility of patrolling the border between Egypt and Israel. This was the beginning of the myth that Canada was the world's pre-eminent peacekeeping nation and that peacekeeping was our traditional role in a world sorely in need of more "Canadas." As we participated in virtually every one of the UN's missions up to the end of the Cold War, the myth became even more ingrained in the Canadian psyche. This, despite the fact that from the beginning, peacekeeping was a very low foreign-policy priority, following our NATO deterrent obligations at sea, on land in Europe and in the skies over North America and Europe. Successive Canadian governments encouraged the myth because it made cutting defence budgets much less controversial. And cut the budgets they did, regularly and predictably. After all, if Canadians could go off and do peacekeeping armed with nothing but a blue beret and a pistol, why was the military clamouring for all those expensive tanks, ships and aircraft?

All of the rules for peacekeeping went out the window at the end of the Cold War, yet the continuing use of the term in Canada and by the UN confused the public even more. In Yugoslavia, the 14,000 strong UN force sent to monitor a ceasefire in Croatia in 1992 arrived six months after the ceasefire had been signed, and the war continued. The force took up positions throughout the war zone and "observed" the war. It had no mandate to intervene and severely limited military capability when it ignored the direction from the UN in New York and tried to do so anyway. Many soldiers were killed and seriously wounded because peacekeeping policy was slavishly applied to a civil war scenario. Venturing back into Sarajevo in June 1992, a tiny UN force of less than a thousand ran a humanitarian airlift and was vilified by the local population, who understandably thought the UN was there to stop the war.

In Rwanda, there were no national self-interests and the Security Council refused to authorize the deployment of the troops that were required to thwart the genocide. The mission in

Somalia became caught up in the 1992 Bush Sr. vs. Clinton U.S. presidential campaign, and the candidate who said he would pull his troops out if he won did just that.

By this time, the only common characteristic of post–Cold War peacekeeping missions was the UN apology that followed each mission—an apology for not doing the job properly and for allowing the slaughter of innocents. Nevertheless, in Canada, faith in peacekeeping and the belief that it couldn't work without us remained. The Canadian Forces continued to be cut in size and funding in search of a "peace dividend." This in spite of the fact that we had cashed in our dividend two decades earlier, during the slash-and-burn years of the outspoken anti-military prime minister, Pierre Trudeau. In our tiny army, the regular infantry shrank to the point where it employed a thousand fewer personnel than the Toronto Police Force. In the months before the terrorist attacks of September 11, 2001, plans were made to eliminate the three light infantry battalions of the Canadian infantry, leaving only six mechanized battalions.

Clearly, the idea of Canada as the world's pre-eminent peacekeeper had lost its currency.

24: A Sea Change: Afghanistan

"Every impulse of Joy, Love, Jealousy, Hope,
Boredom, all the myriad of grand and
petty streams of consciousness that forms
each of us has just been smashed..."

WILLIAM RAY, IN "FIGHTING BLIND"

FOLLOWING ON THE heels of the terrorist attacks of September 11, 2001, Canada committed the 3rd Battalion of the Princess Patricia's Canadian Light Infantry (3 PPCLI) battle group, based in Edmonton, to Afghanistan. This move was in support of Article 5 of NATO's charter, which states that an attack against one member is considered an attack against all. Ironically, 3 PPCLI was one of the light battalions headed for the chopping block as part of the army's forced downsizing—a result of the Liberal government's budget cuts—until Osama bin Laden appeared on the scene.

Canada's commitment followed rapidly on the heels of the UN Security Council's authorization of armed intervention, which was based on the self-defence article of the council's charter. Its deployment, however, was delayed by confusion in Canada about its role in Afghanistan. As a result, there was a lack of strategic lift.

The United Kingdom's Royal Marine Commandos, the first to arrive in Afghanistan, in November 2001, immediately came under fire. Apparently no one had informed the Afghans that NATO was coming to "help them." The plan was that the U.K. troops would leave the theatre in six months and that Canada would take over as lead nation and command NATO's International Security Assistance Force. At an Ottawa conference around Christmas 2001, Turkey volunteered to provide a battalion to the British-led force, but only if it took over command when the British departed. Canada was snookered, and the frustrated commander of the 3 PPCLI battle group, Lieutenant-Colonel Pat Stogran, and his staff returned to Edmonton.

Meanwhile, at the U.S. Army Coalition Forces Land Component Command Headquarters in Kuwait, Canadian Major Jim McKillop was serving as a member of the multinational staff. When he advised the U.S. commanding general that the 3 PPCLI battle group was sitting on its hands in Edmonton, a formal request for forces was sent to Ottawa. On or about New Year's Day, 2002, Colonel Stogran was advised that his battle group would be attached to the 3rd Brigade, "the Rakkasans" of the 101st Airborne Division, based in Kandahar. Seven days later, Colonel Stogran deployed to Kandahar with his key commanders and staff.

That sequence of events should have been followed by the immediate phased deployment of the Battle Group from Western Canada to Afghanistan. But it wasn't. Tragically, the Canadian Forces' strategic capability to deploy troops by sea and air was yet another sacrificial lamb on the altar of reduced budgets for the Defence Department. Since withdrawing its NATO contingent from Germany in 1993, thereby losing its forward

operating base, the Canadian Forces had been reduced to begging rides with U.S. carriers or paying exorbitant fees to rent
ships and/or large Ukrainian Antonov aircraft to move its troops.
In the post-9/11 atmosphere, the increased international military activity resulted in skyrocketing rental prices for ships and
planes. At the same time availability plummeted, so it was February 2002—more than three months after the commitment and
over a month after getting the order to deploy—before the Canadian Battle Group arrived in Kandahar. At the risk of repeating
myself, I must stress that contrary to the information provided
in the majority of media reports, the initial Canadian deployment to Kandahar in 2003 was *not* in a peacekeeping role.

The 3 PPCLI battle group commanded by Lieutenant-Colonel
Pat Stogran formed one-third of a U.S. Airborne brigade operating out of Kandahar airfield and was tasked with seeking out
and destroying elements of al-Qaeda and the Taliban in the
mountains of eastern Afghanistan.

It was reasonable for the United States to assume that Canada
would continue to participate with the U.S.-led mission until the
job was done and the Taliban was defeated. Prime Minister Jean
Chrétien thought otherwise and decided to abandon the mission
after a mere six months, indicating that the Canadian army could
not find the six hundred soldiers required to replace 3 PPCLI.
Many Canadians didn't accept Chrétien's comment about a lack
of personnel and assumed that we withdrew because of the U.S.
friendly-fire incident in Afghanistan that killed four members
of 3 PPCLI and seriously wounded a number of others. In fact,
the prime minister's decision to withdraw from Afghanistan was
made long before that tragic incident. 3 PPCLI returned home to
Edmonton in August 2002, to a well-earned hero's welcome.

Shortly after Canada's departure from Afghanistan, the war
clouds gathered over Iraq as the United States turned up the

heat on the Iraqi president, Saddam Hussein. The U.S. floated a series of justifications for a potential invasion. First came "links with terrorism," but there was precious little evidence to support the allegation. Pictures of Iraqis attacking a gutted Boeing 707 outside of Baghdad could just as well have been video of soldiers practising rescuing hostages rather than terrorists taking them. Next came the "existence of weapons of mass destruction (WMDs)": obviously Saddam had WMDs, because we in the West have the receipts! We sold many of the components—precursors, chemicals and so on—to Saddam during his war with Iran. But the accusations didn't stick with the U.S. public, so the Bush administration went on to justification number three, "regime change," which flamed out with the public as well. In the interests of operating within the confines of international law, the Bush administration returned to the presence of WMDs because that, it could be argued, created "a clear and present danger" and justified intervention, with or without the support of a UN resolution.

On February 5, 2003, U.S. Secretary of State General Colin Powell appeared before the UN Security Council. He pleaded the case for military action against Iraq to eliminate the threat of Saddam's use of WMDs. Undoubtedly he was acutely aware that a resolution would never be forthcoming from the council authorizing such an attack. The UN weapons inspectors could have found a cache of high-yield nuclear weapons at the traffic circle in front of the Palestine Hotel in downtown Baghdad, and still there would not have been even a chance of a resolution authorizing military intervention seeing the light of day. The national self-interests of at least two, and possibly three, of the veto-holding members of the Permanent Five of the Security Council would have seen to that. Russia, France and also China, to a lesser extent, had massive oil interests and investments in

Iraq, and it would only take one of them to veto any resolution authorizing the use of force—and one certainly would.

Using the endless non-productive debates within a dysfunctional Security Council as a fig leaf, on March 18, Prime Minister Chrétien announced that Canada would not participate in the war with Iraq. The lack of Canadian participation would have little effect on the operational capability of the U.S.-led mission; however, the venue chosen by the prime minister to make the announcement was a major diplomatic faux pas that seriously eroded Canada–U.S. relations. Canada had given every indication that it would support the United States in its bid to remove a genocidal dictator from power, yet, in a 180-degree change of heart, Chrétien chose to announce that decision during question period in the House of Commons, and the U.S. leadership first heard about it from the news media.

The rift between Canada and the United States grew even worse in the ensuing months, as a few members of Parliament made fools of themselves and their fellow Canadians by making crude and offensive comments about President Bush and his administration: George Bush dolls were stomped on, and "I hate Americans" became a battle cry for some MPs. No fool, Chrétien looked around for a lifeline and, in spite of saying less than a year earlier that Canada could not find the six hundred troops to replace 3 PPCLI in Kandahar, announced to the surprise and dismay of the military that we would now dispatch two thousand troops to Afghanistan's capital city, Kabul. This new Canadian contingent, cobbled together on short notice, would be employed with NATO's International Security Assistance Force (ISAF) and would patrol the capital city of Kabul and its immediate surroundings. The media inaccurately referred to this as yet another peacekeeping mission, thereby reinforcing the national myth.

The Canadian contingent operated from Kabul for close to two years. During that period, thirty-one of Afghanistan's thirty-four provinces made considerable progress. Three million refugees returned to Afghanistan from neighbouring countries, thousands of schools were built, ten universities were opened, young girls in the millions went to school for the first time and the economy grew at an astounding rate. In the southern three provinces, however, the Taliban and its supporters— some for self-interest, such as the warlords and criminals, and some because they assumed the U.S.–NATO forces would soon depart, leaving them and their families at the mercy of the Taliban—escalated their insurgency. NATO agreed to join the U.S. counter-insurgency operations in the south.

NATO has been around since 1949, and Canada was a founding member. Large numbers of Canadian army and air force units had been stationed on German and French soil as part of NATO's deterrent force, squared off against the Russian-led alliance known as the Warsaw Pact until 1993. Many of the ex-Soviet satellite countries such as Poland and Hungary had joined the alliance after the end of the Cold War. It was all one big happy family, with twenty-six member nations. As described earlier, on its fiftieth anniversary, and searching for a reason to justify its continued existence after the collapse of the Warsaw Pact, which it had deterred for fifty years, NATO found a highly questionable cause. The Kosovo Liberation Army, internationally recognized as a terrorist organization, was ambushing and killing Serbian security personnel throughout the Serbian province. Serbia responded with a heavy hand to this violent independence movement within its own borders. Succumbing to U.S. pressure, led by U.S. Secretary of State Madeleine Albright, NATO sided with the terrorist group and bombed Serbian military, industrial and civilian targets from the safety of

10,000 feet. Largely due to the absence of risk, all NATO members showed up for the Alliance's first "war."

Southern Afghanistan was a completely different kettle of fish. This was a counter-insurgency task, in which NATO troops would be on the ground, taking on the insurgents eyeball to eyeball. This time, NATO members were not lining up to join the fight. Much to its credit, Canada was one of the first to relocate from the relatively safe surroundings of Kabul and moved to Kandahar in the autumn of 2005. NATO's command structure was woefully slow in assuming command in the south because of the delayed arrival of the Dutch and British contingents, so the Canadians operated under the operational control of the United States for their first seven months in Kandahar.

The ensuing operations, conducted by the Canadians as part of the UN-mandated NATO mission, were marked by impressive acts of bravery, outstanding leadership, professionalism and all too much sacrifice. The last resulted from NATO's inability to "convince" enough of its twenty-six member nations to step up to the plate and provide the necessary resources—including personnel, particularly infantry, tanks, artillery, logistics and helicopters—to defeat the insurgency before it could expand. With two to three NATO soldiers per thousand Afghan citizens providing security, rather than the proven requirement for at least twenty soldiers per thousand civilians, the NATO force could not even maintain the status quo. The more than 2,200 kilometres of undefended and uncontrolled border with Pakistan, isolating and protecting the Taliban's sanctuary there, provided the insurgents with an overwhelming advantage. NATO, with its meagre force, less than half of whom were available to fight, was challenged just to keep a lid on the situation. Commanders in the south were dissuaded from requesting large numbers of additional troops and limited their pleas to around

2,500. My estimate of the personnel requirement, after two visits, was around thirteen thousand additional front-line troops. This number was endorsed more than once by commanders on the ground—when they momentarily slipped out from under their political constraints or after they retired.

During this depressing NATO performance, late speaker of the U.S. Congress Tip O'Neill's pronouncement that "All politics is local" took hold in Canada. Much of the Canadian public, woefully ill-informed about the impressive progress being made in most of the Afghan provinces and bombarded with details regarding Canadian casualties, turned against the mission. Within a micro-second of the polls showing dwindling support for the war, the opposition parties jumped on the bandwagon and called for either the withdrawal of Canadian soldiers or a return to "our traditional peacekeeping role." Yet again, the existence of the Canadian peacekeeping myth conveniently kept the debate from reflecting the reality of the situation.

Peacekeeping in southern Afghanistan would be nice, but unfortunately an enemy is active there. The Taliban won't invite us in, and it certainly won't co-operate with an impartial, lightly armed for self-defence-only force. As a result the national focus turned to the silly, non-productive argument of whether supporting the troops meant supporting the mission. All parties joined in this meaningless debate, sending mixed messages daily to the soldiers on the ground, to those who had just returned, to those about to deploy and to all their families. As former U.K. Prime Minister Margaret Thatcher would say, the almost fifty per cent of the Canadian public getting all the attention by the media had "gone wobbly."

Meanwhile, in the sands and mountains of Afghanistan too few soldiers were nevertheless having a series of successes on the battlefield. But their resources were not sufficient to secure each victory. In other words, having won a battle, they had to move on to other tasks in other locations, thereby leaving to the enemy the terrain they had won with blood. The Taliban, soon discovering that it could not defeat the NATO troops in the south in a head-to-head showdown, reverted to the cowardly but effective use of improvised explosive devices, roadside bombs and kidnapping, including beheading local NATO sympathizers, to attack the morale of the soldiers and more importantly the will of the Canadian public. With inadequate numbers of soldiers on the ground, all NATO could do was fight to hold the status quo in the south.

The NATO alliance, in its first real fight in Afghanistan, has come up seriously wanting. It needs, as a minimum, an additional thirteen thousand troops. In 2007, national military personnel contributions to NATO's ISAF, expressed in percentages of each country's regular army deployed in Afghanistan, were as follows: 11%—Canada; 6%—Belgium, Netherlands, United Kingdom; 5%—Estonia, United States; 4%—Denmark, Norway; 2%—Germany, Italy, Lithuania, Luxembourg; 1%—Bulgaria, Poland, Romania; minus 1%—Czech Republic, France, Greece, Hungary, Latvia, Portugal, Slovakia, Slovenia, Spain and Turkey.

For non-NATO contributors, the military personnel contributions are 4%: New Zealand; 3%: Australia; 1%: Sweden; minus 1%: Albania, Azerbaijan, Croatia, Finland and Macedonia.*

It's worth recalling Article 5 of NATO's charter: "an armed attack against one or more of them [member nations] in Europe or North America shall be considered an attack against them all." Does dispatching less than one per cent of your army to help other countries defeat a common enemy meet the demands of

---

* Figures for NATO and non-NATO countries were calculated by dividing their Afghan deployments into the strength of their standing armies.

the charter? I think not, particularly considering the fact that *all* members of the alliance waged war from the sky against Serbia over the Kosovo issue when there had been no attack outside of Yugoslavia against any NATO member country in Europe or North America.

Afghanistan is the first real litmus test for NATO in its almost sixty-year history, and the alliance is failing. Individual countries' governing bodies have got in the way of strategic decision making, as domestic self-interest and the overwhelming desire of parties to stay in power or to gain power trump "doing the right thing" geopolitically. It's perfectly acceptable for opposition parties to question their nation living up to its NATO obligations, providing the justification is sound. But it's totally unacceptable to do this for cheap political gain. In the Netherlands, it was only after four months of parliamentary debate that the decision was made to permit the deployment of their significant and valuable military presence from the relatively peaceful north of Afghanistan to the volatile south. If this laborious, risk-adverse, self-interest-dominated domestic decision-making process is to be implemented in each of its twenty-six members, it does not augur well for NATO coming out on top in any future military confrontation. Paradoxically, the very democratic values that we hope to export and help to encourage abroad thwart timely decision making within the alliance's members at home and may contribute to defeat rather than victory.

When and if NATO finds a way to declare victory by handing off the security role to the Afghans and leaving, both that country's future and the future of NATO will depend on the Taliban. If the Taliban successfully re-emerges to take on and defeat the combination of the Afghan National Army and Afghan National Police created by NATO, and if it returns to power in Kabul or even Kandahar, NATO is doomed. No other victim of aggression, including the member states themselves, will ever again trust the alliance to act as one homogeneous collection of like-minded nations that are standing by to come to the rescue.

During NATO's six decades of existence, there have been times when Canada has been an embarrassment and not pulled its weight within the alliance. Particularly sad was Prime Minister Trudeau's decision to arbitrarily chop our NATO forces in Europe by fifty per cent in the mid-1970s. Canada voluntarily offered up our "peace dividend" fifteen years before the end of the Cold War, before any other nation had, just because a prime minister who had taken extreme measures to avoid serving during the Second World War and who had little, if any, respect for the military thought it was a good idea.

In what might be NATO's final chapter, Canada can stand proud in having erased the memories of its past shortcomings in support of the alliance. When the first true test of NATO's charter was presented to individual members on the heels of 9/11, Canada responded. When the threat became more difficult and dangerous, Canada did not hide behind its three oceans; on the contrary, it increased its commitment to the fight. The sacrifices made by our young men and women in uniform in the hostile deserts and mountains of Afghanistan, in the honourable pursuit of assisting others to have a tiny portion of what we take for granted, has re-established our high standing in the struggling alliance.

I spent the first thirty years of my military career serving in the shadow of the Cold War. As each successive government imposed annual cutbacks on the defence budget, we soldiered on with our contribution to NATO's deterrence role as our number one priority. The strength of Canada's armed forces dwindled from 123,000, on the day of my joining in 1960, to 82,000, on the day of my departure in April 1993. It is down to 60,000 as this is being written. We trained hard for the ultimate, and at times what seemed to be the inevitable, showdown with the Soviets on the plains of West Germany. Training was intense and at times even dangerous. Breaks from the NATO routine were offered up infrequently by six-month to one-year tours of duty with mostly UN-mandated peacekeeping missions in Cyprus, Gaza, Yemen, Lebanon, the Golan, the Sinai, Angola, Syria, Kashmir and a handful of other exotic locales. More than 120 Canadians were killed while serving on these missions, but considering that those missions spanned a period of thirty years, the odds were pretty good that the soldiers would return home in one piece.

The decade following the collapse of the Berlin Wall, the Soviet Union, the Iron Curtain and the Cold War was more dangerous—or exciting, depending on your viewpoint. "In-between" missions such as Croatia, Bosnia, Somalia, Rwanda, East Timor, Cambodia, Macedonia and Sierra Leone, erroneously labelled "peacekeeping," offered up their share of increased danger. In the Balkans alone, twenty-seven Canadian soldiers were killed and more than a hundred were seriously injured—not that the government or the public paid any attention to those losses. No public official or members of the media met the planes bringing the dead and wounded home.

In 2002, Canada went to war for the third time in ten years. The first two times—Gulf War (One) in 1991 and the 1999 NATO bombing of Serbia–Kosovo—didn't count with the media or the public because, for the first time in recorded history, a country participated in two wars and sustained zero fatalities. As they say in the media game, "If it bleeds, it leads." There was no bleeding.

All of that changed with Canada's entry on the ground in Afghanistan. For the first time since the Korean War, Canadian soldiers were no longer training for battle; they were actually in one, on a daily basis. Like surgeons who have trained for thirty years to do open-heart surgery but have never been allowed to operate on someone, those of us who served during the Cold War watched from the sidelines with a certain amount of envy. Now, readers may conclude that I and many of my fellow aging colleagues are a bunch of warmongers longing for a good scrap. Not so—the envy is born of the fact that we missed the opportunity to lead the very best of young Canadians in the most stressful conditions imaginable and in the pursuit of honourable goals.

There is no finer calling than being asked to help those who, through no fault of their own, are one hell of a lot worse off than you are. The abused citizens of Afghanistan certainly qualify for that help. If you find that hard to believe, perhaps this account, written by William Ray, a young Canadian Artillery non-commissioned officer, will cause you to reconsider:

A man dressed in Traditional Afghan garb, dirty and ill kept, his head swathed in the distinctive black headdress of the Taliban religious thought police, pushes a slight, nineteen-year-old girl half his height in front of him into the brightly sweltering Kabul soccer stadium. She is smothered in a blue burka, her hands are bound and she stumbles as the man roughly pushes her to the centre of the pitch. He has an AKM assault rifle, perhaps in the past pried out of the cold hands of some unfortunate Russian conscript, sloppily slung around his shoulder upside down but accessible for his needs. The slackness of his weapon handling, and the careless arrogance of his walk, make it clear this soldier of the margins of Islam fears no contact from armed adversaries today. The crowd is respectably large, made up of men in the earthy brown Dishdas and the rainbow Casper the Ghost knots of women detained in their own anonymity under their all covering raiment.

Brought, perhaps, to remind them of their role in society. The girl's head starts to writhe back and forth beneath her sacking. She must not be able to see much through the restrictive mesh of her burka, the increasingly anticipatory noise and its suddenly swelling volume must be terrifying her as she struggles to breathe against the thick cloth of her heavy hood. The scruffily bearded, slightly inbred-looking minder halts her abruptly on a spot picked out of some twisted qualities deep in his simian brain for centrality and sightlines for the audience; she stiffens and jerks reflexively, her body pumping adrenalin through her system in tendon-bending amounts. He shoves her down hard from the shoulder [and] she sprawls on her stomach, straining to wrench her shoulders around in a vain attempt to look her tormenter in the face, perhaps. Copious amounts of Kabul's thick, cloying dust [are] kicked up in a dense cloud by her fall, rushing through the tiny air spaces in her shroud-like garment. She coughs, spitting the dust back through the clogged venting in her mask.

He struggles to shrug the slung AKM into his shoulder and sloppily sights down its length, steadying his shot as his target goes through her stomach wrenching final exertions. The stinging dust kicks once more into her censored face but there is no more reflex to cough in the central nervous system that once directed this and every other spark of life in this thin, petite young woman, every petty daydream, every impulse of Joy, Love, Jealousy, Hope, Boredom, all the myriad of grand and petty streams of consciousness that forms each of us has just been smashed through by the 7.54 mm Russian-made lead shot that has just finally, and at this point mercifully, removed this young spirit from the terrors of this world. Her crime was to have been unescorted in the company of a man who was not her blood relative.[26]

Lest the reader think that the above is an exaggerated work of fiction, included only for effect: the execution described here, and many others, were clandestinely filmed by La League de Femme. The film was smuggled to the West in 1998.

Why are we in Afghanistan? I, for one, rest my case, conscious of the fact that the obvious question that follows is: "If the gross violation of human rights is sufficient justification for intervention, then why aren't we in Darfur, Zimbabwe, Nepal and God knows how many other countries around the world?" Good question—and the fact is, we should be more interventionist, under the provisions of the UN's Responsibility to Protect. For reasons well beyond Canada's influence, the rigor mortis that characterizes the UN Security Council's decision-making process precludes such action. In the case of Afghanistan, the attacks of 9/11 provided an opportunity to remove one of the most brutal regimes on the planet and at the same time to remove at least one of the sanctuaries for transnational terrorism.

25: "More With Less"

"Canada's less than one per cent of the world's population was doing more than ten per cent of the multinational military 'dirty work.'"

AN OBSERVATION ABOUT THE EARLY 1990S

IT WAS EVER thus.

The coincidence of the end of the Cold War and the expanding profile of transnational terrorism since the attacks of 9/11 presents the Canadian military with new challenges. This in spite of the naive and ill-informed call from many—including some politicians who should know better—that we should "return to our historical role as peacekeepers" as if that were possible.

For the past three and a half decades, the primary concern of every chief of defence staff (CDS) has been the survival of the Canadian Forces. Political parties of all political stripes have regarded defence budgets as discretionary government spending, which can alternatively be made available to fund more attractive vote-getting projects. Starting with Pierre Trudeau's halving of Canada's standing NATO commitments in the mid-1970s and continuing on a downhill slide to the slash-and-burn years of Prime Ministers Jean Chrétien and Paul Martin in the

1990s, the defence budget's real purchasing power was a favourite target in every election.

The military spends its budget allocations in only three ways: new equipment, operations and personnel.

If new equipment contracts are cancelled, hefty penalties must be paid—witness the over $500 million penalty paid as a result of Chrétien cancelling the EH101 helicopter contract on his way to political victory in 1993. Lack of funding in the equipment budget means that equipment well past its "best-by date" is kept in service, even though this policy means exorbitant increases in maintenance costs and a huge deterioration in operational capabilities.

Domestic operations, which are dictated by the government, include military surveillance of the north, coastal patrols by sea and air, search and rescue, and commitments in support of NORAD—all the while maintaining forces at the ready to aid the civil power in the event of emergencies and disasters. Overseas operations are driven by Canadian foreign-policy decisions, which dictate worldwide military commitments—for example, in the skies over Kosovo, in the North Atlantic and in the deserts of Afghanistan. As a rule, governments do not reduce the Canadian Forces' operational demands even when the military leadership disagrees with particular commitments. In 2003, when the military indicated that it was not capable of mounting a two-thousand-strong force for deployment to Kabul without severely jeopardizing the integrity of the army following Chrétien's surprise announcement, the CDS was told to get on with it, no matter what the repercussions.

With little if any direct control over equipment purchases and operations, the CDS of the day was left with only one option to save money and meet Chrétien's diminishing budget—cut people! During the 1990s, soldiers were actually paid a bonus to take an early release. Many highly trained personnel in the critical ranks of sergeant, warrant officer, captain and major took up the offer because they faced a downsizing military and reduced promotion opportunities. Regrettably, these ranks are the most critical to any military. Without them, new soldiers don't get trained and led in the field, and generals don't have viable organizations to task.

During these decades of personnel cuts various CDS were subjected to a good deal of criticism from the rank and file, who saw them capitulating without a fight to government directives that guaranteed a reduction in the Canadian Forces operational capabilities. With the rare exception of General Jean Boyle, who was forced to resign during the Somalia inquiry and who was obviously out of his depth as CDS, the criticisms were blatantly unfair and unwarranted. It was essential for the generals who were appointed as CDS to understand how the political game was played in Ottawa. Without their having that understanding it is not unreasonable to speculate that the Canadian Forces would not exist as a viable military force today. Operational experience in the field was almost non-existent for generals in the Canadian Forces because most Canadian overseas military commitments were too small to justify putting them in charge.

The end of the Cold War ushered in new challenges for the Canadian Forces. A few voices in the wilderness, including my own, opined that greater demands would be placed on the Canadian soldier now that the stabilizing standoff between the U.S./NATO and the Soviet Union/Warsaw Pact was history. We were deemed merely to be angling for increased defence budgets, and our comments were dismissed as irrelevant. Plans to withdraw the Canadian Forces' standing NATO commitment that was stationed in Europe were accelerated, and in 1993 the forces were withdrawn and their overall strength was immediately reduced by the thousands.

What followed was the greatest demand in pure numbers and complexity for the Canadian military since the Second World War—Cyprus, Cambodia, Croatia, Bosnia, Somalia, East Timor, Sri Lanka, Congo, Rwanda, The Golan, Macedonia, Kosovo, Persian Gulf, Kuwait, Iraq/Iran—and the list went on. At one stage in the first half of the 1990s, Canada's less that one per cent of the world's population was doing more than ten per cent of the multinational military "dirty work" with eight thousand soldiers, sailors and air personnel deployed abroad on operational duty.

This ten-year period of intense activity created an ever-growing cohort of middle-rank officers who today, as generals and admirals, make operational capabilities and leadership their number one priority. In some ways, their job has been made easier because the government, the public and the international community are continuously watching and evaluating the Canadian Forces, and therefore the support, be it moral or financial, is more forthcoming. While the defence budget is still woefully lower than called for by Canada's position and obligations in the world, the annual cuts to defence funding that once characterized each federal budget have disappeared—at least for now.

The combination of operationally oriented leadership and increased funding has started the resuscitation of the Canadian Forces. Unfortunately, the devastating cuts to personnel and funding during the 1990s means that too many overdue expenditures are desperately in need of financing, all at the same time. Many major pieces of equipment are beyond both their "best by" and "rust-out" dates: vehicles, helicopters, search and rescue aircraft, fighters, tanks, frigates, destroyers, joint supply ships—all need attention. The public, when it sees quick buys for operationally necessary purchases for the war in Afghanistan, assumes that these acquisitions solve the problem for those types of equipment in the army. Artillery purchases are a good example of this perception. But the numbers purchased are tiny compared with the requirement, since everything is in the shop window in Afghanistan. Similar equipment for training at home and for the other much larger artillery units in Canada are not funded.

General Rick Hillier, appointed CDS in 2005, introduced initiatives strongly supported by Defence Ministers Gordon O'Connor and Peter MacKay. These have set in train a significant transformation of the Canadian Forces with a momentum that will be maintained despite Hillier's retirement, which is scheduled for July 2008. Forces are designated for tasks at home—surveillance and defence in the air and at sea, particularly in the north, search and rescue, counter-terrorism, emergency response, aid to the civil power when requested and the like. Other forces are specifically organized and prepared to take on expeditionary tasks such as the current mission in Afghanistan and Canada's modest commitments in southern Sudan and Darfur.

But it is in the area of expeditionary capabilities that I feel we as a country and as a military are falling woefully short. Certainly the purchase of four C-17 strategic aircraft is a good move and, it is hoped, will wean us from renting ancient Antonov aircraft at exorbitant rates; large aircraft complement expeditionary capability. They cannot, however, provide the strategic heavy lift on their own. That can only be provided by purpose-built ships. This subject is so critical to the operational capability of the Canadian Forces that it warrants its own chapter, which follows.

26: An Army Afloat? Yes, Please!

"Aye, Aye, Sir, and we will be ready to deploy in
about three months—once we arrange the lift and
logistics for our contingent."

NOTIONAL STAFF OFFICER AT NATIONAL DEFENCE HEADQUARTERS

IN 1965 I WAS temporarily assigned to the Infantry School in Camp Borden, near Barrie, Ontario, as an instructor for officer candidates. At the same time I was selected for a career prerequisite company commander's course, but the schedule conflicted with my instructing schedule. The powers that be decided that my instructing duties took priority and that, as a consolation prize for missing the company commander's course, I would attend the first intake of a new, two-month course referred to as "Staff School," which would be conducted in Toronto the following year.

One of the intimidating assignments on the course—and critical to the final grade—was a major writing assignment on a military subject of the student's choice.

In spite of my youth and naïveté, and being one of the few lieutenants on a course designed for captains, I launched into the subject of a particular vanishing and critical capability in the

Canadian military. Word had it that our one and only surviving aircraft carrier, HMCS *Bonaventure,* would be decommissioned within three years. With the *Bonaventure's* loss, our ability to quickly launch the equipment of an expeditionary force would disappear. Only a year earlier, the "Bonnie" had moved the equipment for the first Canadian contingent assigned to serve in Cyprus with a new UN force. This capability allowed our soldiers to patrol their areas of responsibility before those of any other nation in the UN force except the United Kingdom, which had permanent bases on the island.

An expeditionary capability gives a nation the ability to send a self-contained force—in the case of Canada, 1,000 to 1,200 troops, with their combat vehicles, supplies, medical support and air support—anywhere in the world with a nearby coastline. Over ninety-five per cent of the scores of locations Canada sent its soldiers to since the Second World War had the prerequisite coastline. Even with an aircraft carrier, it had to modify the ideal self-contained deployment method and was forced to send soldiers by air to marry up with their equipment, which had been delivered by sea at the destination. That's workable if the situation at the arrival point is relatively peaceful, but it is irresponsible if it's not.

The solution, I wrote, particularly for a nation bordering on three oceans, was to have a genuine amphibious expeditionary capability with purpose-built ships, specialized equipment, trained soldiers, sailors and airmen located on both the Atlantic and Pacific coasts. My paper received a decent mark but was ignored, as were all the other student submissions. This was the norm in Canada's military during the four decades of the Cold War. Writing assignments were just that—writing exercises. They were not considered to be of any potential use to decision makers in the policy world.

For the next thirty years, Canada's capability for deploying its operational forces to overseas missions by using its own resources gradually disappeared. This became a source of considerable embarrassment. Each time our government decided that Canada would participate in a multinational mission, the folks in NDHQ would search the world's inventory of commercial ships available for rent, focusing on the cheapest ones for all the obvious reasons. The best deal might well be in the South China Sea on another contract, unable to make it to Halifax for another month, but it could well get the contract to move our vehicles and equipment. To get our troops abroad, renting massive Ukrainian or Russian Antonov aircraft became the norm. The fact that the troops and their equipment would not arrive together, and that this would be accomplished at an exorbitant cost to the Canadian taxpayer, had to be accepted if we wanted to play with the big boys.

Shortly after my retirement from the Canadian Forces in 1993, I was asked to make a presentation at a military symposium in Halifax. During my speech I launched into a bit of a rant (perhaps a major rant) about our lack of any real expeditionary capability. Since I was speaking in the port city of Halifax, which would be a primary beneficiary of any move to create such a capability, my comments made it into the media. Out in British Columbia, Ralph Fisher, a retired navy commander who had served on two of our long-since-retired aircraft carriers, read the comments and called me. We had spoken a few years earlier about the same subject, but this time we decided to raise the profile of this serious deficiency in our Canadian Forces.

Over the next year, Ralph, his team of retired colleagues and I completed a detailed analysis of the pros and cons of the amphibious expeditionary capability. The study, entitled "Sea Horse," included a number of recommendations that, if implemented, would see such a capability established within the Canadian Forces within five years.

"Sea Horse" envisioned the purchase of purpose-built ships stationed on each coast and designed to carry a battle group of at least a thousand soldiers with their vehicles and equipment. The ships would have a medical facility as well as back-up logistics support for the troops once they were put ashore by both boat and helicopters. If a model was needed, all one had to do was witness the ships being built and used by the United States, United Kingdom, Australia, France, Spain, Italy and many other countries to meet the post–Cold War security challenges.

Realizing that we would probably have to settle for an initial purchase of one ship to prove the worthiness of the concept, we decided that it would be best to locate it on the east coast at the Port of Halifax. I appeared before the Standing Senate Committee on National Security and Defence and outlined the "Sea Horse" concept. I explained that the force would need a mounting facility from which to deploy and that it would be massively expensive to construct. There would be a requirement for a year-round deep port, jetty, crane, long runway, railhead, good road network and accommodation and facilities for over a thousand soldiers. It would take billions of dollars to create such a complex, but they needn't worry because it already existed at the underutilized Canadian Forces Base Shearwater, in Dartmouth, Nova Scotia.

I went on to explain that such a capability would have a very positive impact on the government's decisions about any deployment of the Canadian Forces overseas. Without a true expeditionary force capability, any government had to rush through the process leading to the decision to deploy the forces to an operational theatre. Why? Because once the order was given, the response from the military leadership was along the lines of "Aye,

Aye, Sir, and we will be ready to deploy in about three months—once we arrange the lift and logistics for our contingent."

With the Canadian Forces' expeditionary capability up and running, the government could be more methodical and thorough in its planning for any participation in a particular mission, be it security, humanitarian or disaster relief. During that process, the expeditionary force could set sail and station itself in international waters close to the potential mission area. If the decision was made by the government to participate, the response from the military would be closer to "Aye, Aye, Sir, and we will be there in six hours!" If the government decided against participation, the expeditionary force would weigh anchor and return to its home port or elsewhere.

We decided to submit our recommendations to Prime Minister Jean Chrétien and provide copies to leaders in the opposition and the Defence Department. Relations between the prime minister and me were somewhat strained as the result of an accusation he had made against me the previous year. In response to a question from a journalist who had quoted me as saying the defence budget was too small by half, the prime minister indicated that I was just interested in a bigger lunch with the arms dealers.[27] I was furious, because I had made it a point not to be associated with any lobby group or to join any company selling equipment to the military. I had turned down a number of attractive offers to join the management teams and boards of these companies and had gone out of my way to maintain my independence as a media commentator. I didn't even join my friends in the Canadian Legion, because the Legion had a responsibility to lobby the government on veterans' issues.

I wrote the prime minister a personal letter advising him of my independence and indicating that it was beneath the dignity of his office to make such false and unsupported accusations.

I explained that my comments regarding the underfunding of the military were reasonable and justified and that I would be pleased to participate in any planning undertaken to rectify the situation. I indicated that the prime minister's face-to-face invitation to me to join his team in the 1993 federal election presumably indicated some respect for my opinion on defence issues. When the contents of the letter subsequently ended up in the media, the response from the prime minister's office (PMO) to inquiring journalists indicated that Chrétien stood by his comments.

The "Sea Horse" study was submitted to the prime minister under a covering letter co-signed by me and Vice-Admiral (Ret'd) Harry Porter, a much-respected leader with all ranks in the navy, and a who's who of retired senior officers, including two retired chiefs of the defence staff. The PMO's response was deafening in its silence; however, as the months passed, we noticed that quotes from and references to the study were being mentioned by various individuals in the government and the Defence Department.

The first low point for our initiative occurred during the June 2004 federal election. Stephen Harper's Conservative Party's platform promised to increase the funding for the Canadian Forces, a promise that included the addition of an aircraft carrier to carry troops abroad. The purpose-built ships for deploying troops that "Sea Horse" had recommended were nothing like an aircraft carrier. In most countries, they were referred to as assault ships because their primary role was to deliver troops and equipment ashore. Sure enough, Paul Martin's team saw the obvious flaw in Harper's policy recommendation, flashed a picture of an Argentine aircraft carrier bristling with armed fighter jets on its deck and asked the voters in the television audience, "Do you want better health care or Harper's aircraft carriers?"

When the popular, competent and outspoken General Rick Hillier was appointed chief of the defence staff in 2005, the term "honking big" ship appeared regularly in his presentations regarding the future structure of the Canadian Forces. The "Sea Horse" hearts soared, only to be dashed by the reorientation of defence spending, which was understandably directed to ensuring our troops in Afghanistan had the very best of support.

The final nail in our collective coffin was the unbelievably shortsighted sale of DND property at CFB Shearwater to the Crown's Canada Lands Corporation in 2002. Plans exist to break up the 9,000-foot military runway to provide access to a civilian housing and commercial development. The runway was so highly regarded that it was an alternate for space shuttle use, if need be. To try and stop the destruction, we mobilized support at every level—from the mayor of Halifax to federal cabinet ministers to the Senate of Canada. We were told of a report that concluded $100 million would be required to refurbish the runway. The general manager of the Robert Stanfield International airport, outside of Halifax, visited Shearwater and opined that he wished his airport was in as good a condition as the military's. We asked for a copy of the "$100 million report" and were advised it couldn't be found. Indications to date strongly suggest the study was never done.

At present, thanks to the intervention of Defence Minister Peter MacKay, the engines of the bulldozers aimed at the irreplaceable Shearwater runway are turned off. MacKay was the first politician investigating the subject to recognize the strategic value of this irreplaceable mounting site for an amphibian expeditionary force. The battle is still on to rescue the entire facility from short-sighted destruction and redevelopment; however, the rescue efforts initiated by retired Commander Ralph Fisher over a decade ago are making progress. Thwarting what could and probably would be the most disastrous and short-sighted strategic decision made by the world's second-largest country, especially if it maintains its appetite for foreign interventions in the interests of international peace and security, would be a major achievement. Afghanistan and the Vancouver Winter Olympics are understandably high priorities today, but the value of the Shearwater facility, including the long runway, would be invaluable for generations to come. A wide selection of suitable ship designs are available and proven that could be built in Canada. Leased container ships, modified for military use and with capabilities proven by the U.S. Marine Corps, could fill the void until Canada's own three specially built expeditionary ships were commissioned. In concert with the major equipment purchases currently in the pipeline, a true Canadian Forces expeditionary capability would produce the best little military force in the world.

Epilogue

WHEN I SAT down to write this book, I had no idea that Canada would go to war during the preparation of the manuscript. I've had the good fortune to visit our troops in Afghanistan three times. I have never been prouder of being Canadian than when I watch the Canadian Forces perform their duties under such austere and dangerous conditions. This book is dedicated to the Canadian soldier because he made me look good for thirty-six years, and now he *and she* continue to make Canada look good on the international stage.

As each page of my manuscript revealed itself to me, I was shocked at how much the Profession of Arms dominated my life while in uniform and in the fifteen years since I took it off. For someone who joined up because he needed a summer job to buy a used car, it was a lucky, life-altering decision, one taken much too lightly at the time.

I'm frequently asked, "Do you miss it all?" For years I responded, "Not really, because I'm still intimately involved with the profession as a commentator." A few years ago, I realized I was kidding myself. Dora and I were living in Muskoka at the time, and in February—with the temperature well below zero and a strong wind coming from the west—I was knee deep in snow, attempting to fix a broken step at the entrance to our barn. I stupidly had put only thin dress gloves on, and within minutes my fingers went stiff and started to hurt.

The reasonable solution to my agony would have been to take off the gloves, slip my hands inside my ski jacket and warm them in my armpits. But I hesitated, because for the first time since I'd taken early retirement I realized I missed the army in general and the infantry in particular. The freezing fingers reminded me of the pain that has to be endured in the Arctic, in the jungles, the desert, the mountains—wherever soldiers are required to go in all weather conditions, with everything they need on their back. As technology reduces the weight of weapons, ammunition and equipment, infanteers reap no benefit; they are merely required to carry more. Exhaustion, sleep deprivation and fear all contribute to the pain cocktail. Yet, there are few occupations that can generate the euphoric high that every infanteer experiences with his or her fellow soldiers, when the event that generated the pain in the first place is blessedly over.

I let my fingers freeze a little longer and admitted to myself that yes, I really do miss it all.

Acknowledgements

MANY THANKS TO Scott McIntyre for regularly badgering me during the fourteen years since his publication of my first book, believing that I might have another one in me. To editor John Eerkes-Medrano, who made the editing process an enjoyable and educational experience, which I'm pretty confident is not always the case. To copy editor Ruth Wilson, whose attention to detail is unequalled—for example, Ruth looked back at my storytelling of events that occurred some forty years ago and discovered that I had made a 24-hour mistake in my recollection! And thanks to David Lavin, of the Lavin Agency (www.thelavinagency.com), who inadvertently helped convince me to write this book. David has been my speaking agent for fifteen years, and fourteen years ago convinced me to accept a request to speak on the subject of leadership—which I have done ever since, and which led Scott McIntyre to suggest that I write at least a chapter on the subject.

And, most importantly, a sincere thank you to the soldiers (a term of affection referring to all Navy, Army and Air Force men and women, of all ranks) who worked with me over my thirty-six years in Her Majesty's uniform.

Sources

1   Kofi Annan, Under Secretary-General for Peacekeeping Operations,
      letter to the author, June 28, 1995 (letter in author's
      possession).

2   "Kosovo: The Rambouillet Accords, Interim Agreement for Peace and
      Self-Government in Kosovo," February 23, 1999, chapter 8; online at
      www.kosovo.mod.uk/rambouillet_text.htm, accessed February 3, 2008.

3   Lewis MacKenzie, "Milosevic Strategy Has Ominous Ring," *Ottawa Citi-
      zen Online*, April 8, 1999; online at www.ottawacitizen.com/columnists/
      mackenzie/990408/30516578/16/99, accessed August 16, 1999.

4   ICROSS Canada; online at www.icross.ca/pledge.htm, accessed
      March 20, 2008.

5   Congress of North American Bosniaks (undated open letter
      in the author's possession).

6   Ibid.

7   Congress of North American Bosniaks, "Statements
      Confirming Crimes Committed by Lt. Gen. (ret.) Lewis"; online at
      www.bosniak.org/06/page.php?id=23, p. 3, accessed
      January 2, 2007.

8   Ibid., p. 4.

9   Ibid.

10   Lewis MacKenzie, letter to Judge Branko Peric,
      October 23, 2006 (letter in the author's possession).

11   Carol Off, *The Lion, the Fox and the Eagle: A Story of Generals and
      Justice in Yugoslavia and Rwanda* (Toronto: Random
      House Canada, 2000), p. 176.

12   Ibid., p. 217.

13   Carol Off, "MacKenzie in Sarajevo," in Lieutenant-Colonel
      Bernd Horn and Stephen Harris, eds., *Warrior Chiefs:
      Perspectives on Senior Canadian Military Leaders* (Toronto:
      Dundurn Press, 2001), p. 321.

14   Ibid., p. 322.

15   Ibid., p. 332.

16 Marcus Gee, "Going for the Generals," *Globe and Mail,*
November 18, 2000, p. D12.

17 J.L. Granatstein, "Flaws of UN Peacekeeping Laid Bare,"
Gazette (Montreal), November 25, 2000.

18 Peter Worthington, "The Balkans, in Black and White,"
Toronto Sun, November 16, 2000.

19 Scott Taylor, "The Lion, the Glitch and the Wardrobe,"
Globe and Mail, November 18, 2000, p. D13.

20 Bruce Garvey, "The Tricky Task of Heroism After Sarajevo," *Ottawa
Citizen,* December 3, 2000, p. C16.

21 Bruce Garvey, e-mail to the author, November 21, 2000
(letter in the author's possession).

22 Roméo Dallaire, *Shake Hands with the Devil: The Failure of Humanity in
Rwanda* (Toronto: Random House Canada, 2003),
p. 42.

23 Ibid., p. 233.

24 Ibid., p. 252.

25 Jack Deverell, "Can Disobedience Be a Military Virtue?"
FrontLine Defence, July/August 2007, pp. 30–31.

26 William Ray, "Fighting Blind," excerpt published with
permission of the author.

27 Andrew Duffy, "General to PM: Don't Insult Me," *Ottawa Citizen,*
December 28, 2001, p. A1; Lewis MacKenzie, "Don't Insult Me, Mr.
Chrétien," *Ottawa Citizen,* December 28, 2001, p. A7.

Index

Page numbers followed by "n" indicate footnotes.